D1106281

Practical Exposition of II Peter

Verse by Verse

BY

J. NIEBOER

Evangelist and Bible Teacher

Editor of Monthly Paper
"OUR DAILY WALK"

Author of
PRACTICAL EXPOSITION OF I PETER
PRACTICAL EXPOSITION OF JAMES

OUR DAILY WALK PUBLISHERS
1158 W. 29th Street Erie, Penna.

Printed in United States of America

CONTENTS

INTRODUCTION

After writing on the First Epistle of Peter many have asked, "Where is the Second Epistle?" This persistent demand finally persuaded us to write this book.

Like I Peter, II Peter is a very important book, but sadly neglected. We know of no other book which deals solely with this epistle.

We believe all the Second Epistles have a special message for last days and II Peter is no exception. Like the whole of the First Epistle the first chapter of II Peter is of a very practical nature. Also in this first chapter, Peter gives convincing proof of his authorship by his references to the transfiguration of Christ.

In the second chapter Peter deals with apostasy. As he thunders away he almost sounds like a different Peter. Much of the language here is so blunt and so sharp, that we hesitated to write on it in our usual style. It would be so much easier to soften, or even pass over some of it, but we have felt constrained to treat it no differently than any other portion on which we have written. The apostasy today in many quarters is just as serious as in Peter's day, and we believe he would thunder now, if he was here, as he did then.

The third chapter is primarily prophetic. Scoffers had arisen belittling the coming again of Christ and saying that things had not changed since the creation. Peter proves that there had been great geological changes in the past and states that there would also be great changes in the future. He starts with the creation, mentions the flood, the coming of Christ, and the purging of the present world with fire, and ends with the glorious truth of the new heavens and the new earth to follow. We believe that in this age of the atomic bomb. all will find the study of this third chapter interesting and helpful.

No doubt there will be some things in this book wherewith some of our readers will disagree. Prophetic things have been variously understood down the ages. We have not sought to be obstinate or different, but neither have we compromised with what we consider to be the truth of God. It would be easy to try to word things so as not to bring offense to certain groups of Christians. We have determined not to be men-pleasers, but to state the truth of God as we understand it.

As with our other books, we have sought to present a straightforward, readable exposition of the epistle. We have thought not only of the preacher and the Bible student, but of the average reader as well. We believe, as with I Peter and James, many will find this book suitable for family devotions or daily readings. At the same time, it will give a comprehensive view and understanding of the epistle.

No doubt though, as with our other books, those who profess to get most help from this one will be students, teachers and preachers. We have sought to make it a ready reference work for them. The table of contents, which sets forth in order the main subjects of the epistle, the suggestive paragraph and chapter headings, and also the references on the top of each page, are things which make our books unique in the commentary field. In addition to this we follow the popular verse by verse treatment, skipping or glossing over nothing.

We trust that you, our reader, will find pleasure and help from its pages.

J. Nieboer.

I

AUTHOR AND READERS

(II Peter 1:1, 2)

1:1 "Simon Peter, a servant and an apostle of Jesus Christ, to them that have obtained like precious faith with us through the righteousness of God and our Saviour Jesus Christ."

The first verse of this second epistle is somewhat like the first verse of the first epistle. Both give the name of the author and tell us to whom the epistle was written. There are, however, marked differences. In the first epistle we have only the name Peter, while here we have both of his names, Simon and Peter. He here describes himself as "servant and apostle of Jesus Christ," while in the first epistle it is only "an apostle of Jesus Christ." There is also a marked difference in the way his readers are described. In the first epistle he mentions the places in which they lived, but here he speaks of them as those who "have obtained like precious faith with us through the righteousness of God and our Saviour Jesus Christ." We learn from 3:1 that he addresses this epistle to the same readers to whom he sent the first.

"Simon Peter"

We begin to wonder at once whether there could be a reason for using both of his names, "Simon Peter." "Simon" was his given name, while "Peter" was given to him by the Lord Jesus. "Simon" would remind us of the old Peter, impetuous, but changeable and unstable. "Peter" reminds us of his new life in Christ; not the Peter who denied his Lord, but the one who preached at Pentecost and saw 3,000 saved; the Peter who was unafraid and spoke and lived for his Lord in spite of persecution. When Andrew brings Peter to Christ, the Lord says to him, "Thou art Simon the son of Jona: thou shalt be called Cephas (Peter), which is by interpretation, A stone" (Jno. 1:42). Perhaps Peter discovered, that although he was on the Rock, and his new name meant "stone," yet he had his old nature with him, and he was after all "Simon" as well as "Peter." Many besides Peter have discovered that they do not lose their old nature, even though they have received a new one from the Lord Jesus.

PETER THE AUTHOR

In time past some have questioned whether Peter was the author of the epistle, and whether is should be included in the canon of Scripture. The first epistle has never been questioned, and yet it seems to us that this second epistle has many more internal evidences of Peter's authorship than the first. If Peter did not write it, the author was a rank imposter. Peter's name is not only signed at the outset, but various incidents from his life are mentioned in it. In 1:14 he says, "Knowing that shortly I must put off this my tabernacle, even as our Lord Jesus Christ hath shewed me." This without question, refers to Jno. 21:18, 19. In 1:16-18, the author claims to have been with the Lord Jesus on the Mount of Transfiguration. Only Peter, James and John were there. In 3:1 he claims to have written another epistle to the same Christians, which it would seem could only refer to the first epistle of Peter. In our mind there is no question but that Peter wrote both of these epistles which bear his name.

STYLE AND TIME OF WRITING

This second epistle is somewhat different in style from the first. This is evident especially in the second chapter. There he deals with false teachers, and the difference in subject is without doubt the reason for the difference in style. This second chapter resembles Jude a good deal, and some have thought there may have been copying by one from the other. There is no proof at all of this; they may have both realized the need to be similar, and have been led of the Spirit to write similarly. Both Jude and II Peter were probably written late, 64 to 66 A.D., or maybe even later. Peter knew of at least some of Paul's epistles as we gather from 3:15-16. Paul may have already been executed. We judge from 1:14 that it was written only a short time before Peter's death.

"A Servant"

Peter was one of the chief apostles, one of the first called, and always played a leading part. However, he claimed no priority over the other apostles, and here, like Paul (Rom. 1:1) and James (James 1:1), calls himself a servant of Jesus Christ. "Servant" here is literally "bondman" or "slave." The Roman Catholics have made him out to be the first pope, but he himself claimed no higher place than that of apostle. He calls himself an elder in I Pet. 5:1. There is no scriptural reason to believe that he held any higher office than that of apostle, as our verse says.

One Is Your Master

Peter, James, John and Paul were great men, but they all realized that they were bondmen of Jesus Christ. It would seem they never forgot the lesson the Lord taught them as recorded in Mat. 23:8-12. "Neither be ye called masters: for one is your Master, even Christ. But he that is greatest among you shall be your servant" (Mat. 23:10, 11). Many have not learned this lesson today. Like the Pharisees, they still want the uppermost rooms, the chief seats, and to be called of men "teacher, teacher" (Mat. 23:6, 7). How wonderful they think it to be the pope, or a cardinal, or a bishop, or a priest. A preacher said to an acquaintance of ours, "I went to school for ten years to get my title, and I don't want you to call me 'brother'; call me 'Reverend.' " It seems to us that this man manifested the same spirit as the Pharisees. Is the title "Reverend" any more scriptural than "Cardinal"? A man might not believe in flattering titles, yet manifest the spirit of lordship. Diotrophes carried no title, but he surely demanded and assumed the chief place (III John 9, 10).

Peter's Humility

To call himself a bondman of Jesus Christ demonstrated humility on the part of Peter. He realized his nothingness when compared to the Lord Jesus. He is like John the Baptist, who says, "One mightier than I cometh, the latchet of whose shoes I am not worthy to unloose" (Luke 3:16). It behooves all of us to manifest a true spirit of humility before Him.

SERVANTS OBEY

Peter knew that he was not his own and that he had been bought with a price (I. Cor. 6:19, 20). He realized that he could not do as he pleased; he must do his Master's bidding. He understood that he belonged to the Lord, spirit, soul, and body, and that he had no rights of his own. He puts himself in a position of absolute obedience to the Lord. To serve one so wholly whom you love is not slavery. A father who loves his family serves it freely and gladly, and so, a mother. One who serves the Lord Jesus does not consider it slavery, but a joy and a delight. He is like Jacob, who served Laban seven additional years happily because of love to Rachel (Gen. 29:20).

BLESSINGS OF SERVANTS

There are great blessings connected with being a bondman of Jesus Christ. One could serve no better master. He will see that all the needs of His servants are met. He will give joy in the service and great reward in eternity. To be with Him then forever will be compensation enough. "If any man serve me, let him follow me; and where I am, there shall also my servant be: if any man serve me, him will my Father honour" (Jno. 12:26). The least bit of service, even to the giving of a cup of cold water in His name, shall not lose its reward (Mark 9:41).

"AN APOSTLE"

"An apostle" is the highest Peter ever claimed for himself. "Apostle" means "sent one" in the official sense. Peter's apostleship was never questioned. He rose from a lowly fisherman to one of the leading disciples. He is nearly always the first one named in any list of the apostles. He was one of the three in the garden of Gethsemane, as well as on the Mount of Transfiguration. He was very devoted to Christ, and professed to be ready to die with Him (Mat. 26:35). He did not, however, know his weakness and failed miserably. He denied his Lord three times that very night.

SENT ONES

Some claim to be apostles in the official sense now, but we are sure they are not right in their assumption. Only those who were with the Lord and personally commissioned by Him claimed that in the Scriptures. However, we can all be sent ones of Jesus Christ. As He sent the apostles into the world, so He sends us into the world. He may not send us out of our home town, but He may send us to the other side of the world. If we are truly His servants, we will be ready to go anywhere He may desire.

HE CAN LEAD

"But," you say, "how can the Lord direct us as to where to go?" He can do it in various ways. A number of years ago, we received a letter from the Chicago assemblies asking if we would move there to help in a specific work for the Lord. We wrote back and said we would pray, and see if we could get the Lord's mind as to it. A week or so later I was traveling by car to a distant city for a meeting. While riding along I was thinking, "How can the Lord tell me whether to move to Chicago or not? There is certainly nothing in the Bible about going to Chicago." Only a few moments later, I pulled a road map out of a car pocket fully expecting it to be one of Michigan. But on it in large letters it said "Travel Chicago," a Chicago district map which I had almost forgotten was there. The Lord by His Spirit said, "There are your instructions." Then I was sure I heard someone laugh, but no one was with me in the car. It was the Lord's way of saying, "I could not tell you to move to Chicago, could I?" Needless to say, we moved to Chicago and served the Lord there for nine years. He may not direct you in a similar way, but He can direct you.

"OF JESUS CHRIST"

Peter professed to be "a servant and an apostle of Jesus Christ." By this he surely puts the stamp of deity on our Lord Jesus. Surely he would not consider being a slave of one who was merely man, and one who was not even any longer living on the earth. It showed too, that he believed the Lord Jesus to be alive and able to give him instructions as to where to go and what to do.

NOT JESUS ONLY

Peter, in his epistles, never calls our Lord by the single name of "Jesus." He always links it up with "Lord" or "Christ" and sometimes with both. He does at times use "Lord" alone or "Christ" alone, but never "Jesus." As we noticed in our book on I Peter, "Jesus" is a compound name meaning "God saves," and "Christ" is the Greek for "Messiah," or literally "the Anointed." So Peter, by the use of this name affirms the Lord Jesu the one anointed by God to be the Saviour of sinners. "Jesus" was His earthly name. When we hear a speaker speak of our Lord as only "Jesus," we wonder whether he is thinking of Him only as a man, perhaps a great man, but no more than a man.

To Whom Written

The last half of our verse tells us to whom Peter addresses his epistle. He does not say it is for Jew or Gentile or for any group of Christians living in a certain city or country. It is for those who "have obtained like precious faith with us;" or in other words, all Christians. For this reason we can say without hesitation, it is for us today. However from 3:1, we conclude that it was originally sent to the same Christians to whom the first epistle was sent. There Peter says, "This second epistle, beloved, I now write unto you." From I Pet. 1:1, we know that these were Christians living up in Asia Minor in the country which Paul and his disciples evangelized.

"Obtained Like Precious Faith With Us"

When Peter says, "to them that have obtained like precious faith with us," he is telling his readers that their faith was exactly the same as his own. When he says "with us" some have thought that he meant that his readers had obtained the same kind of faith as the apostles. Others have thought that Peter's readers were mostly Gentile, and that he was hereby telling them that they had obtained the same kind of faith as the Jews. It does not matter much how this is understood, because all, from the weakest to the strongest, whether Jew or Gentile, have the same kind of faith, if they are saved at all. Every saved one has put his trust in the same person, the Lord Jesus Christ. "One Lord, one faith, one baptism" (Eph. 4:5). Right at the outset of his epistle, Peter would put his readers on exactly the same level as himself. This demonstrates real tact and courtesy.

"Faith"

We believe Peter here is speaking particularly of saving faith. There is also a faith which follows salvation, and this differs greatly in various Christians, but saving faith is the same in all. As one realizes he is a guilty sinner, and puts his faith in Christ, he is saved. "Faith" is not the Savior, but it links us up with Him. It is like the water pipe; it is not the water, but it brings the water into our homes. Faith also could be likened to an electric wire; it is not the electricity, but it brings the electricity into our homes. Some seem to think more of faith than they do of the Savior. Faith is important, even as the water pipe and the electric wire are important, but they are all only means by which blessing is brought to us.

"Precious Faith"

While faith is not the Savior, it is important, and Peter calls it precious. It is precious because it links us up with the precious one. Peter calls Christ precious three times (I Pet. 2:4, 6, 7). He calls His blood precious, too (I Pet. 1:19). He also calls the trial of our faith precious (I Pet. 1:7), and speaks of precious promises (II Pet. 1:4). To Peter, the Lord, and all things related to Him, were precious. It should be so with us, too.

Faith After Salvation

Faith after salvation is precious, too. It is wonderful to trust Christ for salvation, but we should trust Him for all things at all times. Even as a parent loves to have his children trust him, so the Lord loves to have His children trust Him too. Can we trust Him to supply us with all our needs? Can we trust Him to care for us in every way? Will we trust Him in time of ridicule or great trial? When He sees His children stand fast in the midst of difficulty, this is indeed precious to Him.

"Through the Righteousness of God"

The expression "through the righteousness of God" may seem strange to some in connection with this verse. What relation to obtaining "precious faith" has "the righteousness of God?" We think of His righteousness as that which demands the punishment of the sinner, and by which we are all condemned. Then we think of the cross of Christ as that which pictures His love and mercy. The cross also pictures His righteousness. Christ met the righteous demands of a sin hating God by dying on the cross for our sins. This is why He is called our "righteousness" in I Cor. 1:30. Now God can in perfect righteousness forgive the sins of the vilest sinner. "To declare, I say, at this time his righteousness: that he might be just, and the justified of him which believeth in Jesus" (Rom. 3:26).

All Done in Righteousness

Everything has been done in righteousness. He has forgiven us all our sins, lifted us from the gates of hell and made us His children, and no one can accuse Him of being unrighteous in the least in it all. He could not now righteously refuse salvation to anyone who would put his faith in the Lord Jesus. He cannot righteously demand payment twice for the same sins, once of His Son, and then again of those for whom He has paid on the cross. So we have obtained our faith through His righteousness, rather than in spite of it, as we might suppose.

"God and Our Saviour Jesus Christ"

The Revised Version has "Our God and Saviour Jesus Christ," so making both "God" and "Saviour" apply to our Lord Jesus Christ. This would appear to be the most accurate translation, and is a definite argument in favor of the deity of our Lord Jesus. Many other Scriptures testify to the Godhood of our Lord Jesus. Romans 9:5 says, "Christ came, who is over all, God blessed forever." In Heb. 1:8 we have, "But unto the Son he saith, Thy throne, O God, is forever and ever."

"Our Saviour"

Our verse calls Christ "our Saviour." Many make Him no more than a helper. They say, "We must do our part and Christ will do His part." One man insisted we had to do good works in order to go to heaven. We asked him then, "Why did Christ have to die on the cross?" He replied, "Christ died on the cross so He could open the gate, and so when we climb up to heaven, we can get in." The Scripture pictures us as hopeless and helpless and unable to do a thing to even help save ourselves. Then it pictures Christ as the Saviour who "is able also to save them to the uttermost that come unto God by him" (Heb. 7:25). Like a drowning man, or one trapped in a burning building needs a savior, so we need Christ to lift us up out of the mire of sin, and lay hold of us ere we slip into hell forevermore.

1:2 "Grace and peace be multiplied unto you through the knowledge of God, and of Jesus our Lord."

In I Peter 1:2, Peter gives almost the same salutation only in our verse he adds "through the knowledge of God, and of Jesus our Lord." This verse is a summing up of the purpose of this epistle. The apostle desires that we may experience the rich unmerited favors of the Lord, and manifest the same spirit of grace. Also that we might have abundant peace in spite of trials and perplexities. He also desires that we grow in the knowledge of God and the Lord Jesus Christ. The more our knowledge of the Lord, the more will grace and peace be multiplied in our hearts and lives. As this is the desire of Peter for his readers, so it should be our daily desire, not only for ourselves, but for all of the Lord's people.

"GRACE"

The generally accepted definition of "grace" is "unmerited favor." God's grace really goes far beyond this. One might show us favor when we have done nothing to merit it, but God shows us favor when we deserve punishment. Sometimes we give our children presents, although they may do nothing particular to deserve them. However, if a boy is bad and disobedient, we may withhold gifts from him. God's grace in salvation reaches the very worst and makes them His children. Even after salvation, much of His favor is entirely undeserved. As children of God we are often miserable failures, but in spite of it all, He showers us with blessings. His heart is much like that of a father who had a very wayward boy. The relatives all said, he should be disinherited and turned out of the house. The father said to him, "Harry, you have heard what they all have said about you, but I would have you know that as long as I have a crust of bread in the house, you will share it with me." This kindness of his father caused this boy to break down in true repentance, and he was led to put his trust in the Lord Jesus. "The goodness of God leadeth thee to repentance" (Rom. 2:4).

"Peace"

Men by nature are at enmity with God. Their hearts, and minds, and wills are set against Him. They love their sin and do not want the Lord to interfere, and will resist any overtures on the part of the Lord or His servants. They have no peace in their hearts, nor are they at peace with one another. However, by the Spirit, many are led to see that they are fighting a losing battle, and they surrender to the Lord. The moment they trust the Lord, they have peace with God.

The Peace of God

After peace with God there follows a peace in the heart, or what the Word calls "the peace of God." It always brings peace to know that sins are forgiven, and that the Lord no longer is against you, but for you. However, some Christians do not have the peace of heart which they might have. This is because their faith is not strong or, as the rest of our verse suggests, they are not acquainted with the Lord to the extent that they should be. Outward circumstances trouble them, and their peace of mind is disturbed. They either forget, or do not believe Rom. 8:28. "And we know that all things (even trials) work together for good to them that love God, to them who are the called according to his purpose."

"Multiplied Unto You"

The expression "multiplied unto you" tells us that it is possible to have grace and peace in various degrees. Our desire should be like the apostle, to have them multiplied. May we suggest a few things to help in this multiplication. Paul suggests in Phil. 4:6, 7 that the way to be rid of care and to have our hearts filled with the peace of God, lies in "prayer and supplication with thanksgiving." We believe other aids are Bible study and fellowship with the Lord's people. The more we know of the Lord and His people the more will the grace of God and His peace fill our hearts and minds.

"Through the Knowledge of God"

Knowledge takes on many forms. Many know much about God, yet do not know Him nor do they know our Lord Jesus Christ. By the hearing of the ear and reading of the newspapers, we know much about the president of our country. Yet we cannot say we know him, if we have never met him. Sometimes people ask, "Do you know brother so and so?" We must reply that although we have met him, we cannot say we know him. Sometimes we meet people often, but yet we cannot say that we know them. If you really meet the Lord Jesus then you can say you know God and also our Lord Jesus. Yet there are various degrees of knowing Him. The better we know Him, the more intimate we are with Him, both in prayer and in Bible study, the more our hearts will be filled with His grace and peace. To know about God may only fill one with fear and dread of judgment, but to know Him takes away this fear and fills one with peace. "And this is life eternal, that they might know thee the only true God, and Jesus Christ, whom thou hast sent" (John 17:3).

Knowledge in II Peter

In our epistle Peter has much to say about knowledge. In our chapter alone besides our verse we have it in verses 3, 5, 6, and 8. It also appears in 2:20 and the last verse in the epistle says, "But grow in grace, and in the knowledge of our Lord and Saviour Jesus Christ." Besides the world "knowledge" we have on several occasions various forms of the word "know." This is all in striking contrast to the first epistle, and some have wondered why. We believe it is because in between the writing of the first and second epistles Peter heard of false teachers who had risen up in some of these churches claiming boastfully that they had superior knowledge of many things. Peter strongly condemns these false prophets in chapter 2. To offset this parading of false knowledge, Peter brings forth the true knowledge of God and of Christ. This true knowledge of the Lord will nourish and develop real faith, and guard one against false teaching. "But the people that do know their God shall be strong, and do exploits" (Dan. 11:32). "Acquaint now thyself with him and be at peace" (Job 22:21).

"JESUS OUR LORD"

Let us not be content with meeting our Lord but once, and so finding salvation. We should desire to know Him better and better, and to walk with Him day by day. We read of Enoch that he "walked with God." As we have constant fellowship with Him, we will become more and more like Him. In our whole life we should own Him as Lord. Peter calls Him "Jesus our Lord." This tells us that if we are to make progress in our Christian life, we must live in constant subjection to Him. We first know Him as Savior, but if we are to experience His grace and be filled with His peace, we must give Him the place of Lord in our hearts and in our lives.

II

HIS DIVINE POWER

(II Peter 1:3)

1:3 "According as his divine power hath given unto us all things that pertain unto life and godliness, through the knowledge of him that hath called us to glory and virtue."

In verse 2 the apostle desires that grace and peace be multiplied unto us. Our verse tells of yet more things that come to us through "the knowledge of Him." Because we know Him, by His divine power, He gives unto us all things needful for our life in Christ, and godliness of life for Him.

"His Divine Power"

In this verse we have "divine power" and in the next "divine nature." It is only by His divine power that it is possible to obtain the divine nature. The word "divine" intrigues us. The original word only appears in these two verses and in Acts 17:29, where it is translated "Godhead." The Greek word "theios" could be literally translated "godlike." It is the godlike power of Christ that gives to us a godlike nature. The word translated "divine" in Heb. 9:1 is a different word and would be better translated "worship." Perhaps our readers have, with the writer, had an unscriptural thought of this word "divine." We have always thought of it as "God Himself" rather than "godlike." The word for God is "theos," not as in our verse "theios." Because of this misunderstanding of the word, and the expression "divine nature" in our next verse, some have almost ascribed deity to the Christians.

Christ's Power

Peter had seen many evidences of the power of Christ. Perhaps the greatest demonstration of His power lay in His self-control. He had complete control over His passions, His words, and His actions. We see this especially at the time of His trial. They accused Him, but He made no defense; they reviled Him, but

He reviled not again; they threatened Him, but He threatened not in return; they abused Him, but He did not call down the wrath of God; they crucified Him, but He said, "Father forgive them, for they know not what they do."

Christ's Power Over Others

Peter saw Christ demonstrate great power over others. He saw many souls saved as well as bodies. He saw wicked sinners changed into adoring saints, such as the sinful woman who anointed Him with the alabaster box of ointment. He saw her sitting at His feet weeping and wiping His feet with her hair. He saw lepers cleansed, the blind have their eyes opened, the lame to walk, and the dumb to speak.

Christ's Power Over Death

Peter likewise saw Christ's power over death. He saw the young daughter of Jairus raised to life; and the young son of the widow of Nain; and then also he saw Lazarus, dead four days, come out of the tomb. The crowning evidence was Christ Himself coming forth out of the tomb on the third day. Peter could not question such mighty evidences of the power of the Son of God.

Christ's Power Over Satan

Peter also saw Christ demonstrate power over Satan. He saw the maniac of Gadara have a legion of demons cast out of him and saw him clothed and in his right mind sitting at the feet of the Lord Jesus. He saw Mary Magdalene have seven demons cast out of her at His command. How devoted this dear soul was to the Lord. Demons had to obey His will. Someday He will cast the devil himself into the lake of fire.

Christ's Power Over Nature

Peter also saw Christ's power over the things of nature. He, with the other disciples, were on the Sea of Galilee when a terrible storm arose. The waves were dashing into the boat, but our Lord lay there fast asleep. They awake Him saying, "Master, carest thou not that we perish." He arose and rebuked the wind and said unto the sea, "Peace be still," and there was a great calm.

Peter also remembered the time when Christ and he too walked upon the boisterous waves. Then there was the coin in the fish's mouth, and the colt upon which the Lord triumphantly rode into Jerusalem. All these things and others demonstrate the power the Lord Jesus had and still has over things natural.

He Still Has All Power

In Mat. 28:18, the Lord Jesus said, "All power is given unto me in heaven and in earth." This means that His power is no less now than it was when He was here. He may demonstrate it in a different way, but it is no less great. Speaking of Himself to His Father in John 17:2 He says, "Thou hast given him power over all flesh." John 1:10, Col. 1:16, and Heb. 1:2 all tell us that Christ was the powerful Creator of all things. Heb. 1:3 states that today He upholds "all things by the Word of his power." His power is still unlimited. "With God all things are possible" (Mat. 19:26).

Power to Save

A young sailor in the Service Men's Center told us one day, "The Lord cannot save me." We asked him, "Why not?" Then he told us a story of trial and difficulty in connection with the navy. He was on one ship torpedoed by a Jap submarine and wounded along with others. He told of Jap atrocities and treachery; then how they once brought a Jap submarine to the surface after badly damaging it. The Japs came pouring out of the conning tower with their hands upraised for surrender, but he and other gunners picked them off as fast as they came out. He thought for this reason the Lord could not and would not save him. We read to him I Tim. 1:15. "This is a faithful saying, and worthy of all acceptation, that Christ Jesus came into the world to save sinners; of whom I am chief." We asked him if he knew who said this and why he called himself the chief of sinners. We explained how Paul had not hated and killed treacherous Japs, but had hated and persecuted and killed Christians, who were not in warfare, but telling out the gospel and living for Christ. If the Lord could save Paul, He surely could save him. The young man was an eager listener, but whether he actually trusted Christ or not we cannot say.

No Case Beyond His Power

Paul could say, "For I am not ashamed of the gospel of Christ: for it is the power of God unto salvation to everyone that believeth" (Rom. 1:16). No case is too hard for the Lord. We can safely bring the gospel to any creature. "He is able also to save them to the uttermost that come unto God by him, seeing he ever liveth to make intercession for them" (Heb. 7:25). We believe His power is shown as much in the redemption of the sinner as it is in connection with creation.

His Transforming Power

One man told us one time, "No use of me becoming a Christian, I could not live the life anyway." We told him, he did not understand the transforming power of Christ. When one trusts the Lord Jesus, the Spirit of God enters into his heart and the man is completely changed. Unconquerable habits fall away, and sinful passions lose their grip.

An Example of Transformation

A woman was saved at some meetings we had. She always impressed us as a very sweet Christian, but we hardly knew her before she was saved. One time speaking to her grown daughter, we mentioned how sweet her mother was. She said, "Yes, mother is sweet now, but she was not always that way. Before she was saved she was cranky, and critical, and provoking. Her salvation surely changed her completely." This divine power working in a Christian makes one more and more Christ-like. The very worst have been changed into the very best.

His Keeping Power

We visited a woman in her home not too long ago. She seemed very interested in the gospel, but said, "There is no use in me getting saved, I could not keep saved anyway." We talked to her for sometime about the keeping power of the Lord; that no one could keep themselves, but that those who trusted in Christ were safe in His hand, and that they would never perish (John 10:27-

30). We also read to her II Tim. 1:12, where Paul says, "I know whom I have believed, and am persuaded that he is able to keep that which I have committed unto him against that day." Suddenly she said, "If that is the way it is, I want it." And quicker than a flash she was down on her knees telling the Lord of her sins, and that she wanted to be saved. When she arose from her knees, she went into an adjoining room where her husband was sleeping and awoke him saying, "Tom, wake up Tom, I'm saved, I'm saved." The Lord is able to save and also to keep.

Benefits from His Power

A realization of the power of Christ should be a great consolation to the Christian. Are we dejected, suffering opposition, or great trial? It is a comfort to know that all is in His plan, for if it were not, by His power He could quickly change it. It is by His almighty power that He makes, "All things work together for good to them that love God, to them who are the called according to his purpose" (Rom. 8:28).

"Hath Given Unto Us"

Our Lord is a great giver. He does not lend, nor lease, nor sell, He only gives. It is entirely by grace, we had nothing and deserve nothing, but with Christ, He freely gives us all things (Rom. 8:32). He gives us all things natural and spiritual. He gives us birth, life, food, clothing and homes to live in. He gives not only possessions, but bodily strength and wisdom. He is the greatest of all givers. May we be givers too.

"All Things"

James says in 1:17, "Every good gift and every perfect gift is from above, and cometh down from the Father of lights." Every good thing in this world comes from the Lord. "All things" in our verse, refers especially to spiritual blessings. "His divine power hath given unto us all things that pertain unto life and godliness." "Life" refers to our life in Christ. He gives everything needful for our Christian life, its commencement, continuance and completion. All these things flow from union to and communion with our Lord. "All things are your's; whether Paul, or Apollos, or Cephas, or the world, or life, or death, or things present, or things to come; all are your's; and ye are Christ's; and Christ is God's (I Cor. 3:21-23). We are indeed rich in Christ.

"THAT PERTAIN UNTO LIFE"

"Unto life" refers to the new life we have in Christ. This life starts with the new birth, but will never end, because it is eternal life. By His divine power, He not only gives that life, but gives everything necessary to foster it and to nourish it. That life will give us entrance into glory and enable us to enjoy His presence forevermore. "Blessed be the God and Father of our Lord Jesus Christ, who hath blessed us with all spiritual blessings in heavenly places in Christ" (Eph. 1:3).

"AND GODLINESS"

His divine power first supplies everything necessary for life, and then also for a godly walk. Some profess to be Christians because they think they lead a godly life, but they have never been born again. It is necessary to be born before one can walk. Life must precede godliness. However, the Lord has also granted everything necessary to godliness. No Christian can excuse himself on the ground that he is weak. The Lord has given the Holy Spirit to dwell in every true believer's heart. He also has given him a new nature. If a Christian is not living a godly life it is not the fault of the Lord, for He has given everything needful for this godliness. It is because the Christian does not avail himself of that which the Lord has provided that he fails. He permits himself to become under the influence of his old sinful Adamic nature.

"THROUGH THE KNOWLEDGE OF HIM"

This is the second time that Peter tells of benefits obtained through the knowledge of the Lord. In verse 2, he desires that "grace and peace be multiplied unto you through the knowledge of God, and of Jesus our Lord." Here it is "all things that pertain to life and godliness." All these blessings can only come through a personal knowledge of our Lord. The better we know Him, the more we will desire to serve Him.

"HATH CALLED US"

Our calling seems to be a favorite subject of Peter. He mentions it five times in first Peter, and also in verse 10 of our chapter, besides in our verse 3. First of all we are called by Christ unto salvation. We hear His call, "Come unto me," and we come to Him. After salvation we are called to various services for Him. All of His calls usually come through the reading or hearing of the Word of God preached.

CALLED INTO BLESSING

We have been called "out of darkness into his marvelous light" (I Pet. 2:9). He has called us out of uncleanness into holiness (I Thes. 4:7); out of affliction into His eternal glory (I Pet. 5:10); out of the power of Satan into His glorious kingdom (Acts 26:18); out of rebellion into fellowship with His dear Son (I Cor. 1:9).

OUR HIGH CALLING

Let us not forget our high calling in Christ Jesus. Let us indeed, walk worthy of this calling wherewith we are called (Eph. 4:1 R. V.). I Pet. 3:9 says that we are called to be a blessing; let us see to it that we fulfill our calling in this, even as our Lord Jesus did. We may even be called to suffering for Christ's sake, as the servant slaves were in I Pet. 2:18-21. Then if we are called to any special service, as was the apostle Paul (Acts 9:15), let us be ready to hear and to do His bidding.

"TO GLORY AND VIRTUE"

Instead of "to glory and virtue" the Revised Version has "by his own glory and virtue." Most contend that this is the better translation, although one would naturally think the King James the most logical. Many other Scriptures tell us that we are called to glory (I Thes. 2:12, II Thes. 2:14, I Pet. 5:10). "Virtue" has been variously translated as "manliness," "bravery," "courage," "energy," "worthiness" and also "power." Certainly we are called to these things, but perhaps by them in Christ too.

HIS GLORY

Peter was much impressed by the glory of the Lord Jesus. The moral glory of the Lord had much to do with his call. He saw the sinlessness of the Savior and His power manifested in His miracles (John 2:11). How impressed Peter was by the great draught of fishes in Luke 5:1-11. The glory of the Lord as manifested on the Mount of Transfiguration left an indelible impression on Peter, as we observe later on in our chapter (II Pet. 1:16-18). Then he saw the Lord in His glory after His resurrection from the dead. No doubt Peter felt this all a part of his call to special service for the Lord.

WE SHALL SHARE HIS GLORY WITH HIM

"Glory" is a hard word to define. It speaks of the highest form of honor and praise. It also speaks of a character of nobility and morality which deserves that glory. Truly our Lord Jesus had and has a noble character and is worthy of the greatest glory. He has now been exalted to the highest pinnacle of glory in heaven. As children of God, we should deport ourselves with the same nobility and dignity which characterized Him, and so already share His moral glory. Scripture everywhere tells us that we shall share His future glory with Him. We may have to suffer a bit with Him now, but "if so be that we suffer with him, that we may be also glorified together" (Rom. 8:17). The knowledge of this should stir us on to faithful endeavor for Him. The better we serve Him now the higher our place in glory.

"VIRTUE"

A few paragraphs back we noticed how "virtue" has been variously translated bravery, courage, power, energy, manliness and worthiness. We generally think of "virtue" now as purity, but that is not the sense of the word in our verse. Whichever definition we take they all fit our Lord very well. Certainly He was brave, manly, and worthy, He had great energy and power. Peter's call no doubt was greatly affected by these characteristics of our Lord Jesus. Many today are drawn to Him because of these things in Him. Again we would say, this character here called "virtue" should characterize us. More of this in connection with verse 5.

III

PRECIOUS PROMISES AND THE DIVINE NATURE

(II Peter 1:4)

1:4 "Whereby are given unto us exceeding great and precious promises; that by these ye might be partakers of the divine nature, having escaped the corruption that is in the world through lust."

"Whereby"

The word translated "whereby" in this verse is in the plural, indicating that it refers back to more than just the last statement of our last verse. It is not that His call "to glory and virtue" alone give us these "exceeding great and precious promises," and cause us to become "partakers of the divine nature," but it is through His "divine power" and the "knowledge of him." It would perhaps be better to start the verse with the expression "through which," so making it plural and applying it to the whole of verse 3. It is through His call, His power, and our knowledge of Him that the blessings of verse 4 come to us.

"Promises"

The "promises" of our verse are not itemized; no particular ones are mentioned. Judging from the rest of the verse we believe it is especially the promises in connection with salvation that Peter has in mind. As we heed the call of the Lord Jesus, and put our trust in Him, we receive "the divine nature," and escape "the corruption that is in the world through lust." What a great promise we have in John 10:28; "And I give unto them eternal life; and they shall never perish, neither shall any man pluck them out of my hand." Of course, the promises of salvation, pardon, eternal life, etc., are conditional. They can only be made real as one feels his need, and is willing to trust his soul into the hands of the Lord Jesus. While the gospel promises are good to any human, the conditions of repentance and faith must be met before they can be claimed. Unless a man realizes the seriousness of his sin, he will never flee to the Lord Jesus for pardon and salvation.

PROMISES FOR HIS OWN

While these promises probably refer to our great and precious salvation, Peter may have had the thousands of promises to the Lord's own in mind also. There are unconditional promises to every child of God, and also many that are conditional upon their faith and conduct. The Bible is so full of promises of every kind, that we might almost call it a book of promises. Besides the promise to pardon from sin, there are promises to sustain in time of trial, promises of guidance in time of darkness, promises of strength in time of weakness, promises to aid in time of need, promises to protect in time of danger, promises to comfort in time of sorrow, promises of His presence in life and also in death. "I will never leave thee, nor forsake thee" (Heb. 13:5). There are promises for the present life and the distant future. To those who die in Christ there are promises of resurrection and immortality. How dark all would be apart from these promises.

"EXCEEDING GREAT — PROMISES"

The promises of the Lord are "exceeding great" and "exceeding precious." They are made by an exceeding great and loving God. If the greatness of them would really grip us, we could not help but shout "Hallelujah." Almost every page of the New Testament contains some exceeding great promise. We just opened our Bible at random, and this great promise immediately struck our eye. "So Christ was once offered to bear the sins of many; and unto them that look for him shall he appear the second time without sin unto salvation" (Heb. 9:28). He is coming back again for His own. We then shall experience that complete salvation, spirit, soul and body; and the sin question will not again be brought up. He took care of that on the cross at the time of His first appearing. Here is another great promise; "Where I am, there shall also my servant be" (John 12:26). If we serve Him now, we will be with Him forever. That means we will be exalted to a place to which no one in this world has ever attained or ever dreamed of attaining. We will be with the ruler of the universe forever.

"PRECIOUS PROMISES"

The promises are not only exceeding great, but also very "precious." We have "precious faith" in verse 1 and now "precious promises." Only as we put faith in the Lord will the promises be for us, and only as we put faith in the promises will we appropriate them to ourselves and enjoy them. To make a promise precious, the thing promised must be precious, but it still will not be precious to us, if we do not believe the promiser can and will keep his promise. Thank the Lord, He is both willing and able, and this is what makes them especially sweet. There would be no hope in sorrow, trial, sickness, or death apart from these promises, they bring the sunshine through the rift in the clouds and this makes them sweet. Only in Christ and the many promises of the Word can a troubled soul find peace.

WHAT IS A PROMISE?

One has defined a promise as an assurance on the part of another of some good for which we are dependent on him. The promise is of no value if the promiser is not able to give. A promise is not compulsory beyond that the promiser is expected to be a man of his word.

WE CAN DEPEND ON HIS PROMISES

If the Lord promises anything, we can be sure He will do it. "God is not a man, that he should lie; neither the son of man, that he should repent: hath he said, and shall he not do it? or hath he spoken, and shall he not make it good?" (Num. 23:19). "For all the promises of God in him are yea, and in him Amen, unto the glory of God by us" (II Cor. 1:20). We heard of a man who constantly put his name in the Bible as he read it. For instance, "Let not your heart be troubled, John; ye believe in God, John; believe also in me, John." In that way he made every promise as well as every exhortation his own. Every promise of the Lord is made binding by the Word of Him who cannot lie. Let us trust them all simply and wholly.

WE CAN TRUST HIS WORD

The Lord Jesus said to His disciples one day, "Let us pass over unto the other side" (Mark 4:35). This was a definite statement and a guarantee that they would pass over the sea and reach the other side. However, He fell asleep on a pillow in the back of the boat, and a great storm arose, and the waves dashed into it. The disciples were afraid, and awoke Him saying, "Master, carest thou not that we perish?" In calm dignity He arose, rebuked the wind and the sea, and there was a great calm. He said to His disciples, "Why are ye so fearful? how is it that ye have no faith?" We too, are making a journey across the sea of time. Storms are bound to come, but remember He is with us, and will see us safely to the other side. If we are fearful, He will need to chide us, as He did His disciples. He said, "I will never leave thee, nor forsake thee' (Heb. 13:5). Cannot we believe His promises?

He Has Not Failed

We could give many examples of how the Lord applies promises in a personal way to a Christian. When the writer first went into full time service for the Lord, he had big ideas of becoming a great preacher. Mingled with this, however, often came fears that we might not be able to continue in the work, because of lack of financial support. I had gone out doing evangelistic work without a salary, and with no guarantee of any kind from anyone. Meetings were held in school houses, homes, or vacant church buildings, as doors opened. One day two prominent preachers and myself were together, and one of them was telling of the wonderful meetings he had had in various places. Immediately there went through my mind schemes on how to become a prominent and great evangelist, too. About that time the conversation drifted to a box of cards on which were printed various Scripture verses. We each drew one from the box. The others read wonderful promises from the Word of God, but I slipped mine back into the box without reading it to them. It said, "And seekest thou great things for thyself? seek them not: for, behold, I bring evil upon all flesh, saith the Lord: but thy life will I give unto thee for a prey in all places whither thou goest" (Jer. 45:5). What a rebuke it was to me, but it also removed fear of lack of financial support as I sought to serve the Lord. By the last part of the verse the Lord definitely promised to take care of me as I sought to serve Him. That was over seventeen years ago, and He has not failed.

PROMISES, BUT ALSO THREATENINGS

The Bible is full of promises, but it also contains threats. To those who refuse Christ the Word pronounces punishment. There is the law with its thunder and lightning. Blessings were pronounced upon the children of Israel if they obeyed, but curses, if they did not. To the Christian who lives for self and the world, there is the promise of salvation, but yet so as by fire. All his works will be burned (I Cor. 3:12-15). We would advise all unsaved to flee to Christ, and to the saved we would say, "Be obedient children, and rejoice in the Lord and His promises."

"BY THESE YE MIGHT BE PARTAKERS"

We believe the expression "by these" refers back to exactly the same things as the expression "whereby" in the first part of the verse. It is by His divine power, and by our call by Him, and our knowledge of Him, that we become partakers of the divine nature. The promises do not give us the new nature, but faith in these promises will cause us to grow more Christ-like and so manifest the new nature. "Having therefore these promises, dearly beloved, let us cleanse ourselves from all filthiness of the flesh and spirit, perfecting holiness in the fear of God" (II Cor. 7:1).

"PARTAKERS"

The Greek word here translated "partakers" is often found in the New Testament. It is also translated as "companion," "partner," and "fellowship." Perhaps the simplest translation would be "sharer;" "sharers of the divine nature." In I Pet. 4:13 we read "partakers of Christ's sufferings," and in I Pet. 5:1, "a partaker of the glory." How closely this all links up with our Lord Jesus.

"PARTAKERS OF THE DIVINE NATURE"

As we noticed in connection with our last verse, "divine" means "Godlike." It does not, as often interpreted, mean that we are given a "God nature," but rather, a God-like nature. This is an amazing statement. When we become children of God we become "sharers of the God-like nature."

DIVINE POWER GIVES THE DIVINE NATURE

There is nothing in man whereby he can lift himself above the natural. If he is to receive a new God-like nature, he must receive it by the power of God. Before we could receive this new nature, the Son of God had to take upon Himself our form of manhood. God became like us, that we might be made like God. The divine one became partaker of the human, that the human might become partaker of the divine. He not only had to become man, but He had to die on the cross to pay for our sins, or we never could have become sharers of His God-like nature. Now the vilest sinner can put his trust in the Lord Jesus, and receive this God-like nature, and so become fit companions for our Lord.

THE OLD MAN AND THE NEW MAN

The Christian has two natures; his old fleshly nature and the new God-like one. The Scripture sometimes calls these natures, the old man and the new man. The old nature is what we have from our birth. It is prone to do evil. It is the only nature the unconverted sinner has. Some try to teach that when one is born again, and receives the new nature, that then he can and must get rid of the old. The Scriptures teach us that we can hold this old nature in check, and that we should consider it dead. Col. 3:9, 10 says, "Seeing that ye have put off the old man with his deeds; and have put on the new man, which is renewed in knowledge after the image of him that created him." Various exhortations in the Word indicate that this putting off of the old man and putting on the new, does not mean that we can be totally rid of the old, but it rather means to put it off the place of authority and prominence, and to put this new man in this place. We can keep sin from having dominion over us (Rom. 6:14), but we will not be wholly rid of it, or rid of our old nature. Only when we are at home with the Lord Jesus will we be free from sin and rid of our old nature. Then we will be like Him forever.

Give the New Nature a Greater Place

The Lord's desire is that we be more and more conformed to His image even now. This new nature should be given a greater place all the time. It will be fully manifested in glory. We see some of that glory now, but the prospects for the future are most glorious. Then that God-like nature will be manifested in all its Christ-likeness. We do not believe though that we will ever lose our individual identity. There will always be a difference between the Creator and the creature.

"Having Escaped the Corruption"

It is the divine or God-like nature in us that enables us to "escape the corruption that is in the world." This new nature knows no lust or sin, and as we submit to it, rather than to our old nature, we escape the pollutions of the world. With divine power to aid us and a divine nature to resist evil, there really is no excuse for a child of God to be again entangled in the pollutions of this world (II Pet. 2:20). Let us show that we really possess a God-like nature by keeping ourselves unspotted from the world (James 1:27). This is the only way we can prove to the world that we have this divine nature.

"Escaped"

This part of our verse is written in the past tense, "Having escaped the corruption that is in the world." Chapter 2:20 tells us that it is possible to be entangled in it again. Some seem hardly to have escaped it at all. If we are to be able to keep clear, we must find refuge in Christ.

Christ Did Not Escape

Christ could not escape; He had to go to the cross. They taunted Him, "He saved others; himself He cannot save" (Mark 15:31). They were wrong in that they questioned His power to come down from the cross, but if He would save us, He could not come down from the cross. Only through Him and His sacrifice on the cross are we able to escape the corruptions that are in the world.

Lot Escaped

Lot escaped from Sodom and all its corruption, but he had to flee. His wife looked back; her heart was there; she turned into a pillar of salt. His daughters escaped the city, but they did not escape its corruptions.

The Children of Israel Escaped

The children of Israel escaped the slavery of Egypt. They were protected by the blood sprinkled on the door posts, and then escaped by passing through the Red Sea. Their passage through the Sea speaks of our passage through death, burial and resurrection, thus putting a separation between us and the world.

Many Have Escaped

Many thousands "have escaped the corruption that is in the world" through fleeing to Christ. We know a gambler who escaped, also a wicked infidel who escaped from his sin and infidelity by fleeing to Christ. We know a man who spent seven Christmases in a row in jail because of drink and thievery; he too escaped. We know another who continually blasphemed God and Christ, who escaped this corruption. We know a woman who was a saloon keeper's daughter, and another who was the pianist at worldly dances; both of these escaped to Christ. We could go on, but may we ask, "Have you too escaped by fleeing to Christ the deliverer?"

"Corruption that is in the World"

Is this world corrupt? We see it on every side. We hear much of corruption in politics. We even hear of judges being bribed. The taverns and gambling dens are full. Fornication, adultery, and kindred pollutions are very common. Man's thoughts are corrupt, his tongue is corrupt, his hands also. A heart surrendered to the divine nature, and strong faith in the promises of God will deliver us from the corruptions that are in the world.

"Through Lust"

It is the lust of the human heart which brings "the corruption that is in the world." "Lust" is an unlawful desire for worldly things and pleasures, and also unlawful coveting for satisfaction of the passions. The new nature stands opposed to all this lust and corruption, but the old nature being weak craves it. It is our bounden duty to hold down these cravings of this old nature, and heed the voice of the new. Peter says in I Peter 4:2, "That he no longer should live the rest of his time in the flesh to the lusts of men, but to the will of God."

Love Not the World

The "new man" in a Christian cannot enjoy the world. If a Christian permits his old nature to drag him into it, he will be a very unhappy man. His new nature will keep him from enjoying the world, and his old nature will keep him from enjoying the Lord. So let us be wise and not grasp for the world, its pleasures, its wealth, its ambitions, but let us seek to love and to live for the Lord. "But thou, O man of God, flee these things; and follow after righteousness, godliness, faith, love, patience, meekness" (I Tim. 6:11). "Love not the world" (I John 2:15-17).

IV

COURAGE AND KNOWLEDGE

(II Peter 1:5)

1:5 "And besides this, giving all diligence, add to your faith virtue; and to virtue knowledge."

The first four verses of our chapter tell of the many blessings we receive from the hand of the Lord. The third verse speaks of the divine power by which has been given to us all things that pertain to life and godliness. The fourth verse tells of the many exceeding great and precious promises, and how we have been made partakers of the divine nature. Now verses 5, 6 and 7 tell us that because of these blessings. we should give forth every effort to develop a strong Christian character. Faith is assumed, without which nothing else could or would follow. Out of this faith we are to develop a string of seven lovely characteristics. It is pictured as our responsibility to see to it that these excellencies are forthcoming. He has done so much for us and certainly, we should do what we can to help along in the situation. "For this very reason *do your best* to add to your faith manliness, and to manliness knowledge" (Montgomery translation).

"Giving All Diligence"

"Diligence" is a word which Peter often uses. In II Pet. 1:10 we have, "Give diligence to make your calling and election sure"; and in II Pet. 3:14, "Be diligent that ye may be found of him in peace, without spot and blameless." The word translated "endeavour" in II Pet. 1:15 is the same word in the Greek. He also uses it in I Pet. 1:10.

What Is Diligence?

The first thought in the word translated "diligence" is haste or speed. So we could translate our verse, "Besides this, giving all haste, add to your faith virtue." It also has the sense of earnestness, and applying ourselves to a matter with all effort and zeal. It further speaks of active, close, steady application to any matter.

Slothful Christians

With many Christians there is a great contrast between their business life and their spiritual life. In business matters they are all zeal and ardor, but in matters of the Lord they are very slow, lax, and careless. There is order in the office, but disorder in the meetings of the church. It is indeed sad to see some Christians consume their energies and time on trifles, and show no diligence in the things of God. So many are like the wicked servant of Mat. 25:24-30, who had a talent given him by his Lord, but hid it in the ground instead of using it to gain other talents.

Diligence Will Succeed

If all Christians were diligent in their Christianity what a blessing it would be. If they were all awake and looking for opportunities to speak for Christ, who knows how many souls would be won in a short time. How alert a salesman is to find prospects for his goods. We need more Christians with the same alertness. We need Christians who dare venture for Christ. Our portion especially mentions diligence in connection with the development of Christian character. We need a fixed purpose to become Christ-like and to battle against sin in ourselves. Diligence makes for growth spiritually, just as physical exercise causes our muscles to grow and to become strong. A diligent Christian, who starts out with Christ and trusts Him for all things is sure to be a successful Christian. One has said, "If Christianity is worth anything, it is worth everything." Let us put our all into it. If the virtues of this and the next two verses are to be attained, we must give "all diligence." They cannot be attained without a struggle.

"Add To Your Faith"

The word translated "add" in our verse is a long one in the original. It literally means "furnish beside." It is a term usually applied to music, and refers to different parts of a band or choir. "Faith" would be the leader of the choir and each virtue, like a member of it, or a part of a grand song. "Add in your faith" would be better than "to your faith." A good translation would be "provide in your faith, virtue, etc." To our faith we are to add one excellency after another, as a builder adds stone to stone in a building. Perhaps it would be better to picture it as growth, as a plant adds cell to cell. The apostle desires that we be like a growing tree with faith as the seed from which the other virtues spring.

"Faith"

All the excellent qualities which the Lord desires us to provide are based on faith. Faith is assumed to be in each of Peter's readers This is the foundation stone of Christianity. Faith in the Lord Jesus is what brings salvation to us; without it none are Christians at all. Without faith there is no beginning of life, and consequently, no further growth. However, faith does not stop with salvation; it should continue on and grow, and from it should bud all other Christian virtues. Faith not only links a sinner to Christ, but it gives him power to develop other excellencies. It is the foundation on which the other virtues are built. We should not be content with the foundation alone; we all want a lovely superstructure.

More About Faith

Faith is a very important subject and what could be written on it is endless. We find it everywhere in the New Testament, also in the Old Testament, only there the word"trust" is used more often to express the same thought. God makes it the beginning, because its opposite, "unbelief," in Adam and Eve was the beginning of sin. It is the beginning naturally too. A child puts faith in his parents before he learns to walk or to talk. Faith in God is to put confidence in His Word and work. One has described it as a telescope which brings near the glories of heaven. If faith is strong we will be able to overcome the world, sin, and the devil.

"Add To Your Faith Virtue"

The first of the seven virtues which are to bud out of faith is "virtue." The word "virtue" has degenerated to mean mostly just "chastity." We also apply the word to any lovely characteristic. For instance we say, "That man has many virtues," meaning "good qualities." It originally meant manliness, courage, valor, vigor or energy. It has also been described as "Christian fortitude" or "energetic faith." A word which we believe translates it quite accurately is "pluck." How badly we need plucky Christians.

FAITH, VIRTUE, KNOWLEDGE

Some might wonder why virtue is the first excellency we are asked to add to our faith. Many would put knowledge first, but Peter puts it second. Much knowledge without manliness or courage to speak and to live for Christ is of little value. Faith should affect our lives before we can acquire great knowledge of the things of the Lord. Courage can be quickly acquired and used after salvation, but knowledge is a much slower process. One may know very little of the Bible and yet speak for Christ and live for Him too. One man could neither read nor write when he was converted through John 3:16. He quickly memorized the verse and went to all his friends, told them of his salvation, then quoted and simply explained John 3:16. The Lord used this to the salvation of some.

A COURAGEOUS CHRISTIAN

An illiterate man was saved and then taught to read the Bible by his wife. He was one of the bravest Christians we ever knew. Often, when he saw a group of people, he would stop the truck which he drove and preach to them out of it. We have known him to stand up in a restaurant and preach to all the diners. One trick he sometimes did, which we did not consider too wise, but surely manifested courage, was as follows: He would get into a small town and just as night fell, he would stand in a dark place with a megaphone and cry out "fire, fire." Crowds would quickly come from everywhere and ask, "Where is the fire?" He would say, "The fire is down in hell and if you do not want to land there, flee to the Lord Jesus Christ." And then he would preach the gospel to them. We first made his acquaintance years ago, but he is still at it. We recently heard that he was down in Florida with a car and a loud speaker telling the story of salvation to all he could reach. No doubt the dear man has greatly increased in knowledge by now, but we doubt if he could increase in bravery from the very first. Knowledge is excellent to add to courage, but alone, apart from courage, it is quite useless.

Historical Heroes

All great men of God were men of courage. This is true of historical heroes as well as Biblical. Martin Luther was a brave man. He did not hesitate to nail his 99 articles on the church door at Wittenburg. He was fearless as he stood before the German court. Many missionaries, like David Livingstone, were not frightened by wild beasts or fierce savages. To these names could be added multitudes who dared, like Daniel, to stand for God.

Biblical Heroes

Almost every Bible character of any note demonstrated great bravery. Think of Abraham, how he dared leave his home city, Ur of Chaldees, and go to a land which he knew not. Think of Elijah, who dared tell wicked Ahab of the drought which was coming, and then face him again and all the prophets of Baal after those terrible three and a half years. Besides Daniel, think of his three friends who refused to bow before Nebuchadnezzar's image even though in danger of the fiery furnace. Then we could mention Joseph, Joshua, David, and many other Old Testament men.

New Testament Heroes

The New Testament too abounds with accounts of real heroes of faith. John the Baptist feared not the wrath of Herodias and king Herod, even though it meant imprisonment and death. There never were more valiant men than Peter, Paul, and the other apostles. Paul lists some of the things he had to undergo in II Cor. 11. As in all other excellencies, none ever exceeded the Lord Jesus in this one. He set His face like a flint to go to Jerusalem and the cross.

Early Christians

It took real courage for the early Christians to trust Christ. To do so meant persecution, perhaps bodily injury, imprisonment, or even death. We see examples of this in the book of Acts and also in later church history. Some could not be intimidated by the threat of death, nor could anything stop them from living for Christ and witnessing for Him. Some were ordered not to speak or to teach in the name of the Lord Jesus, but like Peter and the other apostles, they replied, "We ought to obey God rather than men" (Acts 5:29).

COURAGE TODAY

Many things require Christian courage today. It takes a manly man to follow Christ. The world offers many allurements and temptations, and it takes courage to say "No." Moses had opportunity to be a great man in Egypt. His fleshly nature would say, "Moses, take it," but he had the courage to say "No," and to choose to serve the Lord and His people (Heb. 11:24-26). No doubt it was a difficult decision to make, but he chose against the flesh and the world. If we would be well pleasing to the Lord we too must deny self and walk with Him.

OTHER THINGS WHICH REQUIRE COURAGE

Unexpected trials come; we must learn to bear up under these bravely. Satan will at times thrust in his fiery darts to hinder us. It may be necessary to endure difficulties, sickness, and pain. The Lord may call us to some hard and difficult service. We must bravely go forward in spite of any hindrance or danger.

COWARDICE

Many Christians are too cowardly to witness for Christ, or to live for Him. Such are lowly esteemed by the Lord, and will miss great reward in eternity. "The fear of man bringeth a snare" (Prov. 29:25). It was this fear of man that caused Pilate to condemn the Lord Jesus. It was this also that caused Peter to deny Him. It is this same fear of man which causes many to fail utterly in their Christian life. One has said, "Christianity today is the home of the sick and disabled, rather than the home of the brave and the strong." "The wicked flee when no man pursueth: but the righteous are bold as a lion" (Prov. 28:1).

STRONG FAITH PRODUCES BRAVERY

Strong faith will naturally inspire bravery. It knows that the Lord is in all, behind all, and above all. It also knows that "all things work together for good to them that love God" (Rom. 8:28). Faith assures us that in the end all our enemies will be defeated, and in Christ we already have the victory. It is the weak faith that says, like Jacob, "All these things are against me" (Gen. 42:36). The strong faith says, "I can do all things through Christ which strengtheneth me" (Phil. 4:13).

"Add — To Virtue Knowledge"

This is the third time in these first five verses that Peter brings in knowledge. In verses 2 and 3 he speaks of knowing God and our Lord Jesus Christ. It is first of all necessary to know Christ in this personal way. To this knowledge of Christ we must add a knowledge of His Word, and we believe it is this aspect of knowledge which we have in our fifth verse. We must first of all be brave Christians to speak and to live for Christ, but it is likewise very important to have a good understanding of the Word and spiritual matters. Many of the Lord's people do not read the Bible nearly enough, and consequently do not know it as they should. Too many depend almost entirely upon the preacher; they seldom study the Word for themselves. When the preacher goes wrong, which does sometimes happen, they go wrong with him. Every Christian should seek to have a thorough knowledge of the whole Bible. As time goes by, we should find new heights and depths and breadths in the wonderful Word of the Lord.

We Must Know the Word to Know His Will

If we do not know the Word of God, we cannot know the will of God for our lives. We cannot live for Him unless we know from the Word how He expects us to regulate our lives. Some, however, seem content merely to know the Word, and make no attempt to live according to it. The main purpose in knowing the Word is that we might know how to live to please Him. Our every step should be guided by His Word. As we are ready to act on the Word, the Lord will enlighten us further as to its meaning. "If any man will do his will, he shall know of the doctrine" (John 7:17).

V

SELF-CONTROL, ENDURANCE, GODLINESS

(II Peter 1:6)

1:6 "And to knowledge temperance; and to temperance patience; and to patience godliness."

In this verse we have three more excellencies brought before us. We have temperance or self-control, patience, and godliness. It is well to notice how the apostle links these virtues together. Each one is attached to the preceding one and all attached to faith. Without faith none of these things would be of any avail. Faith is the foundation on which the superstructure is built. To have a finished building we must have all the different parts of the superstructure. To have a well rounded Christian character, we need every one of the excellencies of verses 5-7.

"To Knowledge Temperance"

In present day usage temperance is usually linked with refraining from drinking intoxicating liquors. The original use of the word refers to self-control in any matter. Of course it is important that we use self-control in connection with intoxicating liquors. A self-controlled Christian will not be a drunkard, nor will he be a glutton. In fact self-control forbids excesses of any kind. It will put a check on the lips; there will be no torrent of anger or rage. We will be able to govern our mirth and restrain our fears. All our fleshly lusts will be held in submission. In fact, we will have the mastery over every evil inclination.

Self-Control in All Things

It is often necessary to use self-control in things which are not in themselves wrong. To have a nice home or garden surely is not wrong, yet we need to be on guard lest these things overwhelm us, and hinder our service for Christ. Some put so much time into these things that they have little time to attend meetings, read the Bible, visit the sick, etc. Many let their secular employment bring them to penury spiritually. Automobiles seem to be almost a necessity these days, but unless a Christian uses restraint a car can be a hindrance. Bodily exercise is of some profit (I Tim. 4:8) and we would not deny an indoor worker the privilege of some form of physical pastime, but even in this, self-control is needed. Ball games, golf, or even chess can be a hindrance to one spiritually. This world's pleasures can quickly drown one spiritually. Many today are "lovers of pleasures more than lovers of God" (II Tim. 3:4).

Food and Clothing

We need also to restrain self in connection with food and clothing. We have already mentioned gluttony. Some are not guilty of over eating, but my how they love dainties. One doctor said, "Many people dig their own graves with their teeth." As to clothing one has said, "Some people are like birds of paradise. Their feathers are worth more than their carcases." It is not wrong to have good neat clothing, but let us not go in for finery. May our characters be better than our clothing.

Knowledge and Self-Control

In I Cor. 8:1 we read, "Knowledge puffeth up." There is a danger of even knowledge of the Word puffing us up, so we need self-control to keep humble. Sometimes the lust for knowledge may cause one to lose self-control. We see this with Eve in the garden of Eden. Satan tempted her with the tree of the knowledge of good and evil. "And when the woman saw that the tree was good for food, and that it was pleasant to the eyes, and a tree to be desired to make one wise, she took of the fruit thereof, and did eat" (Gen. 3:6). Her lust for this knowledge caused her to lose her self-control.

Solomon and Self-Control

Solomon was a very wise man. His books, Proverbs, Ecclesiastes, and the Song of Solomon show this beyond a doubt. Yet love of many women caused him to fall into idolatry. With all his knowledge, sexually he lacked self-control. This has been the downfall of many in our time too. Let us be very careful not to fall into this pit. Solomon himself warns of this danger in Prov. 5 and 7.

The Athlete and Self-Control

Paul says in I Cor. 9:25, "And every man that striveth for the mastery is temperate in all things. Now they do it to obtain a corruptible crown; but we an incorruptible." In this connection Paul is speaking of the runners in a race and how they train themselves for the great event. We all know how an athlete in training refrains from smoking and drinking and other excesses. Also how he seeks to get the proper amount of sleep and exercise. The Christian too, is running a race, but a far more important one, and it is far more important that he keep under his body and bring it into subjection (I Cor. 9:27). If we do not, we will not run well, and will not receive the incorruptible crown.

Learn To Say "No"

One of the greatest parts of self-control is the ability to say "no." First of all we must say "no" to ourselves, to every sinful thought and passion. Then Satan too, must hear it. He will do his utmost to hinder our testimony for Christ, but we must resolutely refuse to do his bidding. Perhaps the hardest thing is to say "no" to sinful companions or fellow workmen. A young Christian when in the army was terribly harrassed by his fellow soldiers. They said one day they would compel him to drink some whiskey. Nothing they could do would make him drink it. Finally they said, "If you won't drink it, we will make you smell like it anyway," and they poured the bottle over the top of his head. This is only a small part of what he had to take, but he was resolute in his determination not to walk in their sinful ways. He had real self-control.

Helps To Self-Control

If we are to govern ourselves firmly we will need the help of a stronger hand than our own. We will only be able to rule ourselves as we allow Christ to control us. If we permit Him to be Lord over our lives, He will give us power by His Spirit to rule over ourselves. This of course impresses us with the great importance of prayer. We must keep in touch with Him, or we will utterly fail. We would again impress our readers in this connection with the importance of Bible reading and fellowship with the Lord's stalwart ones. Our own determination to control self is also important to success.

"To Temperance Patience"

Out of temperance or self-control will naturally flow patience or endurance. If we lack self-control we will surely lack patience. Self-control will make us patient with others and cause us to bear trials triumphantly. Self-control will keep us from saying things which offend others, while patience will keep us from being offended when others say things unpleasant to us.

What Is Patience?

"Patience" here would perhaps be better translated "endurance." It has the sense of cheerfulness and hopefulness in it too. One might endure something, but be more or less irritated under it. It is not in this way that we are to endure, but calmly and cheerfully. It also has the sense of perseverance. Many things may arise to try our patience. Difficulty, pain, hardship, affliction, even insult may come our way. How will we behave under it? How to behave under persecution is the principal theme of I Peter. We must bear all these things with cheerful calmness. Waiting also demands patience. How hard it is to wait; it is much easier to go forward and to serve. "Rest in the Lord, and wait patiently for him" (Psalm 37:7). We must patiently go forward in our service even though the time seems very long, and the opposition fierce. One has defined "patience" as "Immovable sweetness mixed with inflexible persistence."

Faith and Patience

Patience is inseparably linked with faith. Faith is the root out of which all other excellencies, including patience, grow. Faith knows we are in the hand of the Lord, and that nothing happens apart from His will, so when trials come it is easy to wait for His deliverance. When one is laboring for the Lord, faith makes the servant patient, realizing that in due time the Lord will act. Faith has confidence in the wisdom, love, and power of God, and can abide His time. Someone has said, "Patience is nothing else but faith spun out. If you would lengthen patience be sure to strengthen faith."

Patience and Hope

Patience and hope are closely linked together. In Rom. 8:25 we read, "But if we hope for that we see not, then do we with patience wait for it." The stronger the hope in our soon deliverance by the Lord, the easier it will be to be patient under the trial. We read in James 5:7, "Be patient therefore, brethren, unto the coming of the Lord." As we hope for His soon coming and the realization that then all will be made right, patience is made easy. In the light of this soon coming, let us patiently endure all difficulties without grumbling or complaining.

Patience and Tribulation

Patience is a splendid virtue, but one not easily acquired. In Rom. 5:3 we read, "Tribulation worketh patience." We can never learn to be patient, or to endure trial and difficulty, until trials come our way. As trials exercise us and cause us to turn to the Lord for help, we learn patience. The most patient souls are usually those who have had many and severe trials. We read in James 5:11 of the patience of Job. Who ever had more tribulation than he? Have you an irritable impatient nature? It is well to pray to the Lord for patience, but do not be dismayed if He sends you tribulation in order to produce patience in you. The price you may have to pay may be great, but the results will be worth it. As we read James 1:3, 4, we conclude that the Lord considers patience as one of the topmost graces.

Patient Endurance

A great part of patience is endurance or perseverance in the things of the Lord. Many start something but soon get weary and quit. We need to be like Carey, the great missionary to India, who said, "I can do one thing — I can plod." We can learn a great lesson from a story told of Columbus. They sailed many days; all his crew were disheartened and urged him to turn around and go back. But he insisted on going further. All he would say was "Sail on, sail on, sail on." His perseverance discovered a new land.

The Hare and the Tortoise

As children most of us heard the fable of "The Hare and the Tortoise." They decided to have a race one day. The hare bounded off to a flying start, leaving the tortoise far behind. He laughed to think of the unevenness of the race. After running some distance, he thought, I will rest awhile and let the tortoise catch up a bit. He fell asleep and while he was lying there, the tortoise passed him. Later the hare awoke and wondered where the tortoise was; but decided to hurry and win the race. To his consternation, he was just in time to see the tortoise cross the finish line ahead of him. The persistent plodder won over the fleet, but spasmodic one. "Let us run with patience (endurance) the race that is set before us." (Heb. 12:1.)

WINNING THE RACE

If we would win the victor's crown, we must let nothing hinder us in running this race. In Heb. 12:1-3, Christ is given to us as one who patiently endured the cross and so has won the victory. He is now "set down at the right hand of the throne of God" (Heb. 12:2).

PATIENCE IS NOT UNCONCERN

Patience is not laziness nor unconcern. Neither is it indifference to sin or troubles in the world. It is concerned about error, and sorrow, and wickedness, etc. A patient soul is concerned about all these things, but they do not cause him to sour, or get discouraged, or to give up. He calmly endures all these evil things for Christ's sake.

PATIENCE NOT APPRECIATED BY MEN

Patience is a great virtue in the eyes of the Lord, but it is not highly appreciated by men. It is mostly a quiet characteristic and so unnoticed and underestimated. If you are looking for the applause of men do not desire patience for they will not praise it. However, if you are looking for the approval of the Lord, nothing will please Him more than to see you have it.

"TO PATIENCE GODLINESS"

The next grace mentioned after patience is "godliness." The more patient a Christian is the more godly he will become. Verse 3 tells us that the Lord has "given unto us all things that pertain to life and godliness." We are to do our utmost to develop this virtue along with the others.

What Is Godliness?

"Godliness" is usually thought of as "God-likeness," but perhaps it is rather "piety" or "reverence toward the Lord." One who is godly delights in, and has real communion with the Lord. He also is filled with reverential trust, or what the Old Testament so often calls "the fear of the Lord." Godliness is really an inward virtue, but it manifests itself outwardly by a life of service, and a desire to be Christ-like. This veneration of the Lord leads to worship and obedience. A godly person loves the Lord and loves His Word, and desires to live a life well-pleasing to Him. He is filled with awe at the thought of the greatness, majesty, and power of God, and makes living for Him his main occupation. To sum it all up, a godly person is a friend and a follower of God. Like Enoch, he is one who walks with God (Gen. 5:24).

Godliness Is More Than Religious Form

Godliness is more than formal worship. Many attend public worship of the church and profess to love it and the Lord, but evidently they know nothing of godliness, and some are not even saved. A godly person will love the public meetings of the church. He delights in the old-fashioned hymns, he loves to hear the gospel preached, and the Word expounded. He will be found at all the Lord's Day meetings and the mid-week prayer meeting too; but he will also manifest an adoration of the Lord and obedience to Him at all other times. His godliness is more than just a form (II Tim. 3:5), as we fear it is with many today. We have met many who could talk much about their church and preacher, but were completely mum when it came to talking about the Lord Jesus Christ. Sometimes the life too, of such, is far from what it should be. We have known of church members who could swear, and drink to excess, and gamble, and go out with other women, etc. Such may be religious, but not godly. They deny by their actions the power of godliness (II Tim. 3:5).

The Fear of the Lord

Malachi 3:16, 17 is a lovely portion. It speaks of those who "feared the Lord." This is practically the same as "godliness" in our verse. "Then they that feared the Lord spake often one to another: and the Lord hearkened, and heard it, and a book of remembrance was written before him for them that feared the Lord, and thought upon his name. And they shall be mine, saith the Lord of hosts, in that day when I make up my jewels; and I will spare them, as a man spareth his own son that serveth him." These who feared the Lord "thought upon his name." In other words, they did nothing without thinking of the Lord and His will. It also says they "spake often one to another." They loved the Lord and consequently their conversation, not only in public meetings, but wherever they met, was about the Lord. True godliness will show itself everywhere all the time. How did this fearing Him affect the Lord? First of all, He listened to and heard their conversation, and the book of remembrance tells us that He would never forget it. The 17th verse tells three precious things; first "they shall be mine;" then, they would be like jewels in His crown when He comes, and lastly they would be spared as a man spares his own son. Truly great things await those who fear the Lord. Let us answer this question squarely, "Am I a godly Christian? Is my main purpose in life to please Him?"

CHRIST AN EXAMPLE OF GODLINESS

If we desire to see a true picture of godliness, all we need do is look at the Lord Jesus. He never had His own interests at heart, but always those of His Father. He could truthfully say, "I do always those things that please him" (John 8:29). In John 8:28 He says, "I do nothing of myself; but as my Father hath taught me, I speak these things." And it was not only in speaking, but in doing, that He manifested godliness. His pure, kind, and lovely character all demonstrated godliness. If we are to be godly, we must be Christ-like. One has well said, "Godliness is Christ made manifest in the lives of His people."

VI

BROTHERLY KINDNESS AND LOVE

(II Peter 1:7)

1:7 "And to godliness brotherly kindness; and to brotherly kindness charity."

In this verse we have the two last excellencies in the chain which we are to add in our faith. They are "brotherly kindness" and "charity." The Revised Version invariably translates "charity" as "love." The word translated into the two words "brotherly kindness" is "philadelphia" in the Greek. This is usually translated as "brotherly love" (Heb. 13:1, I Thess. 4:9). So we could read our verse this way, "And to godliness brotherly love, and to brotherly love love." This of course is a strange expression in our language. There are two different Greek words which are translated "love" and our English Bible makes no attempt to distinguish between them. The one is "phileo" and the other "agape." The first denotes love or affection because of some natural tie, but the second speaks of love in a social and moral sense, which goes out to all humans. It is not too difficult to love those with whom we associate, and to whom we are bound in some way, but it takes a grander and a nobler nature to manifest true love to others. Whenever we read of the love of God the word "agape" is used, thus speaking of love in this grander broader way. Often the Christians are exhorted to love in this same broad, God-like way.

Other Verses with the Same Words

In quite a number of other places we have both of these words used in the one verse. This is true in I Pet. 1:22, "Seeing ye have purified your souls in obeying the truth through the Spirit unto unfeigned love (phileo) of the brethren, see that ye love (agape) one another with a pure heart fervently." The Christians were loving one another in this natural brotherly way, but the apostle desired that they love in this broader and greater sense, which would cause them to be Christ-like in their willingness to sacrifice for one another. In I Thess. 4:9 we have exactly the same two words as in our verse, "But as touching brotherly love (philadelphia) ye need not that I write unto you: for ye yourselves are taught of God to love (agape) one another." We could wish that the English language had two distinctive words to express these two different words, as had the Greek.

"TO GODLINESS BROTHERLY KINDNESS"

Some profess to love the Lord and to be godly Christians, yet do not show much brotherly kindness. It is inconsistent to profess piety, and yet to continually needle other Christians. Some are icy and cold toward those who belong to Christ, yet appear very warm toward the Lord. In our godliness let there also be brotherly kindness. In fact, true godliness cannot help but foster love toward the people of God. If one is sullen and surly, instead of kind, considerate, and loving, we may well question his godliness. Of course, brotherly love must not go so far as to condone evil in our brother and to gloss over sin. Godliness and brotherly kindness must go hand in hand.

BROTHERLY LOVE

We are exhorted to demonstrate brotherly kindness or love in many places in the Word. "Be kindly affectioned one to another with brotherly love" (Rom. 12:10). "Love the brotherhood" (I Pet. 2:17). "Love as brethren" (I Pet. 3:8). If we love the Lord it is natural to love those who are His for we have much in common. We have the same salvation, the same Father, the same Savior, the same nature, the same destination, and the same inheritance. The nearer each of us gets to Christ, the nearer we will be to each other. This brotherhood is a real union; because we are all linked to Christ, we are all linked to each other.

SHOW BROTHERLY KINDNESS TO ALL CHRISTIANS

Man by nature is selfish and does not care for anyone but himself. When he is brought to know Christ and receives a new nature, this old spirit of selfishness should go. We must not let differences of education, or position, or character, or ability, or nationality, hinder brotherly kindness to all Christians. "One is your Master, even Christ; and all ye are brethren" (Matt. 23:8). Differences of doctrine and contending for what is thought to be the truth is often a great hindrance to brotherly love. A spirit of sect or party can be disastrous. We can show brotherly kindness even though there is not complete agreement in all doctrinal matters. Remember, it was Cain who asked, "Am I my brother's keeper?" (Gen. 4:9). A Christian should always seek to help and serve his brethren, and not forget to pray for them.

Brotherly Love Our Responsibility

All the graces of verses 5 to 7 are pictured as our responsibility to develop. It is our responsibility to develop courage, and knowledge, and self-control, and patience, and godliness, but also brotherly love. Instead of noticing every little failing in our brethren, let us contemplate their excellencies and speak of them. Instead of belittling, chiding, and condemning, let us seek to serve them and soon love will increase, too. If the world could see more true brotherly love amongst Christians, no doubt it would be easier to win more for the Lord Jesus.

"To Brotherly Kindness Charity"

As we have noticed, "charity" is invariably translated "love" in the Revised Version. We also noted that it is a different word in the Greek from the one used in connection with brotherly love. It is "agape" rather than "phileo." "Agape" is the one almost always used when speaking of the love of God. It is love that goes out to all alike, related or unrelated, friend or foe. We should have a peculiar love toward the Christians, but because of the love of Christ flooding our souls, our love should go out to all mankind. "Agape" is not so much a love of personal attachment, but a love which seeks the welfare of its object, even though there is no personal attachment. It is doing good to others for no good reason in themselves. In other words, it is demonstrating the love of God. There is no English word which suitably describes it.

Not Stop with Brotherly Love

We must not stop with brotherly love, we must go on to love. Brethren in the flesh may demonstrate brotherly love, but not be men of love. Many fraternal orders pride themselves in their brotherly love, but that does not mean that they are men of love. One such told us one time that he would not sin with a fraternal brother's wife, but that he had no conscience about other women. Another fraternal brother might have had love for his fellow lodgemen, but he had none for me: he deliberately beat me out of $25.00. Beloved, we should have sincere affection for those in our immediate Christian circle, but let us be real men and women of Christ whose hearts go out to all Christians, and to all men. "As we have therefore opportunity, let us do good unto all men, especially unto them who are of the household of faith" (Gal. 6:10).

God Is Love

In I John 4:8 we read, "God is love." In what way has this, and is this, being shown? It is shown every day in nature. The Lord makes His sun to shine and His rain to fall on the just and on the unjust. His love in this respect is as impartial as the sun's rays, which shine on man's filthy dumps as well as on the beautiful gardens. His great love for all mankind is truly demonstrated in the giving of His Son. "For God so loved the world, that he gave his only begotten Son, that whosoever believeth in him should not perish, but have everlasting life" (John 3:16). He not only gave His Son to live in this world, but He gave Him up to die in our room and stead. While His love goes out to all mankind, He loves his own in Christ in a special way.

Results of Divine Love

I Cor. 13 tells us the kind of Christians we will be if this divine love rules within us. There in verse 4 we read, "Charity suffereth long and is kind." No matter how badly we may be treated, we will take it uncomplainingly, without any thought of revenge, and we will not be unkind in return. Verse 4 also says, "Charity vaunteth not itself, is not puffed up." True love will not push self forward, nor do a lot of boasting, and is not filled with pride. I Cor. 13:5 says charity, "doth not behave itself unseemly, seeketh not her own, is not easily provoked, thinketh no evil." Unseemly means in an unbecoming manner or indecent way. One with true love is not only and always seeking his own welfare, but has the interests of others at heart. Some are so easily upset and angered: such actions are not motivated by divine love. Let us not be of those who always think the worst of others; if we love we will always want to think the best. Verses 6 and 7 add other things which love does; "Rejoiceth not in iniquity, but rejoiceth in the truth; beareth all things, believeth all things, hopeth all things, endureth all things." Finally, in verse 8, it says that charity, or this divine love, never fails. Are these wonderful excellencies truly ours? Is this divine love manifest in all our words and actions? If not, we have not attained to the height to which the Lord desires us to rise.

More Results of Divine Love (Giving)

Charity is more than almsgiving, but it surely includes giving. God is a great giver, and one who manifests His love will be a great giver too. He will give to the poor, but also to the work of the Lord. He will give liberally, cheerfully, but discreetly. A sister recently presented Mrs. Nieboer with a $10.00 bill. She was not too well off and Mrs. Nieboer tried to dissuade her, saying, "You probably need this worse than we do." She insisted, however, saying, "Giving is not giving unless it involves some sacrifice."

Divine Love Will Aid All

If one has this divine love, he will seek to aid all classes of people. He will try to teach the unlearned, strengthen the weak, bring back the wanderer, as well as to encourage those who are going on well. Then of course, he will do what he can to bring the gospel to those near at hand and also to those afar off.

Great Importance of Divine Love

I Cor. 13:13 tells us that this charity or Christ-like love is the greatest thing in the world, even greater than faith and hope. It is the highest pinnacle on the ladder of grace; the crown of the Christian excellencies, the roof of the spiritual house. Paul says in Col. 3:14, "And above all these things put on charity, which is the bond of perfectness." Peter says a very similar thing, "And above all things have fervent charity among yourselves: for charity shall cover a multitude of sins" (I Pet. 4:8). Have we attained to this uppermost rung, which the Lord esteems so important?

Love a Commandment

Some think that this love is a desirable thing, and something we should try to cultivate, but they forget that the Lord commands that we have it. If it is not in us we are positively disobedient children. The Lord Jesus says, "A new commandment I give unto you, that ye love one another; as I have loved you, that ye also love one another" (John 13:34). Paul says, "Now the end of the commandment is charity out of a pure heart" (I Tim. 1:5). John says, "And this commandment have we from him, That he who loveth God love his brother also" (I John 4:21).

Love a Proof of Salvation

The first fruit of the Spirit is love (Gal. 5:22). If we do not see this first fruit manifest in some degree, have we a right to believe that the Spirit abides within? Contrariwise, if we do plainly see this divine love in one, we need not question his salvation. "We know that we have passed from death unto life, because we love the brethren" (I John 3:14). This love is also proof to the unsaved that we are true children of God. "By this shall all men know that ye are my disciples, if ye have love one to another" (John 13:35). "God is love; and he that dwelleth in love dwelleth in God, and God in him" (I John 4:16).

Love Is a Natural Fruit of Faith

Like all the other excellencies, love springs out of faith. If faith is strong, love for the Lord will be strong, and also love for our fellow man. Every virtue in this chain springs out of faith and should tend toward love. One has said, "Faith is the foundation, and love the culmination." Faith is the fountain, but love should be the stream which flows from it. Love should bring tenderness to courage, humility to knowledge, beauty to self-control, tenderness to patience, and sweetness to godliness. Just today we saw an apple tree almost breaking down with an abundance of fruit. Are we bowed down, laden with love and kindred fruits of faith? The Lord would love to see everyone of these wonderful links in this chain of graces in each of His children.

VII

FRUITFUL OR BLIND

(II Peter 1:8, 9)

1:8 "For if these things be in you, and abound, they make you that ye shall neither be barren nor unfruitful in the knowledge of our Lord Jesus Christ."

This verse contains the first of three great promises to those who have all the virtues of verses 5-7. It says that such will "neither be barren nor unfruitful in the knowledge of our Lord Jesus Christ." Verse 10 tells us, "For if ye do these things, ye shall never fall." Verse 11 states such will have an abundant entrance into the kingdom of Christ. What happy results we have from developing these excellent virtues.

"If These Things Be In You"

This is literally, "If these things are yours," and indicates something possessed permanently. The blessings are not for those who occasionally manifest some of these virtues, but for those who have them as an abiding possession. To be well-pleasing to the Lord, we need to be well-rounded Christians showing all these qualities. We have a wonderful position in Christ, but we must not be content with that, but must seek to develop the graces that flow from this position. To be merely content with our position is like unto a man being placed on a beautiful farm, only to sit around and say, "This is a lovely place to be." If he intends to raise any crops, he will have to get up and plow, and plant, and cultivate, and harvest. To develop Christian character is not easy work.

"Abound"

How wonderful it would be if each Christian had all the characteristics of verses 5-7 in rich abundance. If we were all filled with manly courage, what an impact this would have on the world. If all were bravely witnessing for Christ, the world would be shaken as in Paul's day, sinners would be convicted and brought to know Christ. Then if all true Christians abounded in knowledge, how wonderful that would be. Oftentimes Christians cannot answer an unbeliever, or silence a member of a false cult. A difficult circumstance arises, and they do not know how to act, because they do not know the Word of God. The Word is the Christian's sword, and only as he knows how to use it will he be a successful warrior for Christ. "Let the word of Christ dwell in you richly" (Col. 3:16). Then how wonderful it would be if self-control and patient endurance filled us; and also godliness, brotherly kindness, and divine love. All of these are extremely important. The Word everywhere emphasizes the last two. "And this I pray, that your love may abound yet more and more" (Phil. 1:9, also I Thess. 3:12, II Thess. 1:3). May we never be content with ourselves until we are overflowing, not with one, but with all seven of these glorious excellencies.

"THEY MAKE YOU"

These wonderful virtues in us will have a very desirous effect upon us. Two are specially mentioned in our verse. First, they will keep us from barrenness or idleness. We will be sure to "abound in the work of the Lord" (I Cor. 15:58). Then they will also keep us from unfruitfulness; we will be loaded down with the glorious "fruit of the Spirit" (Gal. 5:22, 23).

"BARREN" (IDLE)

The Revised Version has "idle" rather than "barren" and is better. No one could have all the qualities of verses 5-7 and be idle. The Lord wants us all to be workers for Him. Apart from this there would be no object in leaving us here. Everything else should be secondary to serving the Lord. Doing His will should be first and foremost in our lives. We should be like the cobbler who said, "My business is to serve the Lord; I fix shoes to pay expenses." Men work hard in this world to become wealthy, educated or renowned, and we should be equally zealous in serving the Lord.

SLOTHFULNESS

The end of idleness is always serious. In Prov. 24:30-34, we read of the slothful farmer whose fields were all over-grown with thorns and nettles, and the wall broken down. "Yet a little slumber, a little folding of the hands to sleep: so shall thy poverty come as one that travelleth; and thy want as an armed man." Many Christians are like that, sleepy, idle, poor. Just sitting idly by and accomplishing nothing for the Lord.

Asleep in Harvest

"He that sleepeth in harvest is a son that causeth shame" (Prov. 10:5). It truly is a shame that so many of the sons of God are asleep in this time of harvest. Souls are perishing all around us and most of the Christians are doing nothing about it. In time of harvest all hands on the farm are expected to do their share toward getting in the crop. "Son, go work today in my vineyard" (Mat. 21:28). If you are a son, the Lord expects you to do your share of the harvesting.

What Can I Do?

Some say, "I would be happy to serve the Lord, but what can I do?" If the seven virtues of verses 5-7 are yours, you will have no difficulty in finding something to do. Perhaps though a few suggestions as to what can be, and what has been done, will help some of our readers.

Personal Testimony

Personal testimony is one of the best forms of service which one can do. Opportunities for this abound on every hand. We are all constantly rubbing elbows with our fellow men, and they often throw the door wide open to speak a word for Christ. The writer has not always availed himself of every open door, but we can truthfully say, we have spoken to hundreds in a personal way and have seen some brought to know Christ as Savior.

Visitation

Visiting in the homes of the unsaved is a very fine work. We would suggest that for this you pick a partner and make it a point to visit at least one such home every week. There should be some point of contact and a definite date made if possible. After arrival swing the conversation as quickly as possible to the things of the Lord, and to their personal salvation. It may be possible to develop some of these visitations into home meetings. If they ask you back, ask them to invite in their friends and neighbors, and at a set time have a regular meeting in the home. We have had many meetings of this kind and the Lord has blessed.

CHILDREN'S WORK

Work amongst children is a very fruitful field. Did you ever think of a Sunday School or children's meeting in your home? Child evangelism classes and Bible clubs are very successful in many places. Object lessons can be easily made, and in some places lantern slides of Bible stories obtained. We have visited in the homes of Sunday School scholars, had the children sing a few choruses and recite a few verses, and then preached to all who were in the house.

OTHER SUGGESTIONS

Tract passing is a great work. We have passed out thousands on the street, door to door, at school houses, in jails, and hospitals. We have helped at open air meetings, and meetings in hospitals, jails, and infirmaries. We have conducted Sunday Schools and gospel meetings in country school houses, and opened up empty country churches. There is no end of opportunities for service if one has the will and the desire to do something.

HE WILL REWARD US

The world, and perhaps even our fellow Christians, will not appreciate what we seek to do for the Lord. Be our service ever so weak and lowly, the Lord will not forget (Heb. 6:10). He will reward for every word spoken for Him, and every sacrifice made for Him. "Well, thou good servant: because thou hast been faithful in a very little, have thou authority over ten cities" (Luke 19:17). Let us not make it needful for Him to ask us, "Why stand ye here all the day idle?" (Matt. 20:6).

"UNFRUITFUL"

The Lord Jesus cursed the fig tree which had no fruit to satisfy His hunger (Mark 11:14). What will He do with us, if we bring forth no fruit to His glory? You say, "He surely will not curse us." No, perhaps not, but He surely will not be well-pleased. He brings home the great importance of fruit-bearing in John 15:1-8.

In verse 8 He says, "Herein is my Father glorified, that ye bear much fruit." The way to bear much fruit is to develop the excellent virtues of verses 5-7. If these things are ours we will bear much fruit. We will manifest the fruit of the Spirit as recorded in Gal. 5:22, 23. We will be Christ-like and be well-pleasing to the Lord. If we know Christ, we are a good tree, and a good tree should bear good fruit. The Lord Jesus says, "By their fruits ye shall know them" (Mat. 7:20). If we bring forth no fruit to the glory of God, who will believe that we really belong to Him?

"In the Knowledge of Our Lord Jesus Christ"

To truly know Christ and yet be idle and unfruitful is contrary to the very nature of things. If we stand in the sunlight, we will surely reflect its rays. Just so, if we bask in the light of Christ, we will spread abroad His glories. We first get to know Christ at the time of our conversion. As we go on in our Christian life and develop Christian character, we will get to know Him better and better. As each of the virtues of verses 5-7 are developed and strengthened, we will also become more Christ-like and our knowledge of Him will become more intimate. A fuller knowledge of Him is the end toward which all these excellencies tend. We know Him, beloved; may we go on to know Him better and better.

1:9 "But he that lacketh these things is blind, and cannot see afar off, and hath forgotten that he was purged from his old sins."

Verse 8 tells of some of the blessings resulting from possessing the virtues listed in verses 5-7. This verse 9 tells what one loses by not having them. Two sad effects are listed. First, those who lack these things are blind and cannot see afar off; then they have forgotten that they were purged from their old sins. Such may not have fallen into immoral practices, but they have made no progress in their Christian lives. They do not seem to appreciate their salvation, and seem to have no joy in Christ. Perhaps there was a first flush of joy and gratitude, but Satan quickly weaned them away from the Lord and His ways. Worldly things loomed up as too important, and the struggle to make a good living too fierce and so no time was left to pray, and to read the

Word, and to attend services. So the Christian life became stagnant and went down instead of up. Consequently, instead of a strong, healthy Christian, we have a sickly, puny child. Some are like a vagabond boy adopted into a nice home and given every privilege, but one who really loved his old life, and haunts, and companions, and so never rose to the level of the others in the home.

"He that Lacketh These Things"

It is a sad fact that many of the Lord's people lack some of these virtues. One has said, "We might better lack an arm, or a leg, or an eye, than to lack even one of these characteristics." Yet some not only lack one, but every one of them. They are like hopeless cripples spiritually and no one seems able to help them. They do not seem to realize that their life as it is, is of no import as far as the Lord is concerned. Satan has blinded their minds almost as effectively as he has the minds of the unsaved (II Cor 3:4).

"Is Blind"

The Greek Word here translated "blind" is the one nearly always used for blindness in the New Testament. This is so whether speaking of natural or spiritual blindness. The word is an interesting one meaning literally "blinded by smoke." It does not always mean total blindness, but may also mean "dim-sighted." This is evidently so in our verse, as is suggested by the next expression, "and cannot see afar off."

Blind Christians

When the Scriptures speak of blindness, it usually refers to the unsaved. "But if our gospel be hid, it is hid to them that are lost: in whom the god of this world (Satan) hath blinded the minds of them which believe not" (II Cor. 4:3, 4). However our verse does not speak of the blindness of the unsaved, but rather of the blindness of some Christians. They are blind to the importance of spiritual things and the importance of developing Christian character. Perhaps when first saved, spiritual things appeared important, but the allurements of the world dimmed this vision, and so they became blind to the great and eternal glories which lie ahead. The world, the flesh, and the devil all unite to dim the sight of the Christian. When Satan loses a soul, he loses a great battle, but he does not stop his work. He immediately starts to hinder the usefulness of the one he has lost. This he does by exaggerating the importance of temporal things, and all too many fall into his snare.

Samson and Delilah

Samson was a Nazarite, separated, and consecrated to the Lord. The Lord gave him great strength and used him mightily. The Philistines and Delilah set about to deprive him of this great strength. Delilah, a type of the lust of the flesh, gets his head in her lap. She persuades him to reveal the source of his strength, and soon he is shorn of his hair, symbol of his Nazariteship, and his strength is gone. His decline is then rapid. He is soon in prison with his eyes gone, grinding corn as a slave. This has been the sad decline of many who started well, but faltered in their purpose to grow into stalwart sons of God.

"Cannot See Afar Off"

The Revised Version has, "He that lacketh these things is blind, seeing only what is near." Young's has "dim-sighted;" others "short" or "near-sighted." It is a sad and sorry fact that many Christians are near-sighted. They can only see a nice comfortable living, with a nice home, and a large car. Their delight and pleasures are all in the things of time. They have no thought of eternal things. They think "A bird in the hand is worth two in the bush." Such may have the assurance of salvation and know what they are saved from, but do not seem to sense what they are saved for.

Who Are Blind?

It was the failure to add the virtues of verses 5-7 that caused the apostle to say that some were blind and could not see afar off. If one has no courage to witness and to live for Christ, he is blind. If he has failed to study the Word and thus increase in knowledge, he cannot see afar off. So also is one who lacks self-control, patience, godliness, brotherly kindness, and love. "But he that hateth his brother is in darkness, and walketh in darkness, and knoweth not whither he goeth, because that darkness hath blinded his eyes" (I John 2:11).

Seriousness of Being Blind

We often stress the seriousness of the blindness of the unsaved, but is it not also very serious to be a blind Christian? Such a one will not lose his soul, but certainly he will be a great loser at the judgment seat of Christ. When we were saved, we were brought into the light, let us see to it that we walk in that light (I John 1:7).

Lot's Choice

Lot made a deliberate choice of the well watered plains of Jordan. This looked like the sensible thing to choose, but he did not consult the Lord, nor consider the fact that there lay wicked Sodom and Gomorrah. He prospered at first and became a great man in Sodom, but when these cities were destroyed he lost all his possessions, his married daughters and even his wife. His two daughters who were spared meanwhile lost all sense of morals in that wicked city. Even so it will be with a Christian, who instead of living for Christ, seeks only worldly advantage. Let us be wise and seek Christ-likeness rather than worldly riches, honor, or pleasure.

"And Hath Forgotten"

What a sad word "forgotten" is. To forget is a very common failure in man. A single injury is long remembered, but a hundred blessings may be quickly forgotten. But what could be more sad or more serious than to forget that happy day when all our sins were washed away? What lack of appreciation, what lack of gratitude to forget such a wondrous salvation. Many have received the divine life, but seem to be content to be merely saved and have no desire to grow in the things of the Lord. They have made no healthy progress in their Christian life because they failed to develop the virtues of verses 5-7.

"Purged from His Old Sins"

One of the chief purposes of our salvation is that the Lord may have creatures to fellowship with Him in glory forever.

However, that is not the only purpose. He desires that this fellowship start already in this scene. He cannot have fellowship with one who is walking in sin. When one is saved, he is "purged from his old sins." That means more than that sins are forgiven. It is literally "a washing off" or "cleansing" as in the Revised Version. "The blood of Jesus Christ his Son cleanseth us from all sin" (I John 1:7). To one who trusts Christ past sins are gone, and as far as salvation goes, present and even future ones are under the blood. We are saved by grace, but let us not make the mistake of some in Paul's day who caused him to say, "Shall we continue in sin, that grace may abound? God forbid" (Rom. 6:1, 2). A Christian may fall into sin, but, it is needless and serious for him to live in sin. Many provisions are made by the Lord to prevent this. He has given us His Spirit, a new nature, and His Word. Study of the Word has a cleansing effect on a Christian's life (Eph. 5:26, Psalm 119:9). If a Christian sins, the road to cleansing is in confession.

Let Us Be Thankful

Let us thank the Lord everyday that we have been saved and so "cleansed from our old sins." If our appreciation is right, this will be easy. Then this continual remembrance of this happy day will be a spiritual tonic to us. We will not then have a desire for the old sins, the lecks, the onions, the garlic, the melons of Egypt.

VIII

FURTHER BENEFITS FROM ADDING TO FAITH

(II Peter 1:10, 11)

1:10 "Wherefore the rather, brethren, give diligence to make your calling and election sure: for if ye do these things, ye shall never fall."

This verse tells us how we may be sure of our calling and election. If we cultivate the virtues of verses 5-7, we need not question our calling and election, and others will not question them either. We do not make our calling and election sure as far as God is concerned, but as far as we ourselves and other humans are concerned. Also, if these virtues are developed in us, there is no danger of falling, or stumbling, as the Revised Version puts it. Not that we need to develop these virtues to keep from losing our salvation, but cultivating them will keep us from backsliding. One who is called and elect will not lose his salvation, but he may lose much of his reward by falling into sinful ways.

"Wherefore the Rather"

The word "wherefore" refers back to verse 9. Instead of lacking the characteristics of verses 5-7 and being blind and near sighted, and forgetting that we are purged from our old sins, let us be diligent to make our calling and election sure, by cultivating them. How anxious the apostle is that his readers go on to fruitful Christian living.

"Brethren"

Unlike James, Peter uses the expression "brethren" but rarely. In five chapters, James uses it fifteen times. This is the only time we find it in II Peter and we have it only three times in I Peter. It is a term used very extensively throughout the New Testament. It is indeed a wonderful thing to be one of the brethren. It is well to remember that every child of God is one of the brethren. We should acknowledge them as such and treat them as such, too. It is a word which denotes nearness and dearness. The apostle desires that his readers realize that he loves them, and is not above them, but closely linked to them in the bonds of Christ. We like to think that the very chiefest of the apostles are our brethren in Christ. A man jokingly said to the writer one time, "Joseph, Joseph; are you any relation to the man they call St. Joseph?" We quickly replied, "Yes, indeed, he is my brother."

"GIVE DILIGENCE"

This is the second time that Peter exhorts his readers to diligence (1:5). How anxious he is that they strive, yea, strain every nerve, to develop these wonderful Christian virtues. The apostle desires that we really work at becoming Christ-like. Remember, the enemy is ever diligent to hinder us, and it takes real alertness to progress in spite of him.

"YOUR CALLING"

From God's side election comes ahead of calling, but from man's side calling comes ahead of election. From eternity past the Lord knew just who would trust Christ and He marked them out for Himself. Man knows nothing of this until he hears the call of the Lord Jesus saying, "Come unto me." When he answers the call and comes to the Lord, then he can be assured of his election. However, there might still be a question if the life remained unchanged, and there was no development in Christian character. There might be such a thing as Satanic deception or misunderstanding. But, when we have the calling and the effects of that calling in a life for the Lord, then we need not question as to the salvation. However, if there is no fruit for the Lord, if the virtues of verse 5-7 are lacking, we may well question the election and salvation.

"ELECTION"

Peter surely believed in election. In I Pet. 1:2 we read, "Elect according to the foreknowledge of God." Paul certainly believed in it too. He mentions it in many places (Rom. 8:28-31, I Thess. 1:4, II Thess. 2:13, 14, etc.). As we noticed in connection with I Pet. 1:2, election is usually linked with God's foreknowledge. Some have not been able to reconcile it with a free proclamation of the gospel, and so have rejected it, or reasoned it away. "Elect" means to choose and so may refer to choosing for salvation, or to choose to some special work for the Lord. "Calling" and "election" are both God's side of salvation.

God's Chosen Ones

It is a wonderful thing to be one of God's chosen ones. It is better to be elected by Him than to be elected by the people as a senator, or even a president. It is like a rich man going through an orphanage and selecting certain children to be adopted into his family. It is wonderful to know too, that when He chooses us it is not for a little time, but for eternity.

Not for the Unsaved to Know

When speaking to the unsaved, we should not mention election. It is enough to tell them that Christ died for them, and that they must trust and receive Him as Savior. When they do this and show that they have divine life by a changed conduct, we can be assured of their election. II Thess. 2:13 tells very graphically of the relationship between election, calling and salvation. "God hath from the beginning chosen (elected) you to salvation through sanctification of the Spirit and belief of the truth: Whereunto he called you by our gospel to the obtaining of the glory of our Lord Jesus Christ." You will notice that the election is by the Spirit, but the calling is by the proclamation of the gospel.

"Your Calling and Election Sure"

Our verse says we can and should make our calling and election sure. From the Lord's side the calling and election of one is always sure, but to the intelligence of the individual it may or it may not be sure. What is certain to God from the beginning is made certain to us by the effect. So our verse is not trying to tell us how to make it sure from the Lord's side, but how to make it sure to our own satisfaction and to the satisfaction of others.

We Can Be Sure

Not long ago a man said to the writer, "You talk as though you know you are saved. No one can be sure of that in this life." Others have said, "To be sure of salvation is pure presumption." We have tried to show such, scores of Scriptures which show us that we can know. Some would put the word "hope" into many verses of Scripture where it really is "know" or "surely." David, in Psalm 23:6, does not say, "I hope goodness and mercy shall follow me all the days of my life: and I hope I will dwell in the house of the Lord forever." He says "surely" and "I will." Such words of assurance are everywhere in the New Testament (I John 5:13 etc.).

Presumption

Of course, it is presumption to say you are saved, or one of the elect, when you never have been saved and are not living a life which proves you are saved. We fear there are many who think they are saved, while all the while they have no knowledge of the Lord at all. This kind of false confidence is ruinous, for one will not seek for that which he thinks he has. If one thinks he is saved when he is not, he will be proud and haughty. Does your life cause others to think that you are one of the elect?

Assurance

Sometimes we see one whom we feel confident is really a child of God, yet seems to lack assurance of salvation. This is injurious to a true Christian and hinders his testimony. He has no peace of mind or heart, and he is not happy, and how can he tell others to trust Christ, if he is not sure that he himself belongs to Him? When there is certainty the mind is set free, the heart is filled with thankfulness and praise to God. He can forget his own case as settled and can pray for and witness to others. Certainty of our election will have a tendency to make us brave in our service to Christ.

Proof of Our Election

I may recall my conversion and testify of this to others, but this will not convince others of my election unless they see a changed life as the fruit of salvation. When I live the life of a Christian, I prove that I am one. One who does not in some measure manifest the virtues of verses 5-7 really has no business claiming he is one of the elect. We know a tree by its fruit. We do not question that an apple tree is an apple tree if it produces apples. Neither do we question that a Christian is a Christian, if he brings forth a Christ-like life. If these Christian excellencies abound in us, we, nor any one else, need be concerned about our election. "The work of righteousness shall be peace; and the effect of righteousness quietness and assurance for ever" (Isa. 32:17). One has said, "We are one of the chosen, if we daily choose the will of God." Another, "To get out of doubting state, get out of idle state."

ELECTION AN URGE TO DILIGENCE

Some might let the knowledge of their election be a reason for sloth and idleness. They might say to themselves, "I am saved, one of the Lord's elect, so the rest does not matter too much." This is the very opposite of our verse. It says, we can only be sure of our election if we are diligent to serve the Lord, and seeking to develop a character like unto Christ. So the knowledge of our election should be a spur to diligence, not to slothfulness. Some seem to think that salvation is only a past work, and forget that it is a life obtained which must be lived. When we live for Christ, we prove that we have life from Christ.

"IF YE DO THESE THINGS"

Believing brings salvation, but the natural effect of believing, and the proof of believing is doing. That is why the Scriptures speak so often of doing the will of God. In Ps. 15:5 we read, "He that doeth these things shall never be moved." The Lord Jesus says, "Whosoever heareth these sayings of mine, and doeth them" (Mat. 7:24). "If ye know these things, happy are ye if ye do them" (John 13:17). James is full of the teaching that we must be "doers of the word, and not hearers only" (James 1:22). Our verse says, "If ye do these things (of verses 5-7), ye shall never fall."

"NEVER FALL"

Instead of "fall" the Revised Version has "stumble." The picture is of a man stumbling in a race. We do not believe it has reference to losing one's salvation. It refers to one falling into sin or becoming backslidden in heart toward the Lord. We believe in the keeping power of the Lord. He paid too great a price for the salvation of the sinner, to let one whom He has redeemed get away from Him again. Paul says, "I know whom I have believed, and am persuaded that he is able to keep that which I have committed unto him against that day" (II Tim. 1:12 also I Pet. 1:5).

We May Fall Like Peter Did

However, it is possible for a true Christian to fall into sin, even as Peter himself did. He denied his Lord three times, the last time with cursing and swearing. At that time he had not yet added to his faith, virtue, or courage. It was because of cowardice that he denied his Lord. If we are not cautious we may do the same. Perhaps because of this failing of his, Peter first mentions courage as needful to add to our faith. As we develop one after the other of these Christ-like virtues, there is less and less likelihood of our stumbling into sin, or getting away from the Lord in heart.

1:11 "For so an entrance shall be ministered unto you abundantly into the everlasting kingdom of our Lord and Saviour Jesus Christ."

Here we have another benefit derived from adding to our faith the virtues of verses 5-7. We will be given not only an entrance, but an abundant entrance "into the everlasting kingdom of our Lord and Saviour Jesus Christ."

"An Entrance"

The Lord Jesus says, "I am the door: by me if any man enter in, he shall be saved" (John 10:9). Christ is the door to heaven. Only as one puts his trust in Him will he be given an admittance there. Our verse puts this admittance as yet future, "So an entrance shall be administered unto you." When are we admitted into this kingdom? In some senses we are in it the moment we are saved, but we believe here it refers to the time of death, or of the coming of the Lord, whichever comes first in our experience. Our verse speaks of more than just an entrance into this kingdom; it speaks of an abundant entrance.

"Ministered Unto You"

The word translated "ministered" is the same as translated "added" in verse 5. As we add virtue upon virtue to our Christian character, so there will be added unto us an abundant entrance into the everlasting kingdom. Our rewards and positions in that kingdom are dependent on how we live for Christ down here.

"ABUNDANTLY"

We like the way the first part of this verse reads in the Revised Version. "For thus shall be richly supplied unto you the entrance into the eternal kingdom of our Lord and Saviour Jesus Christ." We hear some say, "Just so I make it that is all I care about." While some might not say this, yet there every action indicates that this is the way they feel about it. Do we want to be like a boat so badly beaten by the storm that it must be dragged into the harbor; or do we want to be like one with sails all set, colors flying, the band playing, and then to have a grand welcome party waiting for it on the dock? We surely do not want to get in "yet so as by fire" (I Cor. 3:15) with all our works burned up. We desire to go in sweeping through the gates as victors in our battle for Christ.

VICTORY AT DEATH

Some have thought of this abundant entrance as a glorious home going, a victorious deathbed. We have been at very sad deathbeds when unsaved have left this scene, but we have also been at some where the glory of heaven was very apparent. If our life has been one of devotion to Christ, we need have no fear of the dark valley. He will be with us to lead us safely through and home to Himself. One has said, "Every earnest effort to live for Christ is so much sunshine for the dark valley." If we covet this victorious deathbed, let us be careful to develop the Christ-like character as suggested in our chapter.

WELCOME HOME

We do not believe though, that our verse speaks of the approach to death, but rather of the welcome and the reward on the other side. We believe all of God's children will be welcomed home, but we also believe that those who have diligently sought to walk in His ways will have a more glorious entrance than those who were content to be merely saved. Those who have manifested this diligence will not only have an entrance, but an entrance "richly supplied" (R.V.). Such can say with the apostle Paul, "Henceforth there is laid up for me a crown of righteousness" (II Tim. 4:8). One has well said, "The crown worn there, must be won here."

"The Everlasting Kingdom"

The abundant entrance of the diligent is into the "everlasting kingdom of our Lord and Saviour Jesus Christ." Some have made great distinction here between the kingdom and the Father's house. As children in the family, fruit of Christ's work, all are on the same level, and will as such enter into the Father's house. However, in the kingdom, as subjects of the King, the position, rewards, and service will vary. These things are dependent on how we live for Him down here. In Rev. 3:21, the Lord Jesus says, "To him that overcometh will I grant to sit with me in my throne." When the Scriptures speak of His kingdom, it in some way always refers to the government of God.

"Everlasting"

Earthly kingdoms soon fade away and are gone, but the kingdom of our Lord is everlasting. "Of the increase of his government and peace there shall be no end" (Isa. 9:7). Some have thought of this kingdom as the millennium kingdom, but that is only for 1,000 years. The kingdom here mentioned is forever, it will never pass away. There will never be any revolutions, or elections in this kingdom; our Lord will reign over it throughout eternity. Satan will make one last desperate effort to overthrow it, but he will fail (Rev. 20:7-9). Whatever rewards we receive from Him in that kingdom will be eternal, even as the kingdom and the King are eternal.

Christ the King

It is nice to realize that our Savior will be the King in that kingdom. He is entitled to reign as the King not only in His own right, but because He has been the mighty victor. He has conquered sin, death, hell, and the grave. He has defeated the great impostor Satan, and will soon have him out of the way. "That through death he might destroy him that had the power of death, that is, the devil" (Heb. 2:14). Some have thought from

I Cor. 15:24-28 that the time would come when Christ would cease to reign, but we believe this refers to Him as the Son of man. As the Son of man, He shall some day deliver the kingdom into the hands of the Father, but as the Son of God, He shall continue to reign through all ages to come. "The throne of God and the lamb shall be in it" (Rom. 22:3). "His dominion is an everlasting dominion, which shall not pass away" (Dan. 7:14). Do we now see the importance of cultivating the excellencies of verses 5-7? Our position and rewards in this everlasting kingdom will be according to the way we have advanced in these virtues.

IX

PUT YOU IN REMEMBRANCE

(II Peter 1:12-15)

1:12 "Wherefore I will not be negligent to put you always in remembrance of these things, though ye know them, and be established in the present truth."

In verses 5-11, the apostle has been exhorting his readers to diligence. Now in 12-15 he tells how he too, as a servant of the Lord, desired to be diligent in his service for Christ. He felt it his special duty as long as he remained in this scene to stir them up and to establish them in the things which they already knew.

"I Will Not Be Negligent"

Negligence is an awful thing. A man neglects his business and his business soon goes. It is the same with a farmer and his farm, or even a home owner with his home. Some have discovered that neglect can even lose a wife and family. Many have neglected salvation and so were lost forever. Christians have suffered from neglect too. They have neglected their Bibles, or the meetings of the Christians, and have suffered spiritually. They have neglected to add the wonderful virtues of verse 5-7 and so will miss the abundant entrance mentioned in verse 11. As a servant of the Lord, Peter did not intend to be negligent in the work to which the Lord had especially commissioned him. "Feed my sheep,—tend my sheep." May we, who are the Lord's servants, not neglect to teach, to exhort, to warn the people of God. The Lord says to us, as He said to Peter, "Strengthen thy brethren."

"Always in Remembrance"

Christians need to be constantly reminded of the fundamental things of Christianity. They will not think a thing important unless it is continually brought to their attention. Peter feels that to bring things to the remembrance of the Christians is of vital importance. Some preachers think they must constantly bring something new to the people, but Peter was content to remind them of the old things. We must not forget that new converts are continually coming up and they need to be firmly grounded in the fundamental truths, lest they be carried away with every wind of doctrine. The fact that Christians must walk in the ways of the Lord, must also constantly be brought to their attention.

The Mind

The human mind is a wonderful thing. No one fully understands it. It is remarkable how memories are retained there. The remembrance of some things remains for years, while others are quickly forgotten. It is usually things which have been forcibly brought to the attention that stay in the mind. Other things would be soon forgotten if not constantly brought to remembrance. Peter desires to always remind them of the important things of Christianity lest they forget.

The Bible a Remembrancer

If we preach all the counsel of God, the Lord's people will be constantly reminded of all things necessary. We believe it a fine practice to go straight through the Scriptures, teaching things as they are brought before us and then nothing will be neglected. As we go through the New Testament, every important truth is stressed in its right proportion. In the Gospels we have the life of Christ, His death and resurrection. In the Acts and the epistles we have the purpose and importance of these events stressed. In some places one would hear very little of the coming again of the Lord Jesus; yet the New Testament refers to it hundreds of times. Other important truths are stressed over and over in order that we may not forget them.

The Lord's Supper

When the Lord Jesus instituted the Lord's supper he said, "This do in remembrance of me" (Luke 22:19). The purpose of this feast is that we might be constantly reminded of His person and His work for us. The bread reminds us of His body and the wine of His outpoured blood. There is little danger of a group of Christians ever going modern as long as they have this remembrance feast every week, as they apparently did in the early church. In one large church, it was customary to have the Lord's supper once every three months. The preacher hated that day and wanted to get rid of it. He said to his board, "How can we ever get rid of that blood religion as long as we have the Lord's supper every three months?" Of course, those who really love the Lord Jesus and believe in Him as the Son of God want to remember His work on the cross, and are very thankful for His shed blood.

"Though Ye Know Them"

When Peter says, "though ye know them," he is showing that he is not writing to young and unlearned Christians. He commends them for knowing the truth; they were well taught. In spite of this, he would stress the old truths, that they might have them indelibly impressed on their minds, and that they might walk according to them. "Then said he unto them, Therefore every scribe which is instructed unto the kingdom of heaven is like unto an householder, which bringeth forth out of his treasure things new and old" (Mat. 13:52).

"Established"

It is wonderful to be established in the truth; to know what you believe and why you believe it. False teachers will not be able to lead such astray; they are too well grounded. Peter desired that they might be yet further strengthened, so he goes over these important things again and again. He would have them be like what Paul writes to the Colossians, "Rooted and built up in him, and stablished in the faith, as ye have been taught, abounding therein with thanksgiving" (Col. 2:7).

"In the Present Truth"

Instead of "in the present truth" the Revised Version has, "in the truth which is with you." It is well to remember that when Peter wrote, the truths of the gospel were all comparatively new. They were new to both Gentile and Jew. When he said "established in the present truth," he meant that they were established in the truth of the gospel and in all New Testament truth. How thankful we should be that we know these truths.

Many all around the world, and even in our own enlightened land, do not know them. May we do what we can to propagate these truths. May we also be ready to walk according to them.

PETER WAS A GOOD SERVANT

This whole portion tells us that Peter was a good servant of the Lord. Paul says to Timothy, "If thou put the brethren in remembrance of these things, thou shalt be a good minister of Jesus Christ" (I Tim. 4:6). Peter did not serve for praise, or riches, but only for Christ and the good of the Christians. One has said, "A good servant will not seek the church's goods, but the church's good."

1:13 "Yea, I think it meet, as long as I am in this tabernacle, to stir you up by putting you in remembrance."

"I THINK IT MEET"

Instead of "I think it meet" the Revised Version has, "I think it right." Some have translated it, "I think it fitting" or "important." Peter felt that as long as he was left in this scene the best work he could do was to stir up the Christians to a strong faith and a godly life; not to teach them a lot of new things, but to remind them of the important things which they already knew. Peter was getting old and he knew the time of his departure was fast drawing near, and he wanted to use his time and gifts to the best advantage. He realized that after he was gone the only way he could be of service would be through what he had written.

"THIS TABERNACLE"

Peter here calls his body a tabernacle or a tent. When he says, "as long as I am in this tabernacle" he meant as long as he was in his body in this world. This must have been a common expression at this time because Paul used it too in II Cor. 5:1-4. "For we know that if our earthly house of this tabernacle were dissolved, we have a building of God, an house not made with hands, eternal in the heavens" (II Cor. 5:1). The body is a tent, a frail dwelling place, for the spirit of man. This tells us that the body is not the most important part of man, as the tent in which a man lives is not as important as the man who lives in the tent. Since the spirit is more important than the body, we should not seek the welfare of the body before the welfare of the spirit. Yet many, even Christians, make this very mistake. Folks swarm after one who professes to heal the body, but they do not swarm in the same way after one who preaches the pure gospel which aims at reconciling the spirit to God.

Strangers and Pilgrims

In I Peter 2:11, Peter calls the Christians strangers and pilgrims. What more fitting for strangers and pilgrims than that they live in a tent? We are making a journey through this scene. This is not our eternal home; heaven is our home. We will soon be through with this journey, we will pull up stakes, roll up our tent and leave it behind until the resurrection day. Of course, the Lord may come and then we will not leave our tabernacles behind, but our bodies will be made like unto His glorious body.

"Stir You Up"

Peter felt the need of stirring up the Christians. Out of love to the saints and a desire to fulfill the commission which the Lord gave him, he would warn them of the danger of forgetfulness and sloth. It is so easy to get into a rut, and come to a standstill. It is a real gift and much needed, to be able to stir others out of this condition of inactivity. Perhaps some of our readers are not as active in the Lord's work as they once were; perhaps they are not living as close to Him, nor as clean as at a former time. We desire to be a spoon in the hand of the Lord to stir you to renewed purpose and activity in His service. "Therefore we ought to give the more earnest heed to the things which we have heard, lest at any time we should let them slip" (Heb. 2:1).

"Putting You In Remembrance"

This is the second time Peter uses the expression, "putting you in remembrance" (vs. 12). We have it again in 1:15 and 3:1. He feels that the way to stir them up to a renewed life for the Lord was by reminding them of the vital things of their Christian faith. We should learn from this to stir up the people of God by the same method.

1:14 "Knowing that shortly I must put off this my tabernacle, even as our Lord Jesus Christ hath shewed me."

PETER'S DEATH

Peter knew that the time of his departure was fast approaching. The Lord had told him very plainly that when he became old he would die, and that his death would be swift and violent. The Lord had said to him, "When thou wast young, thou girdest thyself, and walkest whither thou wouldest: but when thou shalt be old, thou shalt stretch forth thy hands, and another shall gird thee, and carry thee whither thou wouldest not. This spake he, signifying by what death he should glorify God" (John 21:18, 19). Tradition says that Peter was crucified head downward, and that he requested this, saying he was not worthy to die in the same way the Lord Jesus had died. There is little question but that he was crucified. Peter was old now and he felt his predicted death could not be far away, and he was anxious to make the very best use of his remaining days. He went forward to meet this death with courage and dignity.

"I MUST PUT OFF"

We like the way Peter says, "I must put off this my tabernacle." It is like a man putting off a suit of clothes, or moving out of a house. There is no thought here of soul sleep; Peter moves out of his tent, but he lives on. Death does not end it all, nor does a man's soul sleep until the resurrection day, as some teach. When Paul speaks of sleeping in I Thess. 4:13-17, he is thinking of the body, not of the soul. He says in Phil. 1:23, "Having a desire to depart, and to be with Christ; which is far better." In II Cor. 5:1-8 Paul also talks of the body as a tabernacle, and shows that while we are here in the body we are absent from the Lord, but when we say good-bye to the body we are present with the Lord.

THE DYING OF SAINTS

Have you ever seen a real child of God go home to heaven? As the writer's first wife went over the line, you could see a look of amazement on her face as she beheld the glory of the Lord. She could not speak, but she pointed upward to heaven, to assure us that she would soon be at home with Him. The wife of a dear friend as she was dying said, "I see Him, I see Him," then she fell back on her pillow and said, "He is so precious to me" and was gone.

OUR TIME IS COMING

We cannot, like Peter, foreknow the time or manner of our death, but if the Lord does not come, we shall surely die. Someday a storm will come along and blow our tent down, or years will take their toll and it will become uninhabitable. The stakes of our frail tent can be quickly and easily removed. Peter's time was short, and at best, ours is not long. Someday our dear ones will call the undertaker, some preacher will preach our funeral sermon, and they will lay our bodies in the grave to return to dust. Ah, you say, "I have many years yet to live." You know nothing about it; today may be your dying day. In comparison to eternity, even 70 or 80 years is a very short time. Let us redeem what little time we have. Let us make living for Christ the main business of our lives.

> "Only one life, twill soon be past,
> Only what's done for Christ will last."

1:15 "Moreover I will endeavor that ye may be able after my decease to have these things always in remembrance."

In view of his soon death, Peter was not thinking of his own welfare, but only of the Christians whom he was leaving behind. His desire was that they might be firmly established and that he leave them a strong impression of truth which they would not easily forget.

"I WILL ENDEAVOUR"

The word here translated "endeavor" is exactly the same as the one translated "diligent" in verse 10. He would do everything in his power to see to it that the important truths were firmly embedded in his reader's minds, so that they might always be remembered. Do we show a similar concern for others? Is it our aim to propagate and perpetuate the great truths of Christianity? Is it our chief ambition to see souls saved and strengthened in the things of God? Will the world be better for our having lived in it? Will souls rise up in glory and call us blessed? Oh, beloved, these are the great important things in life, the things which are really worth while.

"AFTER MY DECEASE"

The word Peter here uses for "decease" is not the ordinary one used for death. It is "exodus" in the Greek, the same word used to name our second book in the Bible. If literally translated, it would be "a road out." It has the sense of "going out." In the book of Exodus the children of Israel went out of Egypt. Peter did not believe he would cease to exist at death, nor that his soul would sleep until the resurrection. He was moving out of his temporary house, and going home to be with the Lord. In verses 13 and 14, he speaks of the tent of his soul and in our verse 15, he talks of moving out of the tent.

TABERNACLE AND DECEASE

It is interesting to notice that Peter uses two words in these few verses which are also used in connection with the transfiguration of Christ. He writes of the transfiguration in the next few verses. Peter said to Christ at the time of the transfiguration, "Let us make three *tabernacles;* one for thee, and one for Moses, and one for Elias" (Luke 9:33). He uses the same word "tabernacle" in connection with his own body in verses 13 and 14. In our verse 15, he speaks of his own *decease.* In Luke 9:30, 31, we read, "And behold, there talked with him two men, which were Moses and Elias: who appeared in glory, and spake of his *decease* which he should accomplish at Jerusalem." This word "*decease*" is used only in these two places in the New Testament. Peter was present at the transfiguration, and the use of these two words just before he writes of the transfiguration, is convincing to us that Peter is surely the author of this second epistle.

A COMPOSED DEPARTURE

How calmly Peter speaks of his death. Though it was to be violent and painful, he calls it a departure, and manifests no concern or fear. He realized that it was a sweet release, "absent from the body, present with the Lord." Sometimes we see Christians today equally composed as they face eternity. They too counsel dear ones as to various things after their decease. Some plan their own funerals, and advise as to all things concerning the temporal and spiritual welfare of those left behind.

ARE WE PREPARED? ILLUSTRATION

An old story tells of a king and his jester. One day when the king was highly pleased with his jester, he gave him a wand saying, "You are the greatest fool in the world; if you ever find a greater one, give him this wand." One day the king was very sick and he said to his jester, "I am going on a long journey." "When are you coming back?" "I will never come back." "Have you made any preparation for this journey?" "No," said the king, "Absolutely none." "Here is your wand" said the jester, "You are a greater fool than I am." Everyone of us may at a moment's notice be called upon to make this long journey. Have we made preparations? If not, how foolish. If saved, let us be wise and live in the knowledge that at any moment we may have to say good-bye to this old world and face our Lord.

A GOOD INFLUENCE

Everyone leaves a mark on future generations, either for good or bad. If we are leaving a good impression on them by our counsel and life, we are leaving them a legacy of more value than silver or gold. If Christianity is to advance in the world it is needful that each Christian propagate it by lip and by life. One toils night and day to establish a reputation, another a business, yet another an estate, but like Peter, we should be anxious to bequeath to the world an influence which shall ennoble and enrich lives to the glory of God. If you influence one soul for good, he may in turn influence another, and that one, still another, and so you may start a long chain of good. "Now also when I am old and greyheaded, O God, forsake me not; until I have shewed thy strength unto this generation, and thy power to every one that is to come" (Psalm 71:18). May we have an ambition similar to the writer of this Psalm.

PETER'S EPISTLES

When Peter wrote this verse he may have been thinking especially of his written ministry, hoping that it would be an influence which would keep the important things of Christianity in the minds of Christians. He probably had no thought that his two epistles would be of help to all succeeding generations as well as to those to whom his epistles were originally written. Through his speaking he won many to Christ, but through his writings he won many more. While living, he influenced many Christians for good, but through his epistles he has helped many more. He lived for 60 or 70 years, but his books have lived for nearly 1,900 years. Like Abel, "He being dead yet speaketh" (Heb. 11:4).

WRITTEN MINISTRY

Many have done the church and the world much good through their written ministry. If any have this gift they owe it to posterity to write. Much that is written is of use to only the present generation, but some of it has lived on for many years. Think of the untold good done by books such as Bunyan's "Pilgrim's Progress," and gospel booklets such as "God's Way of Salvation" by Alexander Marshall. The only thing which stirs us on in our writing is the knowledge that some of the Lord's own have been helped thereby.

X

HIS POWER AND COMING

(II Peter 1:16-18)

1:16. "For we have not followed cunningly devised fables, when we made known unto you the power and coming of our Lord Jesus Christ, but were eyewitnesses of his majesty."

In verses 1-4 Peter tells of the blessings we have in Christ. In 5-7, he tells of the practical virtues which we should add in our faith because of these blessings. Now in verses 16-19, he brings in the glory of Christ Himself, as an added incentive to live for Christ. He tells of this glory by citing the wonderful event generally called the transfiguration.

"Cunningly Devised Fables"

No doubt, some in Peter's day, as now, accused the apostles of following cunningly devised fables. They preached of the power of Christ and His coming again, but some said they had hallucinations or wild dreams. Peter says, "Not so, on the Mount of Transfiguration we had a preview of His coming in power. We are not basing our teachings on fables, but on solid evidence." We trust we are all convinced that the Lord will come and reign.

"Eyewitnesses"

The apostles everywhere attested to the fact that they were eyewitnesses of Christ in His glory. John says in his first epistle (1:1-3), that they had declared unto them the things which they had seen, and heard, and handled of the Word of life. Paul, too, tells how he saw Christ in His glory on the Damascus Road. Matthew, Mark and Luke all tell the story of the transfiguration. It seems unlikely that so many men of good report would join together for the purpose of spreading as truth, that which was only a pretty myth.

Would the Apostles Tell Out Fables?

As we read of the apostles, they seem to be men of integrity, who would not be guilty of deception. They were spoken of as being "unlearned and ignorant men" in Acts 4:13. Such are not likely to be clever impostors. What did they stand to gain by broadcasting cunningly devised fables? They met opposition everywhere and were accused of folly and madness. As we read portions like Acts 3:6, we must conclude that gaining money was not their aim. If it was, they certainly did not get it. Instead, they were persecuted, imprisoned, and all but John met martyrdom for their convictions. Every unprejudiced man must admit that if the apostles were telling out cunningly devised fables it was because they were themselves deceived.

Who Wrote Them?

If the Bible is full of fables, as some say, who wrote them and why? Would priests write them when they so often condemn wicked priests? Rich men would not write them either, because they are everywhere spoken against. The Bible also condemns worldly wisdom, so it is not likely that learned men would write them. And what poor man would have the time or ability to so write?

Other Proofs of the Bible's Veracity

If the Bible is composed of cunningly devised fables, these fables have been most beneficial to man. Even today through faith in Christ and the Word, thousands of lives have been transformed from sin to righteousness. Where the light of its pages enter, not only individuals, but whole nations are lifted. This, no cunningly devised fables could do. The striking unity between its parts, and the fact that unbelief of a bitter kind has not been able to overthrow it, also prove it to be the Word of God.

The Transfiguration

We read of the transfiguration in Mat. 17:1-9, Mark 9:1-10, and Luke 9:28-36. Shortly before this time the Lord began to teach His disciples that He would go to Jerusalem and there be tried, condemned, and crucified. This greatly upset the disciples, and we believe one of the main purposes of the transfiguration was to assure them that even though He was to be crucified, He would rise from the dead and come again in glory to rule and to reign in His kingdom.

His Glory

Peter, James, and John were the three privileged ones with the Lord on the mount. We read in Luke 9:29 that as He prayed, He was transfigured before them. If we would pray more perhaps we would more often behold and also manifest His glory. This transfiguration was truly glorious. Light emanated from His body and caused all His clothing to shine and glisten. We believe this is the way the Lord appears now in glory and will appear when He reigns. For the most part, while here, His glory was veiled.

Moses and Elijah

While upon the mountain the Lord had two well known visitors from the glory. Moses and Elijah appeared and talked with Him. Moses died on Mount Pisgah, as we read in Deut. 34:1-7, but Elijah never died at all, but was taken to heaven in a fiery chariot (II Kings 2:11). Some have seen in Moses a picture of those who have died in the Lord, and in Elijah a picture of those who shall be translated to heaven without dying at the time of His coming. As Moses and Elijah appeared with Him in glory, so all saints who have died will appear with Him in His future glory, and also all those who are translated at His coming.

His Death and Glory

It is interesting to note that the three on the mountain spoke of the decease that our Lord "should accomplish at Jerusalem" (Luke 9:31). So on the Mount of Transfiguration we have the necessity of the cross emphasized as well as a picture of His glory. Moses represents the law. In his writings, he told of Christ's death and also of His glory. Elijah was a representative of the prophets. They also tell of Christ's death and glory. The Lord took Peter, James and John up on the mountain so that they might be firmly impressed with the importance and necessity of the cross, as well as have a personal testimony concerning His glory.

"The Power"

The transfiguration especially impressed Peter with two things, "The power and coming of our Lord Jesus." That these two things were especially intended by the Lord is evident from Mark 9:1. "Verily I say unto you, That there be some of them that stand here, which shall not taste of death, till they have seen the kingdom of God come with power." Peter says that this is exactly what he saw in preview on the Mount of Transfiguration. Some translate the expression "power and coming" as "coming in power." The Lord says just that in Mat. 24:30. "And they shall see the Son of man coming in the clouds of heaven with power and great glory." Some were questioning this coming with power of our Lord Jesus, for we read where they ask, "Where is the promise of his coming?" (II Peter 3:4).

His Present and Future Power

Christ often demonstrated His great power while here on earth. He had power over sin and sickness, also over the things of nature, such as the wind and the waves; He raised the dead and He Himself came forth from the grave. When He was about to ascend into heaven He said, "All power is given unto me in heaven and in earth" (Mat. 28:18). When He comes again His power will be demonstrated in even a greater way. In addition to the powers he showed when He was here the first time, when He sets up His kingdom, He will have power over the nations. He will sit on the throne of His father David (Luke 1:32). "He shall have dominion also from sea to sea, and from the river unto the ends of the earth" (Psalm 72:8).

His Coming

Peter says that when he saw Christ on the Mount of Transfiguration, he had a preview of Him as He will appear at His coming again. Some try to apply "the power and coming of our Lord Jesus Christ" to His first coming, rather than to His coming again. The word for coming here is "parousia" which is almost always used in connection with His future glory. We believe the three on the mountain had an actual sight of Christ as He will appear in the glory of His kingdom.

We Will Share His Glory

On the mount, we see not only the glory of the King, but we have the voice of the Father. We have Old Testament saints,

Moses and Elijah, and New Testament saints, Peter, James, and John. Some seem to think that the kingdom will be solely for the Old Testament saints and will be entirely Jewish. They say that the church is the bride of Christ and it is composed of a heavenly people, and so will have nothing to do with the earthly kingdom. While it is true that the Christians of this age are a heavenly people and the bride of Christ, we still believe they will share the glory of the kingdom. Peter, James, and John were certainly part of the New Testament church, and they were on the Mount of Transfiguration. The bride will share the glory of the bridegroom, just as a queen shares the glory of the king. In Zech. 14:5 we read, "And the Lord my God shall come, and all the saints with thee." "And the armies which were in heaven followed him upon white horses, clothed in fine linen, white and clean" (Rev. 19:14). According to Rev. 19:8, it is the bride who is clothed in this white linen, and it speaks of the righteousness of saints. In Rev. 19:11-16, we have the coming of Christ in glory, and these saints clothed in white linen are the ones following Him. We love to think that all of us, all New Testament saints, as well as Old Testament ones, will be in the grand army which will share His great glory at the time of His coming to rule and to reign in this world.

He Shall Rule

Many Christians do not believe at all in the coming again of our Lord Jesus. The Bible speaks of this coming hundreds of times in both the Old and New Testament. How such can profess to believe the Bible we cannot understand. Others believe Christ is coming back again all right, but believe it is only to wind up the affairs of the world and to bring speedy judgment upon it. They do not believe He will set up His kingdom here for a period as we read so plainly in Rev. 20, and all through the Old Testament prophets. All these Scriptures they explain in a figurative sense and spiritualize them. We believe they should be taken literally to mean that Christ shall actually sit on the throne of His father David in Jerusalem, and that He actually shall in person reign over the earth. Certainly Rev. 20 is an earthly scene, as we must conclude from verse 8. Zech. 14:4-8 certainly speaks of the coming again of our Lord Jesus, and then in verse 9 we read, "And the Lord shall be king over all the earth; in that day shall there be one Lord and his name one." This whole chapter in Zechariah, and many another, testify to the fact that the Lord will actually come and rule and reign.

1:17 "For he received from God the Father honour and glory, when there came such a voice to him from the excellent glory, This is my beloved Son, in whom I am well pleased."

In our last verse Peter states that he had been an eyewitness of Christ's power and glory on the Mount of Transfiguration. In this verse he tells of having heard the voice of the Father testifying to the fact that Christ was His Son and that He was well-pleased with Him.

"HE RECEIVED FROM GOD THE FATHER"

Peter here emphasizes the fact that Christ had received special honor and glory from His Father on the Mount of Transfiguration. Moses, the great law giver was there, and he had been greatly honored. Elijah was a great prophet, and he too had been greatly honored. Now God the Father was honoring Christ way above either of these. Moses and Elijah had both been great servants, but now the Father says that Christ was more than a servant; He was a "beloved Son." The Father also testifies to the fact that this Son always pleased Him, and that it was He whom the people of God should hear. Peter does not mention this last truth, but Matthew, Mark and Luke all tell of it.

"HONOUR AND GLORY"

The Lord Jesus says, "All things are delivered unto me of my Father" (Mat. 11:27). Also "All power is given unto me in heaven, and in earth" (Mat. 28:18). God the Father will gather together in one in Christ all things in heaven, and on earth (Eph. 1:10). Every knee shall bow to Him, and every tongue shall confess Him as Lord (Phil. 2:10, 11).

"Christ shall have dominion over land and sea,
Earth's remotest regions shall His empire be."

These truths are everywhere manifest in the New Testament. Especially John's gospel is full of things Christ has and will receive from His Father. Honor was given to Christ on the mount by the voice of the Father. The cloud which the Father spoke from probably was like the Shekinah glory which hung over the tabernacle and temple in Old Testament times. This cloud resting upon Christ would symbolize that all the glory of God was now centered in Him.

His Glory Is Our Glory

It is well to remember that His honor is our honor, and His glory is our glory. The Lord Jesus says in John 17:22, "And the glory which thou gavest me I have given them." As the bride of Christ, the church will share His honor and glory. This should keep us from seeking the paltry honors of this world, and cause us to seek only to bring honor to His name.

"A Voice — From the Excellent Glory"

The voice of the Father came to the Lord Jesus on two special occasions; first at His baptism and then at His transfiguration. Peter does not mention the baptism because he was not there. At the transfiguration he was there, and personally heard the voice of the Father as he especially mentions in the next verse. Our verse emphasizes that the voice came from the excellent glory. The Revised Version translates this the "majestic glory." No doubt this refers to the bright cloud out of which the Father spoke. Peter was thoroughly convinced by this voice and this wonderful glory that Christ was the Son of the Living God.

"This Is My Beloved Son"

God the Father says, "This is my beloved Son." Moses and Elijah were very high in the estimation of the Lord and also of the Israelites. Peter had said, "Let us make here three tabernacles; one for thee, and one for Moses, and one for Elias" (Mat. 17:4). In this way Peter thought to honor the Lord Jesus equally with Moses and Elijah. In Luke's gospel (9:33) we have the statement that Peter did not know what he said. The Father says, "This is my beloved Son," as if to say, "Peter, Moses and Elijah were great servants, but the Lord Jesus is more; He is my Son. He is far above the level of Moses and Elijah." So God the Father, the greatest authority, exalts Christ to the pinnacle of glory, far above any of the great men of God of either Old or New Testament times. This also exalts Him above the angels, because He never calls the angels sons in this way. "For unto which of the angels said he at any time, Thou art my Son, this day have I begotten thee?" (Heb. 1:5).

"My Beloved Son"

We do not wonder that the Father calls Christ, His beloved Son. We love our sons just because they are our sons, but we love them more when they are obedient sons. Christ was a most obedient Son. He was "obedient unto death, even the death of the cross" (Phil. 2:8). "Therefore doth my Father love me, because I lay down my life, that I might take it again" (John 10:17). It must have been difficult for Him to leave the glory of the mountain and to descend to the shame of the cross, but He was willing to go in order to please His Father, and so become the Savior of poor lost sinners. And for our sakes the Father was willing to permit His Son to lay His glory aside and die on that awful cross. How thankful we should be to such a Father and to such a Son. Their love for us must have been very great indeed, or they never would have gone to such extremes to save us.

He Loves Us As His Children

When we accept Christ as our Savior we too, become sons of God, and of course He loves all His children in a special way. In the sense that we are obedient children and well-pleasing to Him, could He say of us, "My beloved son" or "daughter" as the case may be? Let us forget the favor and applause of men, but let us seek to be the kind of children who are easy for Him to love. The more we are conformed to the image of His Son the more He will love us.

"In Whom I Am Well Pleased"

The Father was well-pleased with every word and every action of His Son from the manger to the glory. He was well-pleased with His birth, His life and His death. It pleased Him that His Son, by His life, showed the character and the heart of His Father. Perhaps more, that the Son was willing to lay down

His life as an atonement for the poor lost sinner. Way back in Isaiah 42:1, we hear the Father say of Him, "Behold my servant, whom I uphold; mine elect, in whom my soul delighteth." Christ could say, "I do always those things that please him (His Father) (John 8:29).

IS THE LORD WELL-PLEASED WITH US?

The Father is well-pleased with His Son and certainly we who are saved are well-pleased with Him too. We trust, dear reader, that the Lord is well-pleased with us as well. Are we like the apostle Paul who said, "Wherefore also we make it our aim, whether at home or absent, to be well-pleasing unto him?" (II Cor. 5:9 R. V.). Already, at his conversion Paul asks, "Lord, what wilt thou have me to do?" (Acts 9:6), and from then on he sought to do His will day by day. Oh, that we may be more like this dear servant of the Lord, or better still, more like the Lord Jesus Himself. He never sought to please Himself, but only His Father. The more we seek to please Him here, the more He will glorify us when we get home with Him in heaven.

1:18 "And this voice which came from heaven we heard, when we were with him in the holy mount."

We like the Revised Version of this verse; "This voice we ourselves heard borne out of heaven, when we were with him in the holy mount." Thus Peter lays stress on the fact that he, and James, and John actually heard this voice from heaven and so were not following any cunningly devised fables.

"WE HEARD"

In verse 16, he states that they "were eyewitnesses of his majesty." Here he emphasizes that they actually heard this voice and understood exactly what the Father said. In fact, the message of the Father was addressed to them. "This is my beloved Son, in whom I am well pleased; hear ye him" (Mat. 17:5). In Mat. 17:6 we read, "And when the disciples heard it, they fell on their face, and were sore afraid."

WE SHALL SEE HIS GLORY

John says in his gospel (1:14), "And we beheld his glory, the glory as of the only begotten of the Father." How favored these three, Peter, James, and John were, to actually see His glory and to hear the voice of the Father. We are not privileged now to see Him in His glory, but we can, as we read the Word, hear His voice, and thank God, understand it too. The Lord pronounces special blessings to those who have not seen, yet have believed (John 20:29). Although we are not now as privileged as these three apostles, when he comes again, we will also see Him in all His glory.

"THE HOLY MOUNT"

Peter calls the Mount of Transfiguration "the Holy mount," because there he had a sight of the glory of Christ and of His Father. The presence of the Lord is what makes a place holy. When the Lord speaks to Moses out of the burning bush, He says, "Put off thy shoes from off thy feet, for the place whereon thou standest is holy ground" (Ex. 3:5). When Joshua was in the presence of the Lord, he heard similar words; "Loose thy shoe from off thy foot; for the place whereon thou standest is holy" (Joshua 5:15). Because of the presence of the Lord, Zion, the temple site in Jerusalem, is also called a holy mountain (Zech. 8:3, Psa. 87:1, 2). Mt. Tabor is generally thought to be the mountain upon which the transfiguration took place, but there is no certainty as to this.

XI

THE PURPOSE OF PROPHECY
(II Peter 1:19)

1:19 "We have also a more sure word of prophecy; whereunto ye do well that ye take heed, as unto a light that shineth in a dark place, until the day dawn, and the day star arise in your hearts."

Peter now turns from the transfiguration to prophecy which also tells of the power and coming of Christ. Some might say, "Peter, you had a dream or an hallucination, we do not know whether to believe you or not." "All right," says Peter, "If you will not believe me as to this, perhaps you will believe what the prophets say about the coming again of our Lord Jesus. If you give good heed to them you will believe that He is coming again."

"A More Sure Word of Prophecy"

"A more sure word of prophecy" is literally, "We have the prophetic word more firm." The Revised Version puts it, "The word of prophecy made more sure." The way our Authorized Version reads, it would seem that Peter is comparing prophecy with the transfiguration and leaving the impression that prophecy was more important than his testimony of the transfiguration. However, he may have meant that the transfiguration made more sure or confirmed the truth of prophecy. At all events, the Father's proclamation cannot be of less value than the voice of the prophets, although it might be that some of Peter's readers would be more ready to believe the prophets than Peter's testimony. Both were the Word of God.

"Prophecy"

We generally think of prophecy as foretelling, but this is not always so. A prophet is one who speaks for another; he is a spokesman for God. God says to Moses in Ex. 7:1, "Aaron thy brother shall be thy prophet." He also says to Moses of Aaron in Ex. 4:16, "He shall be thy spokesman." Moses, in telling of Christ says, "The Lord thy God will raise up unto thee a Prophet from the midst of thee of thy brethren, like unto me; unto him ye shall hearken" (Deut. 18:15). So we have Aaron called Moses' prophet, but Moses is also called a prophet, and Christ too. All of these did predicting, but the great bulk of their work was exhorting the people of their times. A prophet may tell of the past, the present, or the future. Here of course, Peter is referring primarily to the predictions of the prophets concerning the power and the coming of our Lord Jesus Christ.

THE WONDERS OF PROPHECY

When Peter speaks of prophecy he is referring to Old Testament prophecy, as is evident from verse 21. Prophecies already fulfilled are convincing proof of the inspiration of Scripture. Think of Psalm 22 with all its statements concerning Christ on the cross, and then remember that David lived 1,000 years before Christ was born. Isaiah lived 700 years before Christ, yet his book is full of prophecies concerning the person and work of Christ. His 53rd chapter alone should convince any doubter of the truth of inspiration. Such prophecies just could not have been invented by man. Besides the hundreds concerning Christ, we have prophecies already fulfilled of Judas, John the Baptist, and Mary; of Israel, Babylon, Egypt, and many others. Prophecy starts way back in Gen. 3:15, where the Lord says to the serpent (Satan), "I will put enmity between thee and the woman, and between thy seed and her seed; it shall bruise thy head, and thou shalt bruise his heel." This tells of the struggle between Christ and Satan in which Christ gained the victory.

PROPHECIES CONCERNING HIS COMING

Both the Old and New Testaments are filled with prophecies concerning the second coming of Christ. Our portion is particularly interested in Old Testament prophecy, so we desire to touch on a few of these. One of the plainest, Zech. 14:5, we have already quoted. "And the Lord my God shall come, and all the saints with thee." In Deut. 30:3 we read, "That then the Lord thy God will turn thy captivity, and have compassion upon thee, and will *return* and gather thee from all nations, whither the Lord thy God hath scattered thee." We know that the regathering of the children of

Israel into Palestine is a part of the work to be done in connection with the return of our Lord.

OTHER PROPHECIES

We love the testimony of Job. He says in chapter 19:25-27, "For I know that my redeemer liveth, and that he shall stand at the latter day upon the earth: and though after my skin worms destroy this body, yet in my flesh shall I see God." This could only be fulfilled at Christ's second coming when Job is raised from the dead. There are hundreds of Old Testament references to Christ's glorious reign upon the earth. A good example is Psalm 72. Verse 6 says, "He shall *come down* like rain upon the mown grass; as showers that water the earth." Verse 8 says, "He shall have dominion also from sea to sea, and from the river unto the ends of the earth." Practically all the prophets refer to this glorious reign to some extent.

THE VALUE OF PROPHECY

Besides proving the inspiration of Scripture, prophecy has many other valuable uses. It shows us how our mighty God has a foreknowledge of all things. It also warns the unsaved of the times of judgment which are ahead, and advises them to turn to Christ before it is too late. It teaches the Christian to work "while it is day: for the night cometh, when no man can work" (John 9:4). It enlightens the Christian as to the future and so separates him from the evils of the world.

"YE DO WELL THAT YE TAKE HEED"

Our verse says that we do well when we take heed to this prophetic word. We should not only read it, but give it our closest attention and let it affect our every action. What our verse says of prophecy should be true of the whole Word of God. We should make both Old and New Testaments our constant study and guide. "Thy word is a lamp unto my feet and a light unto my path" (Psalm 119:105). "I have more understanding than all my teachers: for thy testimonies are my meditation" (Psalm 119:99). "They received the word with all readiness of mind, and searched the scriptures daily, whether those things were so" (Acts 17:11).

Civilization has risen or fallen in the measure in which the Word has been welcomed or rejected.

"A LIGHT THAT SHINETH IN A DARK PLACE"

Peter pictures prophecy as a light or lamp which shines in a dark place. What would we know of the past, or present, or future if it were not for this lamp? We would be completely in the dark. We would know nothing of the origin of things, nor their purpose, nor their end. Without the Word of God, we would know nothing of God and our creation by Him. Without it we would know nothing of His plans for us or for the world. And certainly, we would know nothing of the consumation of the matter. Thank God for everyone of us who have come to know Christ and His salvation. We truly have been "called out of darkness into His marvellous light" (I Pet. 2:9).

THIS LAMP GUIDES US

This lamp enlightens the Christian's path before him and causes him to see in spite of total darkness all around. As the pillar of fire was a light and a guide to the children of Israel as they journeyed through the darkness of the wilderness between Egypt and Canaan, so the Word is a light and guide to us as we journey through the darkness of this life to the glory land. Let us more and more avail ourselves of this brilliant light. We need never walk in the dark if we take it with us wherever we go.

"A DARK PLACE"

The word translated "dark" in our verse could be translated "dry" or "squalid." This indicates that the lamp not only dispels the darkness, but exposes the dirt and filth. It is like a dark room filled with trash and filth. This is not noticed in the dark, but when the lamp is lit it all comes to light. The world is not only in the darkness of ignorance, but also in the darkness of sin and corruption. Much of this would pass unnoticed except for the shining of the lamp.

THE PROPHETS WERE LIGHTS

Every prophet was a light who showed up the sin and squalor of his time. Joseph was a prophet who exposed the sin of his brethren. Elijah shined the light of God upon the sin of king Ahab and the people of his time. Isaiah, Jeremiah, Daniel, Amos, etc., were all lights exposing the corruption of their times. In many ways this is a beautiful world which manifests the hand of a marvelous Creator, but for the most part it has been ruined by the corruption that is in the heart of man.

Christ the Light

The greatest light of all times was the Lord Jesus Himself. He said, "I am the light of the world: he that followeth me shall not walk in darkness, but shall have the light of life" (John 8:12). "The dayspring from on high hath visited us, to give light to them that sit in darkness and in the shadow of death, to guide our feet in the way of peace" (Luke 1:78, 79). None ever exposed the squalor of His times like the Lord Jesus. While He spoke mostly in a tender way, yet He had a way of convicting sinners of their sins which caused them to be pierced to the heart. It caused many to turn to Him for salvation, but others to hate Him even unto death. He especially showed up the sins of the religious, but hypocritical, Pharisees, and this caused them to cry out for His blood.

Ye are the Light of the World

Christ, the great light, has gone back to heaven. The Word of God is here to shine out and to dispel the darkness and to expose the squalor. Each Christian now should be an aid in dispelling the darkness. Many in the world seldom read the Bible, but a Christian should witness and live for Christ and so be a light in the world. The Lord Jesus says in Matt. 5:16, "Let your light so shine before men, that they may see your good works, and glorify your Father which is in heaven." In Eph. 5:8 Paul says, "For ye were sometimes darkness, but now are ye light in the Lord: walk as children of light." May we, like the moon, reflect the glorious sunlight of the Son of God.

"Until the Day Dawn"

The sun arose on this scene when our Lord Jesus was born in Bethlehem, but it quickly set again at Calvary's cross, and now it is dark. Perhaps not quite as dark as before, because of the light from the Word and the reflection of Christ, though dim, by the Christians. When our Lord Jesus comes again the day will again dawn. "The Sun of righteousness shall arise with healing in his wings" (Mal. 4:2). Our present times and the times when He is here, will be as different as night and day. All will be clear when the sun shines. Prophecy was a lamp in the darkness, but we will not need a lamp when the Son shines. What a grand day that will be; it will be the day of all days. The Lord is soon coming. "The night is far spent, the day is at hand: let us therefore cast off the works of darkness, and let us put on the armour of light" (Rom. 13:12). "Ye are all the children of light, and children of the day: we are not of the night, nor of darkness. Therefore let us not sleep, as do others; but let us watch and be sober" (I Thess. 5:5, 6).

"THE DAY STAR ARISE"

Shortly before the break of day a bright star appears in the heavens. Our verse refers to this as the day star. In other places it is referred to as the morning star. Christ says in Rev. 22:16, "I am the root and the offspring of David, and the bright and morning star." So this bright and morning star represents the Lord Jesus. Many have seen in this the glorious coming of our Lord Jesus Christ for His church. As the morning star appears shortly before the daybreak, so the Lord will appear first of all to receive His own to Himself, and then shortly after that He will appear as the rising sun to bring a new day to Israel and the world. Before the world sees Him as Lord of Lords, we will be with Him in glory, at least, so we understand it. We believe I Thess. 4:13-18 speaks of the rapture of the church. As we read this over carefully, we see a marked difference between it and other passages such as Mat. 24:27-31. The one is a meeting with Christ in the air, the other, His coming to the earth with great power and glory. We believe the rapture of the church precedes the coming of Christ in glory, even as the morning star appears before the day break.

"IN YOUR HEARTS"

The expression "in your hearts" at the end of our verse might cause some to say, "The day star arising has nothing to do with the coming of the Lord. It is a matter of arising in our hearts." Many interpreters believe that "in your hearts" refers back to "take heed." In other words we are to take heed in our hearts to this "more sure word of prophecy." They would make the words in between these two phrases a parenthesis as follows: "We have also a more sure word of prophecy; whereunto ye do well to take heed, (as unto a light that shineth in a dark place, until the day dawn, and the day star arise) in your hearts."

He Shines Into Our Hearts

However, the person of Christ and the hope of His coming, should shine into our hearts. The lamp of prophecy is intended to throw light on our path, but also into our hearts. We are walking in the midst of darkness, but it is not dark in our hearts. The joy of the light of Christ shines in before the day breaks. The Christian anticipates the glorious day which is coming, and is not a child of the night, but of the day (I Thess. 5:5, 6). "For God, who commanded the light to shine out of darkness, hath shined in our hearts" (II Cor. 4:6). He is the bright and morning star for our hearts as well as for the rapture of the church.

This Should Wean Us from the World

If the truth of Christ and His coming really shines into our hearts, it will wean us from the world. We will care for none of its pleasures, or honors, and certainly not for its sinful ways. "And every man that hath this hope in him purifieth himself, even as he is pure" (I John 3:3). In many ways this is a night of trial and sorrow, but the light of this bright and morning star shines in to fill our hearts with joy. Has this glorious light shined into our hearts?

XII

THE ORIGIN OF PROPHECY

(II Peter 1:20, 21)

1:20 "Knowing this first, that no prophecy of the scripture is of any private interpretation."

As this verse reads in our Authorized Version one might think that it refers to the reader's right to interpret the meaning of the Old Testament prophecies. The Catholic Church has taught from it that the average Christian is unable to understand the Bible, and so should make no attempt to interpret it, and even has discouraged him from reading it. We believe that this verse and the next cannot be separated, and that the first teaches the negative side, while the second teaches the positive side of the same truth. In other words it is a matter of the origin of prophecy rather than its interpretation. Perhaps we could translate the whole portion this way; "Knowing this first, that no prophecy of the scripture is anyone's own unfolding of things, for the prophecy came not in old times by the will of man: but holy men of God spake as they were moved of the Holy Spirit."

"Knowing This First"

We believe Peter, when he says, "Knowing this first," would impress us with the fact that the inspiration of the Scriptures is one of the primary and most important truths for a Christian. He applies it to the Old Testament Scriptures, but we can safely say this is true of both Old and New. Without inspiration we bog down into hopeless bedlam. Many question the truthfulness of some parts of the Word today and, as a result, they are hopelessly at sea. If some parts are not trustworthy, how can one be sure which parts are trustworthy? This leaves one with absolutely no foundation on which to stand. It is like undermining a beautiful building and soon the whole thing crashes to the ground. Let us plant our feet firmly on this primal truth; the Bible, the whole of it, is the Word of God.

"PRIVATE INTERPRETATION"

The word "private" would perhaps be better translated "one's own" or "personal." The word "interpretation" has been variously understood and interpreted. It is literally "unloose" or "unfold," so we could read, "No prophecy of the scripture is of one's own unloosing." We can readily see how this could be translated both in connection with the reader or the prophet. What Peter is trying to say is that no prophecy of Scripture is the prophet's own mind or opinion of a matter, but that it is a message he has received through the Spirit of God. These prophecies were not of human origination, but expressions of the mind of God. In Num. 16:28 we read, "And Moses said, Hereby ye shall know that the Lord hath sent me to do all these works; for I have not done them of *mine own mind.*" This is exactly the thought of our verse; the prophets did not prophesy of their own mind. Jeremiah says in his book (23:16) of false prophets, "They speak a vision of their own heart, and not out of the mouth of the Lord." All prophecy, yea all Scripture, is given by inspiration of God (II Tim. 3:16).

HOW TO STUDY PROPHECY

It is a very good thing to make a careful study of prophecy, as our preceding verse indicates. However, we must be very cautious as to our interpretation. Let us always approach them with a sense that they are not merely man's words, but revelations from the Lord Himself. This will lead to careful study rather than to the neglect of it, as the Papists advise. As we study it, let us seek help from the Author, the Holy Spirit. He will not lead us astray. Let us not jump to conclusions from isolated texts, but learn to compare Scripture with Scripture. One portion is sure to throw light on another. If you would learn truth about the second coming of Christ, read carefully all the portions you can find which deal with it. Do the same with other truths. Do not expect to understand everything about prophecy. The prophets themselves did not always understand their own prophecies (Dan. 12:8 etc.).

EXAMPLES OF ERROR

Many have jumped to conclusions concerning prophecy and time has proved them wrong. There is especially danger in connection with setting dates concerning the return of the Lord. One otherwise sound gospel preacher said over the radio, "The Lord just cannot stay away longer than 1937." Of course he was wrong as time has proved. We one time heard a quack prophet say over the air, "The Bible says that no one knows when Christ is coming back again, and even Christ Himself said He did not know, but I know." And then he proceeded to tell when Christ was coming back again.

FURTHER CAUTIONS

Some seem to see some Bible prophecy fulfillment in almost every important event that happens in the world. We need to be very cautious in this or we may have to take back our words. Your author himself has made some mistakes along this line and this has taught him the necessity of extreme caution. It is wise when teaching prophecy not to be too dogmatic. If there is any question about a matter it is wise to say, "It seems to me that this is the truth of the matter," or some such expression, rather than to say, "this is it."

1:21 "For the prophecy came not in old time by the will of man: but holy men of God spake as they were moved by the Holy Ghost."

This is a continuation of the thought of the last verse. The first part is still putting the matter in a negative sense, while the last part puts it in the positive. Old Testament prophecy did not come by the will of man, but "Men spake from God, being moved by the Holy Spirit" (R. V.).

"PROPHECY CAME NOT — BY THE WILL OF MAN"

Peter here repeats that the Old Testament prophecies were not the result of religious meditations. Man's promptings or suggestions had nothing to do with it at all. Of course, this is true of the whole Bible, not only of the Old Testament prophets.

"HOLY MEN OF GOD"

Many of the Old Testament prophets were called "men of God." Moses was so designated many times (Deut. 33:1, Josh.

14:6), Elijah also (I Kings 17:18), and Elisha (II Kings 4:7), and David (II Chron. 8:14). All the penmen for the Lord could be thus designated. They were not only "men of God," but "holy men of God." Not that they were sinless and never erred, but they were men of good character, set apart by God for a special purpose. They were men especially commissioned and used of the Lord to speak forth and to write His mind. The word "men" here is emphatic. It is well to remember that although the Bible is God's book, He used men to write it. Paul says, "But we have this treasure in earthen vessels, that the excellency of the power may be of God, and not of us" (II Cor. 4:7).

Are We Men of God?

What a wonderful thing to be called a "man of God." It is something every servant of the Lord should covet for himself. What do the Christians think of you? Do they look upon you as a man of God? More important yet, do the unsaved in the world look upon you as such? How about your next door neighbors, what is their thought of you? Let us seek so to walk in this scene that all may see something of Christ in us. He was truly a man of God. Of course, He was God manifest in the flesh.

"Spake As They Were Moved"

The expression "spake as they were moved" gives some hint as to the method of inspiration. They were not self-moved, but moved by the Spirit even as a sail boat is moved by the wind. "Moved" could be translated "driven." The prophets were driven to speak and to write by an irresistible force, the Spirit of God. They could do nothing else but speak and write those things which He would have them to do. David says, "The Spirit of the Lord spake by me, and his word was in my tongue" (II Sam. 23:2). Zacharias says, "As he spake by the mouth of his holy prophets" (Luke 1:70).

"Moved by the Holy Ghost"

The prophets were moved by the Holy Spirit. They were under His direct power and influence. The Spirit was the author, man the instrument. The exact method used is not definitely known.

We can see the character of the man in his writings, but also the influence of the Spirit. We believe the very words of Scripture to be the very words of the Spirit. "All Scripture is given by inspiration of God" (II Tim. 3:16).

The Spirit Indwells Us

As "men of God," we too can be moved by the Spirit of God. We do not mean in the same inerrant way that the prophets and others were led to write the Scriptures. But if we lean upon the Lord and seek His help and guidance, He too will lead, and guide, and manifest His power in and through us, and we will be a great blessing to saint and to sinner. We see this very plainly at Pentecost and throughout the Acts and the epistles. "For as many as are led by the Spirit of God, they are the sons of God" (Rom. 8:14). Every true Christian in this dispensation is indwelt by the Spirit (Rom. 8:9). However, every Christian is not filled with the Spirit, but is exhorted to be so filled (Eph. 5:18).

Testimony of Various Scriptures

Many New Testament Scriptures testify to the fact that the Old Testament Scriptures were given by the Holy Spirit. In Mark 12:36 we hear the Lord Jesus say, "For David himself said by the Holy Ghost, The Lord said to my Lord, Sit thou on my right hand, till I make thine enemies thy footstool." In Acts 28:25 we read, "Well spake the Holy Ghost by Esaias the prophet unto our fathers" (Also Acts 1:16, 3:18). We have similar language three times in Hebrews (3:7, 9:8, 10:15). "The Holy Ghost this signifying, that the way into the holiest of all was not yet made manifest" (Heb. 9:8).

The Prophet's Own Testimony

The prophets and all Old Testament Scriptures everywhere testify to the fact that they were inspired by the Lord. We often hear the prophets say, "Thus saith the Lord" or similar statements. In connection with Moses, 51 times we read, "Then the Lord said unto Moses" and 72 times, "The Lord spake unto Moses." In I Peter 1:10-12 we read that much which the prophets wrote was not for themselves at all, but for future generations.

THE BIBLE NOT ONLY CONTAINS BUT IS THE WORD OF GOD

We one day read an article by a supposedly fundamental preacher. He said, "The Bible contains the Word of God, but not all of it was inspired by Him. When Paul writes to Timothy 'Drink no longer water, but use a little wine for thy stomach's sake' (I Tim. 5:23), that was Paul's advice to Timothy, but was not inspired by God." We believe even such statements as the one in question was inspired by the Lord. It is a well-known fact that grape juice and wine make a fine tonic for some forms of stomach trouble. Some might say, "Why did not Paul suggest grape juice rather than wine?" We must remember that in those days they had no way of keeping grape juice from quickly fermenting. The Bible not only contains the Word of God, but it is the Word of God. This is the only safe ground on which to stand.

NO OTHER BOOKS INSPIRED BY THE SPIRIT

Some times we hear something like this: "O yes, the Bible is an inspired book, but so are many other books." And then they will tell you of some great poets and authors whose writings they believe also to be inspired. There are no books inspired in the same way as was the Bible. None others have the Holy Spirit for their author.

A WONDERFUL BOOK

This inspired volume of God is a wonderful book. All classes of people love it and use it, although others hate and abuse it. Children love its touching stories. Housewives read it and are helped in the managing of their children and homes. Soldiers carry it in their knapsacks and resort to it in time of danger. Statesmen study it so they can quote from it to embellish their speeches. Judges use it as a text book on law. Old people find that time is not heavy on their hands when they pour over its pages. It is a great comfort to the oppressed, the sick; and the dying use it as their pillow. It has brought rest, peace, joy, and salvation to millions. There is no other book in the world which can begin to compare with it. It is inspired of God.

OTHER WONDERFUL THINGS

This precious book has found its way into all languages, nations and places. Although fierce enemies have determined to destroy it, it continues down the ages unchanged. While everything else blossoms for a time and then fades away, the Bible continues to spread farther and farther and to influence hearts and minds for good in yet more dark and distant lands. It never becomes out of date; it always is abreast of the times. Man, with his ever increasing knowledge, never surpasses the Bible. The majesty of its style and language has astounded the most learned. While it is a book primarily for the heart and life, yet matters of geography and science are stated with great accuracy. Apart from it we would be utterly in the dark about the most fundamental things of life. Many of these things only God could reveal to man.

CHRIST IS THE PRINCIPAL THEME OF THE PROPHETS

The principal theme of the prophets, yea, and of all Scripture, is the Lord Jesus Christ. Isaiah 7:14 predicts that He was to be born of a virgin. Micah 5:2, that Bethlehem would be the place of His birth. Many details of His crucifixion can be found in the prophets. For instance in Psalm 22:16, "They pierced my hands and my feet." Verse 17 tells how not a bone of His was broken, and verse 18 how they divided His garments and cast lots for His cloak. Psalm 69 is also a remarkable Psalm of the cross. In verse 21 we read, "In my thirst they gave me vinegar to drink." Isaiah 53 over and over tells of the purpose of the cross. We believe verse 9 tells of the two thieves and also of the rich man, Joseph of Arimathea, who laid the Lord in his own new tomb. Zechariah has much to say of Christ, His person and work. In Chapter 13:6 they ask Him, "What are these wounds in thine hands?" Then in 12:10, "They shall look upon me whom they have pierced."

THE PROPHETS AND CHRIST (Cont.)

We could go on to tell of the offerings, and the hundreds of things and characters which in one way or another typify Christ and His work, such as the Passover lamb, etc. As we noticed previously, all the prophets speak of His glories, especially as the coming reigning King. How the Spirit of God delighted to exalt the Lord Jesus. Note carefully Luke 24:44, "All things must be fulfilled which were written in the law of Moses, and in the prophets, and in the Psalms concerning me." (Also Luke 24:24-27). These fulfilled prophecies concerning our Lord Jesus Christ prove conclusively that He was the divine Son of God. They also certainly prove that the Bible is the divine Word of God.

XIII

FALSE TEACHERS

(II Peter 2:1)

2:1 "But there were false prophets also among the people, even as there shall be false teachers among you, who privily shall bring in damnable heresies, even denying the Lord that bought them, and bring upon themselves swift destruction."

In chapter 1:19-21, Peter has brought in the true prophets of the Old Testament. In this first verse of chapter 2, he brings in the false prophets of the Old Testament, and uses them as a starting point to speak about false teachers who would appear in the Christian church and cause no end of trouble. This second chapter is a dark appalling one. From verse 1 to 22, there is no let up in his scathing hot condemnation of these deceived deceivers. The only other chapter in the Bible which begins to compare with it in the fierceness of its storm, is the one chapter of the little book of Jude. As we see the lightning flash and hear the awful rumbling of the thunder, we almost wonder, "Is this the same Peter who wrote the first chapter and also the first epistle?" How tenderly he speaks elsewhere, but here he minces no words. Almost every verse has a scathing rebuke or pronounces some awful judgment. He starts with "damnable heresics" and ends in verse 22 with a dog "turned to his own vomit again." The first verse starts with doctrinal error, but these false teachers are soon entangled in moral filth.

"False Prophets"

While there were many true prophets amongst the Old Testament people of God, there were also some who were false. Peter especially mentions Balaam in verse 15. In I Kings 22, we read of Micaiah, the true prophet, but Ahab believes the nice things said by the false prophets to his own destruction. We read of the false prophets of Baal in I Kings 18, and the false prophet hired by Tobiah and Sanballet in Neh. 6:12-14. Moses mentions these false prophets (Deut. 13:1-3), also Isaiah (Is. 9:15, 56:10, 11).

Jeremiah speaks of them often. "I have not sent these prophets, yet they ran: I have not spoken to them, yet they prophesied" (Jer. 23:21). "The prophets prophesy falsely, and the priests bear rule by their means; and my people love to have it so" (Jer. 5:31). How sadly true that even today there are many who profess to be teachers come from God, but He never sent them, yet they are respected and honored by many.

"False Teachers Among You"

The false prophets were from amongst the people, and so the false teachers were to come from amongst the Christians. There always seems to be tares amongst the wheat. One has said, "Wherever God erects a house of prayer, the devil always builds a chapel there." False teachers usually arise from amongst the true children of God. Someone hears the truth but is not genuinely saved. He then has ambitions to become a religious leader and begins to propagate his error. Followers then rise up to carry on the falsehood, and so we have a false cult of somekind or other. The number of these today are legion, and they parade their falsehoods as the greatest truths.

Christ Told of these False Teachers

We are not surprised at the multitude of false teachers around us today. Our Lord Jesus, as well as Peter, prophesied of them. Three times we have Him do so in Mat. 24 (verses 5, 11, 24). "There shall arise false Christs, and false prophets, and shall show great signs and wonders; insomuch that, if it were possible, they shall deceive the very elect" (Mat. 24:24). These things are literally so today.

Other Writers

Many other places in the New Testament we have prophecies concerning false teachers. Paul says to the Ephesian elders in Acts 20:29, 30, "For I know this, that after my departing shall grievous wolves enter in among you, not sparing the flock. Also of your ownselves shall men arise, speaking perverse things, to draw away disciples after them" (also II Cor. 11:13-15, I Tim. 4:1-3). John says in I John 4:1, "Beloved, believe not every spirit, but try the spirits whether they are of God: because many false prophets are gone out into the world" (also I John 2:18, 19, Jude 18). As we look about us and see these prophecies so literally fulfilled, we are not surprised, nor cast down, because the Lord knew years ago they would come.

"Who Privily Shall Bring In"

False teachers seldom bring in their heresies in an open and quick way. They, like Satan himself, are cunning, stealthy, and underhanded. They first bring in a lot of truth and a very little error. Then they slowly bring in more and more error, and less and less truth. Many of the false cults got their start in this way, and so do modernists creep into a fundamental church. "Beware of false prophets, which come to you in sheep's clothing, but inwardly they are ravening wolves" (Mat. 7:15). In Gal. 2:4 Paul says in connection with some who were seeking to have the Christians circumcised, "False brethren unawares brought in, who came in privily to spy out our liberty which we have in Christ Jesus, that they might bring us into bondage."

"Damnable Heresies"

The word "damnable" would be better translated "destructive" as in the Revised Version. "Heresies" is an untranslated Greek word coming from a word signifying "choice." As here, it is usually to be taken in the bad sense, so speaking of wilful insubordination. It is translated "sect" in Acts 24:5. It is a wilful choice to go on in one's own way, irrespective of the authority of the Lord Jesus. It indicates wrong action as well as wrong belief. It is unsound doctrine coupled with evil practice. As we go on in the chapter we will notice that Peter lays as much stress on their evil actions as he does on their evil teachings. These destructive heresies oppose and would seek to destroy the truth.

Present Day Heresies

Present day heresies are legion, and take on a great variety of forms. Most all of them err right at the most important place. They belittle the person and the cross work of Christ. They either deny that He is the divine Son of God, or they deem His work on the cross of little value, and insufficient for salvation. Some separate Christ's work almost entirely from the seriousness of sin

It is certainly heresy to teach that one can be saved apart from conviction of sin, and also to teach that one can be saved and still live a life of sin and corruption. When one is born again, he is cleansed by the Spirit of God and given the power to live for Christ. It is the solemn duty of every true Christian to constantly guard against these attacks of error and evil.

FALSE CULTS

Many false cults start out with the heresy that God will not punish sin. They do not seem to see that God is holy and righteous, and that this very nature of His makes it essential for Him to punish evil doers. We must begin with the absolute purity and holiness of Christ. False cults forget the scene in Isaiah 6, where the seraphim covered their faces and their feet in His presence and cried, "Holy, holy, holy, is the Lord of hosts." Until one sees this truth of God's holiness, and that He must punish sin, he will not feel the need for forgiveness and the necessity of Calvary. One only sees the blackness of his sin in the light of the absolute purity of God and Christ. A lessening of the sense of sin is one of the first steps in a downward course toward evil.

WRONG TEACHING BRINGS DEPRAVED LIVES

The special heresy in Peter's mind seems apparent from verse 19. These false teachers were promising their followers liberty: not liberty from the thraldom of sin and Satan, as Paul preached, but liberty to sin, as some professed that Paul taught. "Why" they said, "Paul teaches that Christians have liberty, so go and sin in any kind of way you please." Naturally this would bring widespread corruption. These wrong teachings would result in depraved lives and cause the Christian faith to be evil spoken of. There are many today who teach and act very much like these heretics. They claim that a mental assent is sufficient for salvation, but never mention sin as a serious thing to the unsaved, or to those who profess to be Christians.

"DENYING THE LORD"

It is heresy to deny the person and work of Christ; it is also heresy to deny His claims. In the light of Peter's denial of Christ, it must have hurt him to use the same words of these heretics.

Peter denied Him in a moment of weakness and fear, but these were denying Him openly and blatantly in the worst sense. One has said, "It is bad to slight Christ, worse to forget Him, yet worse to forsake Him, but fearful to deny Him." How fearful to deny, not a man, or a parent, or even an angel, but the Lord of heaven and earth. "But whosoever shall deny me before men, him will I also deny before my Father which is in heaven" (Mat. 10:33). "If we deny him, he also will deny us" (II Tim. 2:12). Let us not forget that all sin is in a sense a denial of Christ and His authority. If He sits on the throne of our hearts as He should, sin will not in any sense rule over us.

"The Lord that Bought Them"

The word translated "Lord" is a strong one, from which comes our English word "despot." The thought is of one who is absolute ruler or master. The picture is of a great man buying slaves at a slave market, who then mutiny against their master and refuse to obey him. These false teachers apparently were not true Christians at all, but yet Peter claims that they were bought by Christ. The payment that Christ made on the cross was sufficient to buy everyone in the world. In the parable of the treasure in the field in Mat. 13:44, Christ buys the whole field, but it is in order to obtain the treasure in the field. "The field is the world" (Mat. 13:38) but the treasure is the church. So not only the true Christians owe Christ abject obedience, but every man in the whole world does. Of course the unsaved, like these false teachers, disown Christ's rights and authority over them. "He is Lord of all" (Acts 10:36).

Christians Must Own His Authority

A Christian has been both bought and redeemed by Christ, and he should own this in word and by deed. We should not only call Him Lord, but let Him be the Lord of our lives. In I Cor. 6:19, 20, we have, "Ye are not your own, for ye are bought with a price: therefore glorify God in your body, and in your spirit, which are God's." The apostles all acknowledged that they were the property of the Lord Jesus. Peter, Paul, James, and Jude all called themselves servants of Jesus Christ, and the word "servant" is "bondman," or "slave" in the original. If we are Christ's servants we should not live to serve man primarily, but Him (I Cor. 7:23). We should seek to do His will and to live clean lives which will bring glory to His name.

"Bring Upon Themselves Swift Destruction"

These false teachers, who brought in these destructive heresies, were to bring upon themselves swift destruction. They were the cause of their own downfall. Sin brings its own reward. They who seek to destroy others, will themselves be quickly destroyed. Haman, in the book of Esther, sought to destroy all the Jews, especially Mordecai for whom he built a special gallows. The Jews were not destroyed, and Haman himself died on the gallows made for Mordecai. "His own iniquities shall take the wicked himself, and he shall be holden with the cords of his sins (Prov. 5:22).

"Swift Destruction"

God may delay judgment, but when it comes it comes quickly and unexpectedly. It comes swiftly even as the ground opened up suddenly and swallowed up rebellious Korah, Dathan and Abiram (Num. 16). It will come swiftly, unexpectedly, like the coming of the Lord. "He that being often reproved hardeneth his neck, shall suddenly be destroyed, and that without remedy" (Prov. 29:1). How sad when the Lord Jesus says, "And if the blind lead the blind, both shall fall into the ditch" (Mat. 15:14). Let us be careful not to follow Satan's pernicious ways, but seek to be followers of the Lord Jesus Christ and to be led by the Spirit.

An Old Pirate Story

The story is told of a mean old pirate captain, who gleefully took the warning bell off a buoy, which warned of dangerous rocks just under the surface of the water. Sometime later, he and his ship went down after hitting those very rocks. By seeking to destroy others, he destroyed himself.

XIV

FALSE TEACHERS LEAD ASTRAY

(II Peter 2:2, 3)

2:2 "And many shall follow their pernicious ways; by reason of whom the way of truth shall be evil spoken of."

The prophetic statement of this second verse has also certainly come true. Many have followed these false teachers in their destructive heresies and ruinous ways. [As a result, many are confused as to the right way. They say, "Christianity is divided into so many different groups and we hear so many different things; how can we know the right way?"] Then the lewd practices of some who profess Christianity bring reproach on the whole cause of Christ.

"Many Shall Follow"

[It seems hard to get people to follow the truth, but crowds will follow after a false teacher who makes the way of life easy.] The Lord says that only a few are saved, but many seem ready to follow any crack-pot who comes along with any brand of fakery. [A display of knowledge which does not demand a new birth and a clean life, can quickly gain a huge following.]

Heresy Spreads

Heresy is like leaven. "A little leaven leaveneth the whole lump" (Gal. 5:9). How quickly evil doctrine can corrupt a whole work for God. Many churches a few years ago were thoroughly fundamental, but now are steeped in modernism. Let a modernistic preacher get into such a fundamental place and very soon the whole church is ruined. The weak and uninstructed are quick to follow in these ruinous ways.

False Cults

The number of false cults today is legion, and some of them have large followings. Mormons have passed the 1,000,000 mark. Russellites, now Jehovah's Witnesses, have exceeded 144,000. Catholics number about one-sixth of the population of the U.S.A.,

25,000,000. Adventists are making progress all over the world. Christian Science is strong amongst the rich and the educated. Modernists have wormed their way into almost all kinds of Protestant churches. Truly, many have followed the way of error. There is great reward promised to those who win one soul to Christ. How great must not the punishment be of those who lead many to destruction.

LET US USE CAUTION

All Christians need to be very much on guard, lest they too, be quickly led away by error. The safe thing is to keep very close to the Lord Jesus. Let Him be our head and then no false leader will be able to lead us astray. If any of us are leaders, let us be very careful to teach only the truth of the Word of God, and also let us by our daily walk set a good example to all of the Lord's dear people.

"PERNICIOUS WAYS"

The nearest literal rendering of the Greek word here translated "pernicious" is "ruinous." Some Greek manuscripts use a different word here which would be best translated "lascivious" or "exciting lust." This would lay emphasis on their evil practices rather than on their evil teachings. We know from the rest of the chapter that Peter had this form of sin in mind in connection with these teachers (verses 10, 14, 18, 19). Usually false teaching quickly leads to corrupt living, and many false religions lean toward this unclean form of living.

HOW TO TEST TEACHERS

One of the first things to notice about those who profess to be religious teachers is, what do they think of the Bible? Do they believe it to be the very Word of God? The next thing is what do they think of Christ? Is He the only begotten Son of the Living God? Then what do they think of the cross and the blood of Christ? Do they believe that He alone can save from sin and hell? Many think of the atonement as something completely out of date, and Christ no more than a great man.

EXAMPLES OF UNBELIEVERS

We have had occasion to visit many so-called Christian book stores to show them our book on I Peter. Many have treated us wonderfully and shown us every consideration, but some have laughed and even sneered at us. "Who in this enlightened age would care to read a book of this kind" was the question of one? Another said as he looked through the book, "I see you write about lust; our preachers never preach on things of that nature any more. I am sorry, but no one who patronizes our book store would be interested in a book which believes in the Bible the way you do." We wonder why some still profess to be Christian leaders, when they do not believe the Bible at all. They do not believe in repentance toward God, nor confession of and forgiveness of sin. They do not believe that sinners need the mercy of God, and so Christ's atonement is an unnecessary thing to them.

"BY REASON OF WHOM"

Such unbelievers do the church of Christ much harm. The unsaved are not able to distinguish between the true believer and the one who merely professes to be a Christian. We recently heard a Jewish Christian tell of his experiences. He was born and raised in Austria where even as a boy he was hated and abused by professing Christians. He believed that all Christians were hard and cruel and that Christ must have been so too. The Lord graciously showed him that Christ was different than he supposed and that true Christians were not hard and cruel either. Now he is saved and a missionary to his own people. He said that the actions of many of these false Christians caused many of his people to curse the name of Christ.

IMMORAL ACTIONS BRING REPROACH

Especially when false doctrine leads to immoral action, does reproach come upon the way of truth. An immoral man should never claim to be a Christian, because his actions bring reproach on the name of Christ. Sometimes even true Christians do great harm to the work of the Lord by an immoral act. May the Lord keep our every word and every action pure.

"THE WAY OF TRUTH"

Peter here calls Christianity "the way of truth." "The way" is a very common title for Christianity in the Scriptures. Peter calls it so twice more in this chapter (vs. 15, 21). It is very common in Acts (9:2, 16:17, 18:25, 26, 19:9, 22:4, 24:14). The Lord Jesus says in John 14:6, "I am the way, the truth, and the life: no man cometh unto the Father, but by me." He also speaks of the narrow way and the broad way in Mat. 7:13, 14. Few seem to realize that the way into heaven is not in religious form, or creed, or even in a manner of life; but in the person of Christ, the Son of God.

ONE HUNDRED WAYS TO HEAVEN?

A man visited preachers of various kinds, Catholic priests, Jewish rabbis, Y.M.C.A. secretaries, etc., and asked each one the way to heaven. He then sat down and wrote his findings in a book, and titled it "One Hundred Ways to Heaven." If we read our Bibles rightly there is only one way to heaven and that is in the person of our Lord Jesus Christ. Only as sinners come to God through Him, will they be saved.

"EVIL SPOKEN OF"

The word here translated "evil spoken of" is "blasphemo" and should be translated "blasphemed." It is sad to think that because of false teachers and loose living professors of Christianity, the way of truth should be blasphemed. We cannot help what these hypocrites bring about, but let each of us be very much on guard lest our actions give the enemies of truth an occasion to blaspheme. David did that because of his sin with Bathsheba and Uriah her husband. Nathan says to him, "By this deed thou hast given great occasion to the enemies of the Lord to blaspheme" (II Sam. 12:14). Paul says to the Jews in Rom. 2:24, "For the name of God is blasphemed among the Gentiles through you." We know the world hates the Lord Jesus and is looking for an occasion to speak evil of Him. Let us not give them occasion to do this.

2:3 "And through covetousness shall they with feigned words make merchandise of you: whose judgment now of a long time lingereth not, and their damnation slumbereth not."

In this verse we have the reason why these false teachers taught as they did, and also the means by which they would seduce their followers. It was because of covetousness, the desire to enrich themselves in this world, that they were ready to teach smooth and pleasing things. Oftentimes false teachers are excellent orators and very clever talkers. They will say and profess anything to gain and convince listeners. The latter part of our verse emphasizes the fact that sentence upon these false teachers has been pronounced long ago, and that execution of it would soon come.

"COVETOUSNESS"—

Covetousness is a terrible sin. It speaks of being avaricious for gain; being even ready to defraud others for monetary advantage. It has ever been a besetting sin, and is surely so today. Some men will do most anything to obtain money. Paul says to Timothy, "The love of money is a root of all kinds of evil" (I Tim. 6:10 R.V.). It is a bad sin in any man, but unspeakably bad in a religious leader. Sometimes worldly men become ministers for no other reason than personal advantage. A friend of ours asked a young man, evidently unsaved, why he was studying to be a preacher. He replied something like this; "It is a nice easy job, with good pay, and folks look up to you." The love of the Lord and the souls of men apparently had nothing to do with it; he only had himself in mind.

AN OLD SIN

The Law already says, "Thou shalt not covet" (Ex. 20:17). It evidently was very prevalent in Old Testament times. Verse 15 of our chapter tells of Balaam's convetousness. We have the story of Achan in Joshua 7. What trouble he brought on the children of Israel through his covetousness. The prophets complain a great deal of this sin. Isaiah says (56:11) of the watchmen of Israel, "They are greedy dogs which never have enough: — they all look to their own way, every one for his gain, from his quarter." Then in Micah 3:11 we read, "The heads thereof judge for reward, and the priests thereof teach for hire, and the prophets thereof divine for money." (See Jer. 6:13, Ez. 13:19).

In New Testament Too

Covetousness was also a prevalent sin in New Testament times. This sin plus a desire to be highly thought of, constrained Ananias and Sapphira to hold back part of the price of their land (Acts 5:1-11). Paul says in I Tim. 6:10, "While some coveted after they have erred from the faith." And in Rom. 16:18, "For they that are such serve not our Lord Jesus Christ, but their own belly; and by good words and fair speeches deceive the hearts of the simple." How similar this is to our verse in II Peter.

A Servant Must Not Be Covetous

[No man who serves the Lord in any capacity should be an avaricious, covetous man. One of the qualifications of both elders and deacons is that they be "not greedy of filthy lucre" (I Tim. 3:3, 8)]. Paul could say, "I have coveted no man's silver, or gold, or apparel" (Acts 20:33). He also asks the Corinthians, "Did I make a gain of you by any of them whom I sent unto you? — Did Titus make a gain of you?" (II Cor. 12:17, 18). Rather than be accused of being covetous or greedy, Paul went to work making tents to supply his own needs and those of his co-workers.

No Covetousness in our Lord Jesus

How utterly without covetousness was our Lord Jesus. The whole world was His by right, and yet we never hear the slightest word that would indicate that He expected the least thing from anyone whom He helped. We, who are servants of the Lord, should never do a thing that savors of covetousness. Let us, like Paul, seek to serve the Lord as He would have us do it, leaving the fact of remuneration entirely up to His care. If we serve Him faithfully, He will see to it that our needs are met. [Let us seek not our own profit, but the profit of our hearers.]

Covetousness and Error

One has said, "Back of every system of error is the sin of covetousness." Our verse in II Peter would seem to bear this out. In Titus 1:11 we read of some who were "teaching things they ought not, for filthy lucre's sake." It might not always be lust for money which causes some to advocate error; it might be lust for power, or lust for honor, which are but other forms of covetousness. We believe though that if the money question was left out, many false cults would soon cease to exist. The richest organization in the world did not get that way because it taught the truth.

"WITH FEIGNED WORDS"

The word "feigned" is one which literally means "molded," and by implication "artificial" or "false." These heretics were deceiving their followers with cunningly formed words, which sounded very nice and plausible, but really were deceiving and destructive, and had no solid foundation. They talked so nicely, as though they wanted to be a great help to their hearers, but back in their minds was only the thought of how to fleece them. They were like Absalom in II Sam. 15, who stole the hearts of the children of Israel with sweet words in order to steal the kingdom from his father. Absalom really did not have the children of Israel's welfare in mind at all, but was only thinking of his own welfare. These false teachers of our portion were like Judas, who pretended to love the Lord Jesus a great deal, and threw his arms around Him, and kissed Him, but all the while he was betraying Him for thirty pieces of silver.

HERESY AND HYPOCRISY

Heresy is usually linked with hypocrisy. The untruth is dispensed in eloquent language. Heretics are really not Christians at all, but they wear the clothes and use the language of the Christians. One has likened them to pirates who hang out the flags of other nations in order to deceive the unwary. They are like a man offering a dog a piece of meat which has been saturated with poison. The special heresy of those mentioned in our chapter seems to have been offering their hearers licentious living in the name of Christian liberty. There are foul teachers today who use fair speeches to lead the simple astray.

"MAKE MERCHANDISE OF YOU"

What an awful thing we have pictured here: wicked men by fair speeches selling souls, as a merchant sells his wares. There is much religion today which is no more than what the world calls a racket. Joseph's brethren sold him into slavery for twenty pieces of silver. There are those who would sell the souls of their fellow men into hell for little more. Speaking of the merchandise of Babylon, we read in Rev. 18:12, 13, "The merchandise of gold, and silver, — and horses, and chariots, and slaves, and souls of men." Babylon probably does not refer solely to Rome, but certainly their teaching on purgatory is a wicked thing which has no foundation in Scripture, and brings in vast revenue to their church. We believe it is trafficking in souls. When we think of the value of a soul, how serious it is to mislead. To destroy a soul through wrong teaching is worse than murder.

Influenced by Money

There is a great danger even of true Christians and saved preachers being influenced by money. Some seem to be afraid to tell the whole truth, or to speak against sin, for fear that it will in one way or another influence their income or position. Let us be bold to stand firm for the Lord and His Word, trusting that He will be with us and take care of us. Certainly, let us never sink to preaching error because of base gain. Let us never give our Lord occasion to say, "Take these things hence; make not my Father's house an house of merchandise" (John 2:16).

Manhood on the Market

Others who may be thought of as putting manhood on the market are liquor dealers, writers of obscene literature, atheistic orators and those who have a part in the white slave traffic. Anything done for money which has a tendency to lower man morally or spiritually can be called making merchandise of man. Of course, nothing is as bad as Simony, the sale of souls.

"Whose Judgment — Lingereth Not"

The Revised Version has this last part of our verse thus, "Whose sentence now from old lingereth not, and their destruction slumbereth not." The thought seems to be that these sinners were sentenced a long time ago, and the carrying out of the sentence was soon to take place. We know how this sometimes goes in a law court; the sentence comes long before the execution. Men are sentenced to die in the electric chair or on the gallows, but the time of their death is set for months later. Now the sentence pronounced against these false teachers is about to be executed.

JUDGMENT NOT DELAYED

The expression "lingereth not" is literally "is not idle" and could be translated "is not delayed." The sinners of our portion were living prosperously and when their judgment did not speedily come they probably thought they would go free. Men under sentence often hope something will arise and they yet go free, but our verse says nothing about pardon. Only judgment awaits these sinners. "For when they shall say, Peace and safety; then sudden destruction cometh upon them, as travail upon a woman with child; and they shall not escape" (I Thes. 5:3). No doubt if individuals amongst them did repent and turn to Christ for forgiveness, even this heinous sin would be forgiven.

"THEIR DAMNATION SLUMBERETH NOT"

"Damnation" would be better translated "destruction" as in the Revised Version. "Slumbereth not" is literally "does not nod;" figuratively "is not delayed." God's judgment will not sleep. The Lord does not slumber nor sleep when it comes to watching over His own (Ps. 121:3, 4). Neither will He be found sleeping when it comes time to execute judgment upon guilty sinners. Men probably said in Noah's time, "Look how long Noah has been telling us of that flood. It will never come." But when the appointed time arrived it came. Let sinners beware; God makes no idle threats.

XV

GOD SPARED NOT

(II Peter 2:4, 5)

2:4 "For if God spared not the angels that sinned, but cast them down to hell, and delivered them into chains of darkness, to be reserved unto judgment;"

This verse tells how angels who sinned were cast down to hell. It is the first of three examples of how sinners were overthrown in judgment. The next verse tells of Noah and the sinners overthrown by the flood, and then in verses 6-9 we have Lot and the destruction of the wicked Sodomites. These illustrations from past history are given to show that the guilty heretics mentioned in our chapter need not expect to escape the righteous judgment of a sin hating God. This whole portion pictures the certainty of the future punishment of the unrepentant sinner.

"God Spared Not"

Many do not seem to know that God is righteous and holy and that He must punish sin. They think that they can live about as they please in this world, and that yet somehow God will spare them and not send them to hell. Peter here is doing his utmost to show that God will not spare the unrepentant, unbelieving sinner.

"God Spared Not the Angels that Sinned"

The fact that "God spared not the angels that sinned" tells us that He will not spare because of any excellency in any of His creatures. The angels greatly excel us in strength and knowledge, but when they sinned judgment was immediately pronounced upon them. One may be a great man in the world, a king, a president, a statesman, an industrialist, a scientist, or a capitalist, but none of these things will cause God to spare in the day of judgment. Only if as sinners they come to the Lord Jesus for pardon, will they be spared.

SPARED NOT THE OLD WORLD

Our next verse 5, uses the same expression "spared not." There it speaks of the sinners who lived before the flood. How many perished in the flood we cannot determine, but one thing is certain, a great number of souls lost their lives at that time. Because they were many did not cause the Lord to spare them. The sixth verse mentions the destruction of Sodom and Gomorrah. Although Peter does not use the same expression, "spare not," yet the thought is still the same. None in these great cities were spared excepting Lot and his two daughters. Sin swept them all away.

HE SPARED NOT HIS OWN SON

In Rom. 8:32 we read, "He that spared not his own Son, but delivered him up for us all, how shall he not with him also freely give us all things?" Sin is such a terrible thing that before a single sin could be forgiven, or a single sinner pardoned, Christ had to die on the cross to pay for that sin, and die in the room and stead of that sinner. Now God can righteously spare the sinner who puts his trust in Christ and His work on the cross. "To declare, I say, at this time his righteousness: that he might be just, and the justifier of him which believeth in Jesus" (Rom. 3:26). If God spared not His own Son, let not the unrepentant, Christ rejecting sinner, think for one moment that God will spare him.

"ANGELS"

Before writing of the angels who sinned, we would like to note a little of the lofty place and work of unfallen angels. The Scriptures abound with references to them. The word "angel" means "messenger," and this is perhaps their principal work. They are messengers of God. We see them at this work in many places. They announced the birth of Christ (Luke 2:11). Heb. 2:2 says that they brought the law to Moses. We see them bring messages to Daniel, etc. They are serving spirits; "Are they not all ministering (serving) spirits" (Heb. 1:14). They ministered to Christ at both the temptation and in Gethsemane. One brought Elijah food in I Kings 19:5, and another shut the lions' mouths so they could not hurt Daniel (Dan. 6:22). They guard children

(Mat. 18:10). An angel delivered Peter out of prison (Acts 12:7). They worship the Lord (Neh. 9:6 etc.). They fight the battles of the Lord (Psalm 68:17 etc.). They are great in power and might (II Pet. 2:11, Rev. 5:2). They will play a great part in the end time (Mat. 13:39, 16:27, 24:31).

"Angels that Sinned"

We might wonder why angels would ever sin, but they were the first transgressors. Everything was in their favor. They had no evil environment or circumstances, yet they rose up in rebellion against the Lord. They had no tempter as did Adam and Eve. One would think that their happiness in heaven would be unalloyed, and that they would crave nothing different. Satan evidently was the first sinner. Isaiah 14 tells us that it was his desire to be as high as the Almighty, which caused him to rebel. "The devil sinneth from the beginning" (I John 3:8). "He was a murderer from the beginning, and abode not in the truth" (John 8:44).

Special Class of Fallen Angels

The nature and time of the sin of the fallen angels of our verse is not revealed. It would seem they followed the lead of Satan. These seem to be a special class of sinners, because they are bound in the pit, while Satan and many of his followers are loose and free to roam the earth. We see this in connection with those out of whom the Lord cast demons. Some think these angels of our verse are those who sinned in that they took human wives and are the sons of God of Genesis 6. We are inclined to doubt this theory, as we explained in connection with I Peter 3:19. The number of these fallen angels, and why they are chained, is not revealed.

We Stand In Christ

Though angels fell, the saints of God are made to stand, though not in themselves, but only in Christ. Although Christians still fall into sin, sin does not have dominion over them. Their new nature hates it, and the Spirit of God within gives them victory over it in a measure.

GOD DEALS IN GRACE WITH MAN

God deals with man according to grace, but in strict justice with angels. This is because man had a tempter, and also, all but Adam and Eve were born after sin came into the world, and so were not responsible for its coming. He gave Christ to die for man's sin, but this has no efficacy for the sins of angels.

"CAST THEM DOWN TO HELL"

The word for "hell" here is "tartarus." This is the only place it is used in the Word. It is generally conceded to be the deepest abyss, or pit of hell, a gloomy dark place of punishment. This is probably the same bottomless pit into which Satan will be cast during the millennum (Rev. 20:1-3). We read that hell was prepared in the first place for the devil and his angels (Mat. 25:41). Some of them were the first inhabitants of this dread place. In Luke 8:31, in the story of the man out of whom the Lord Jesus cast a legion of demons they request, "that he would not command them to go out into the deep." This may be the same deep or Tarturus of our verse. It would seem that this Tartarus is the final abode of Satan and all fallen angels. In Mat. 8:29 they ask of the Lord, "Art thou come hither to torment us before the time?" They were fearful that the Lord might cast them into this pit before the appointed time.

HELL A REAL PLACE

While hell was prepared for the devil and his angels, let not unbelieving sinners think that they will escape that dread place. Hell is a real place, and all those who insist on following Satan, rather than submit to Christ, will find their place therein along with the fallen angels (Mat. 13:42, 25:46, Luke 16:23 etc.) There is no mercy, no forgiveness, no restoration for fallen angels, but for man all these things may be had, but only while in this life. The only escape from this dread place is to trust Christ now. Fallen angels not only lost heaven, but deserved hell.

NO PURGATORY. ILLUSTRATION

The Bible knows of only two places after death; heaven and hell. We were talking with a preacher's wife on a train. She was returning from her girlhood home in New York state. While there she said she visited the church of her childhood and the young preacher delivered a rather strange sermon. He said, "Some people are not good enough to go to heaven, but not bad enough to go to hell, so there just must be a purgatory." Then she added, "I thought maybe he had something there." We then told her that none are good enough to go to heaven, and all are bad enough to go to hell, but that God had provided a way whereby any who would trust Christ would escape hell and go to heaven. We preached the gospel to her for about an hour, and when she left the train she said, "I never heard anything like that before."

"Delivered Them Into Chains of Darkness"

In verse 7, we read how God *delivered* just Lot out of Sodom; here we read of fallen angels *delivered*, not from danger, but into hell. They are "delivered into chains of darkness." Rev. 20:1, 2 tells how an angel came down from heaven with a great chain in his hand, and bound Satan for 1,000 years and put him in the pit. Chains speak of bondage; the darkness, of misery. Into what a terrible place these sinful angels land. How utterly foolish it is for anyone, whether angel or man, to rise up in rebellion against the Lord.

"Darkness" Illustration

A friend of ours was touring one of the giant caves of Kentucky. The guide said to the party, "If you would like a thrill, all of you turn off your flash-lights, and leave them off until I tell you to turn them on." The place was suddenly plunged into a terrible darkness. No one dared move, and there was a feeling of utter aloneness. When the guide said, "Turn on your lights," there was a sigh of relief. The guide said, "You people did well, I have had women scream before I told them to turn on the lights." I am glad I am not going to those dungeons of darkness where the lights will never be turned on.

"Reserved Unto Judgment"

These fallen angels are already in chains of darkness, but are reserved unto the day of judgment. There is no sign here of annihilation or hope of pardon. Their condition is utterly hopeless. If God so punished the angels who sinned, the false teachers of our chapter need not expect better treatment. Verse 9 says, that the unjust of our day are also reserved "unto the day of judgment to be punished."

2:5 "And spared not the old world, but saved Noah the eighth person, a preacher of righteousness, bringing in the flood upon the world of the ungodly."

Here the apostle takes another example from past history of God's judging hand. In the last verse we see how He spared not the angels who sinned. Here he tells how He spared not the old world of sinners who lived before the flood. Probably more people died in the judgment of the flood than in any other catastrophe which ever struck this world. It is generally thought that that flood came over 1,500 years after Adam and Eve were created. With the longevity of man at that time, and all those years, there probably were millions of humans in the world. They all perished, except the eight souls who were in the ark. This shows how greatly God is displeased because of sin.

"NOAH"

Peter said the Lord "saved Noah." Many today do not believe that there ever was a flood, and question whether there ever was a man named Noah. They call it all a nice piece of fiction. Peter believed that there had been a flood and that Noah was a real man. The Lord Jesus also believed it. He said, "And as it was in the days of Noe, so shall it be also in the days of the Son of man. They did eat, they drank, they married wives, they were given in marriage, until the day that Noe entered into the ark, and the flood came, and destroyed them all" (Luke 17:26, 27). It is interesting to note that Peter brings in Noah and the flood, and then Lot and Sodom, just as the Lord Jesus did (Luke 17:26-29).

"BUT SAVED NOAH"

The Lord told Noah of the flood which was coming, and instructed him to build the ark. "Noah, being warned of God of things not seen as yet, moved with fear, prepared an ark to the saving of his house" (Heb. 11:7). It is interesting to notice that grace is first mentioned in the Bible in connection with Noah (Gen 6:8). This would tell us that, although the Lord calls

Noah "a preacher of righteousness," he still was not sinless, or he would not have needed the grace of God. This also teaches us that God will not destroy those who trust Him along with the wicked. We like to think of the ark as a type of Christ. All who entered the ark were saved from the flood. All who trust the Lord Jesus are saved from sin and hell.

"THE EIGHTH PERSON"

The expression "The eighth person" no doubt refers to the fact that Noah was one of the eight persons saved from the flood by entering the ark. The Revised Version has "preserved Noah with seven others." There is no word for "person" in the Greek. It is literally, "Noah the eighth" implying that he was one of eight. In Jude 14 it speaks of Enoch the seventh from Adam. This is chronologically correct. Some have thought that Peter meant that Noah was similarly the eighth from Adam, but this is not chronologically correct, since Noah is the tenth in line from Adam. Since there were just eight souls saved by the ark, it is natural to believe that Peter meant one among eight. Greek scholars say this is in accordance with a well-known Greek idiom.

ONLY A FEW SAVED

This all agrees with what Peter says in his first epistle (3:20), where we read, "wherein few, that is eight souls were saved." Out of the great mass of humanity at the time of the flood only eight souls were spared. If the righteous be many or few, all of them, but they only shall be saved.

"A PREACHER OF RIGHTEOUSNESS"

In Gen. 6:9 we read that "Noah was a just man and perfect in his generations, and Noah walked with God." Then in Gen. 7:1 the Lord says to him, "For thee have I seen righteous before me in this generation." But we nowhere read in Genesis that Noah did any preaching. This is an added word of inspiration by Peter. Noah could hardly refrain from preaching while building the ark. Many would ask him, "Noah, what are you building this ark for?" So he would be compelled to explain about the flood which was coming. No doubt Noah's words, his building the ark, and his exemplary life all preached to the sinners round about him.

Noah Warned the World

Every word which Noah preached and every board he put into the ark was a warning to the world that judgment was coming. Noah preached and built for 120 years, so the world had plenty of time to repent. How gracious the Lord was to warn them so long before the flood really came. It mostly fell on deaf ears, because when it came time to go into the ark, none went in save Noah and his wife, and his three sons and their wives. You say, "My how discouraging, all that preaching and all that building and only seven believe the message." It is well to remember that the Lord will not reward because of success, but because of faithfulness. One said one time, "Noah did not do so badly. At least his whole family was saved, and that is more than some preachers are able to say."

"Bringing In the Flood"

In Gen. 7:16 we have, "And they went in — and the Lord shut them in." When the Lord shut Noah in the ark, He shut all others out. After the terrible flood started to come it was too late for those outside to gain admittance. No doubt some pounded on the door, but Noah could not open that which God had shut. The flood swept them all away. As with the five foolish virgins, they knocked on the door but it was too late. "Every living substance was destroyed — and Noah only remained alive, and they that were with him in the ark" (Gen. 7:23).

"The World of the Ungodly"

Noah was a preacher of righteousness in a time of general corruption. It is greatly to his credit that he was willing to preach to such sinners and for so long a time. He did not get discouraged, even though they did not heed and probably even laughed and scorned. The extent of the corruption is suggested in Gen. 6:5, 11-13. Gen. 6:5 says, "And God saw that the wickedness of man was great in the earth, and that every imagination of the thoughts of his heart was only evil continually." The stench of it all rose up to heaven and God washed it all away by the mighty flood.

XVI

SODOM AND LOT

(II Peter 2:6-8)

2:6 "And turning the cities of Sodom and Gomorrha into ashes condemned them with an overthrow, making them an ensample unto those that after should live ungodly."

Now Peter brings in Sodom and Gomorrha as examples of the judging hand of God. The old world He destroyed by water, wicked Sodom and Gomorrha by fire. These cases from history are advanced as a warning to wicked doers of all ages.

"The Cities of Sodom and Gomorrha"

Sodom and Gomorrha were thriving cities in the Jordan valley not far from the Dead Sea. Abraham offered Lot the choice of the land when it became necessary for them to separate. Lot chose these well watered plains of Jordan because they were as the garden of the Lord (Gen. 13:10). Then as now, prosperous country-side produced prosperous cities. Along with this great prosperity went great wickedness. This is often so today. Good times produce immorality rather than higher morals. No doubt, when Lot made his choice he thought he was wise, but time proved that the wickedness of these cities made his choice a very bad one.

Their Wickedness

The wickedness of the citizens of Sodom and Gomorrha was so great that God could no longer tolerate it. The terribleness of their degradation is pictured in Gen. 19:4-11. To think that they actually surrounded Lot's house and demanded that he bring out to them his two visitors, that they might abuse them in order to satisfy their fleshly lusts. No wonder the Lord says to Abraham, "Because the cry of Sodom and Gomorrha is great, and because their sin is very grievous: I will go down now, and see" (Gen. 18:20, 21). Sin is very grievous today too, but we know of no instance in modern times, where it was so open and unashamed.

"TURNING THE CITIES - - INTO ASHES"

God sent down fire and brimstone from heaven and turned these wicked cities into ashes. How suddenly the hand of judgment fell, and they were gone with all their prosperity. The Lord proved that He could suddenly destroy by fire as well as by water as in our last verse. While He has promised that He will not again destroy civilization with water (Gen. 9:11-15), He has said that He will destroy it by fire (II Peter 3:10). Scoffers have sneered at the story of Sodom and Gomorrha and its destruction by fire and brimstone from heaven. If man can burn up a whole city with a few atom bombs, what folly to say that God could not do the same. Let no city, or people, or individual suppose that he is out of the reach of God's arrows of judgment.

"CONDEMNED THEM WITH AN OVERTHROW"

The fact that the Lord reduced these cities to ashes showed that He disapproved of their lewd actions. Their sins were terrible and their judgment equally so. God still hates and condemns the sin of the world, and it is folly to think that He will not condemn the unrepentant sinner. Some say, "God is love and He will not condemn the sinner." Perhaps some Sodomites had similar thoughts, but the day came when the judgment fell. Many think you should never say anything about hell or judgment, and that one who does is old-fashioned. It never is out of date to say that the unrepentant sinner is already condemned by God, and will someday experience His wrath in judgment.

SINKING NATIONS

Not only Sodom and Gomorrha have been judged because of sin, but also Babylon, and Nineveh, and Greece, and Rome. "Sin is a reproach to any people" (Prov. 14:34). A sinful nation will as surely sink as will a sinful person. Let modern nations beware, lest they too feel the judging hand of God. No doubt the recent war was His hand in judgment upon the sins of the nations.

"MAKING THEM AN ENSAMPLE"

Sometimes, when a certain crime becomes prevalent and vile, the judge, in order to check it, will be very severe with a few outstanding cases, making them examples to other offenders. The Lord did that with these wicked cities. Their sin was great and the Lord meted out severe judgment in order that other offenders might beware; not only offenders of that day, but offenders of all ages. Many would shelve the story of Sodom and Gomorrha as a bit of ancient history. They would be wise to let this history speak to their hearts. What God has done He will do. He punished the sinner of the past, and He will punish the sinner of the present and the future. In Sodom we have a picture of what the persistent sinner may expect. There is only escape from judgment by fleeing to the Lord Jesus. This portion is especially addressed to false teachers of Peter's time, who taught that carnal living was Christian liberty. Let such or kindred teachers of today especially beware.

2:7 "And delivered just Lot, vexed with the filthy conversation of the wicked."

In this verse Lot is brought in to show that, although God will punish the sinner, yet He will deliver the righteous, be they ever so few. We have some statements here concerning Lot which we would not know by only reading the account of him in Genesis.

"Delivered Just Lot"

The Lord pictures Lot's rescue out of Sodom as a deliverance. The angels first warned him of the judgment, and then practically had to force him to leave the city. "And while he lingered, the men laid hold upon his hand, and upon the hand of his wife, and upon the hand of his two daughters; the Lord being merciful unto him: and they brought him forth: and set him without the city" (Gen. 19:16). He seemed reluctant to go, and then objected when they told him to flee to the mountains, and was given permission to flee to the little city of Zoar. Although declared a righteous man, it would seem, to a great extent, his heart was in Sodom.

Only a Few Saved

This would again teach us that only a few are saved. Only eight were saved from the flood, but only four were saved from Sodom, and Lot's wife was changed into a pillar of salt. There are not many saved in our day either. "Enter ye in at the strait gate: for wide is the gate, and broad is the way, that leadeth to destruction, and many there be which go in thereat; because strait is the gate, and narrow the way, which leadeth unto life, and few there be that find it" (Mat. 7:13, 14).

ABRAHAM AND LOT

Our verse suggests that Lot was delivered from Sodom because he was a just man. As we read the latter part of Gen. 18 we would be inclined to think that it was mostly because of Abraham's intercession. No doubt both are true. Lot was a righteous man in a wrong place, Abraham pleaded for him and the Lord delivered him. Perhaps if we would pray more for worldly Christians more of them would be delivered out of Sodom.

"JUST LOT"

The Spirit's testimony of Lot here is that he was a just man. As we read the account of his life in Genesis we certainly would conclude that at best he was a worldly child of God; one whose faith was weak. He chose wicked Sodom because of worldly advantage. No doubt at first he prospered greatly. We find him sitting in the gate of Sodom, considered a great place in Bible times; the place where the judges sat. He probably was a man of great wealth. This choice did not end well. Some of his daughters married Sodomites and were lost in its overthrow. When he fled Sodom, he left all his wealth behind to be consumed. His wife's heart was in Sodom and as they fled, contrary to instructions, she looked back and was changed into a pillar of salt. Two of his daughters were delivered, but they lost all sense of morality in this wicked city, and we see them do a shameful thing with their own father. He entered Sodom a prince, but came out a pauper. It is an evil thing for a Christian to go in for worldly advantage.

LOT'S RIGHTEOUSNESS

In spite of all this, Lot was one of the Lord's own, righteous in His sight because of faith in Him. This is emphasized three times in our verse and in the next. Besides being "just," he is called a "righteous man" having a "righteous soul." That he had more than imputed righteousness is evidenced by the fact that he reprimanded the Sodomites for their wickedness. He says, "I pray you, brethren, do not so wickedly" (Gen 19:7). There is no evidence that he in any way partook of their extremely wicked ways. He was a just man in the midst of corruption and injustice. It must have been a struggle to maintain a moral life in the midst of such great evil.

Temptations While In the Army

We remember how it was with us in the army during the first world war. It would have been easy to have fallen into the ways of our evil companions, but the Lord had His eye on His newly born child, and gave strength to overcome. Some fell by the wayside. We were made sad by seeing a preacher's son engulfed in the evil.

Lot Failed but was Delivered

Lot is not listed amongst the heroes of faith in Heb. 11. His lack of faith caused him to choose Sodom. He was a righteous man in a wrong place. Many a child of God today is living in the world. Let us, as Abraham interceded for Lot, pray that the Lord may deliver these worldly Christians. Lot was only one righteous among many corrupt sinners, but God was careful to deliver him, even though there was much about him which could not be commended. It is interesting to note that here the Lord commends Lot's faithfulness, but says nothing of his sin.

"Vexed"

The word translated "vexed" in our verse is a very strong one. It elsewhere is translated "tormented." It is literally "tortured." The Revised Version has "sore distressed by the lascivious life of the wicked." It would seem that the apostle would stress real mental misery, because of the awful sin surrounding Lot. A child of God living in the world is not happy. He will be grieved with himself and with the sinners round about him. A Christian should not hate man, but should hate his evil deeds. Are we grieved by the sinful actions of those round about us? If not, beware lest we soon sink into similar practices. Evidently

Lot was paying a price for living in Sodom even before he ever fled out of it.

"FILTHY CONVERSATION OF THE WICKED"

"Conversation," as elsewhere in the New Testament, would be better translated "manner of life." It is not only that their speech was filthy, but all their actions were so. "Filthy" is variously translated as "lawless," "lasciviousness" and "abandoned." "But the men of Sodom were wicked and sinners before the Lord exceedingly" (Gen. 13:13). They not only broke the laws of God, but the very laws of nature.

FILTHY LIVES TODAY

We believe the lives of many today are as filthy as the Sodomites, although not as open and defiant as theirs. If we knew how serious it really is, perhaps we would, like Jeremiah, weep over the sins of the people. "Oh that my head were waters, and mine eyes a fountain of tears, that I might weep day and night for the slain of the daughters of my people!" (Jer. 9:1).

2:8 ("For that righteous man dwelling among them, in seeing and hearing, vexed his righteous soul from day to day with their unlawful deeds;")

This verse is an expansion of our last one. It adds that Lot, dwelling amongst them, both saw and heard their wickedness. Also, that the vexing of his soul was a daily occurrence.

RIGHTEOUS LOT

Some might ask, "Was this righteousness of Lot an imputed righteousness or a practical one?" We believe it was both. "Abraham believed God, and it was counted unto him for righteousness" (Rom. 4:3). We believe this was true of Lot, too. In fact, faith in Christ now is the beginning of righteousness as far as God is concerned. He considers none righteous unless right with Him (Rom. 3:21-28).

PRACTICAL RIGHTEOUSNESS

However, practical righteous living should follow imputed righteousness. We believe Lot was a righteous living man in the midst of the corruption of Sodom. Evidently there were none other righteous ones in the whole city of Sodom. One has said, "It is better to be righteous with one single Lot, than to perish with the whole of Sodom." If the reader would like more on the subject of righteousness, we would advise a careful study of the book of Romans.

"DWELLING AMONG THEM"

Chronologists figure that Lot dwelt in Sodom at least 16, perhaps 20 years. In all that time he did not get hardened to the awful conditions around about him, and in it all he maintained his integrity and righteousness. No doubt his righteousness accounts for his advancement in Sodom. While the world does not like the pure life of the Christian, nevertheless it puts a Christian in responsible positions, because he is trustworthy.

SOME CANNOT STAND RIGHTEOUS CHRISTIANS

Sometimes a Christian's righteous life works against him. The writer at one time was discharged from a good position, because, as our superior later confessed to a friend, "I just could not stand that Christian around." Many wicked men do not relish a "righteous man dwelling among them." We believe the righteousness of Christ was the main reason why He was bitterly hated and finally driven to the cross.

"IN SEEING AND HEARING"

Poor Lot not only had to hear filthy language continually, but the Sodomites were so open and blatant in their evil that he had to continually view their filthy actions. These sinners did not even try to cover their shame from the eyes of others. In spite of this Lot did not become contaminated, he remained just. The contacts of a preacher, like your author, are mostly with moral Christian people, yet often we hear vile things, and sometimes even view them. Perhaps many of our readers hear and see a great deal more than we do. We would advise each one to avoid as much of this as possible. Lot did not have to stay in Sodom, and ofttimes the Lord's people can avoid seeing and hearing these wicked things.

"VEXED HIS RIGHTEOUS SOUL"

The word "vexed" here is the same as in verse 7. It is literally "tortured," often translated "tormented." Being righteous he naturally hated evil. Sin grieves the Lord, and being His children, we should be grieved by that which grieves Him. We read in Mark 3:5 of our Lord, "Being grieved for the hardness of their hearts." We believe it was the sins of His creatures which caused our Lord to be a "man of sorrows" (Isa. 53:3). Many of God's saints have been grieved by the sins of those round about. The Psalmist says, "I beheld the transgressors, and was grieved" (Ps. 119:158). Ezra said, "And when I heard this thing I rent my garment and my mantle" (Ezra 9:3). Daniel prayed for the sins of the captives in Babylon (Dan. 9:3-19). Isaiah laments because of his own sins and those of his people (Isa. 6:5). We wonder if the sins of our friends and relatives, to say nothing of our enemies, ever cause us to be grieved and to be humbled before the Lord. Unless we are grieved by their sin, we probably will do little or nothing to win them for Christ.

"From Day to Day"

The expression "from day to day" would tell us that Lot was not spasmodically grieved by the sins of the Sodomites, but that it was a daily affair. Time did not make him callous to the wickedness around him. Perhaps daily he pled with these sinners and prayed for them too. At least we should do no less today. Above all, in the midst of corruption, let us keep ourselves clean. May we shine as lights in a dark world.

XVII

THE WAY OF THE UNJUST

(II Peter 2:9, 10)

2:9 "The Lord knoweth how to deliver the godly out of temptations, and to reserve the unjust unto the day of judgment to be punished."

[Here we have simply stated what we have pictured in verses 4-8. Peter has shown how the Lord delivered righteous Noah and Lot, but also, how He punished sinning angels, the antediluvians, and the sinners of Sodom and Gomorrha. He knew how to deliver Noah from the flood and Lot out of Sodom, and even so He can deliver His own from trial today. Sinning angels and sinful men did not escape righteous judgment, so let rebellious sinners living today beware.]

"The Lord Knoweth"

The Scriptures in many places tell of the great knowledge of our Lord. He knows all about us, our every action (Ps. 139:3), our every word (Ps. 139:4), yea, our every thought (Ps. 139:2). He not only knows those who are His (II Tim. 2:19), but He also knows all the trials which ever beset them. "For the Lord knoweth the way of the righteous (Ps. 1:6). He knows the way of the ungodly too. "Such knowledge is too wonderful for me; it is high, I cannot attain unto it" (Ps. 139:6).

"Knoweth How to Deliver"

[The Lord not only knows when one of His own is in difficulty, but He knows how and when to deliver him out of it. Perhaps far more often than we realize, He keeps His own from getting into trouble. He knows just when for their own good, to let them get into trouble, just how long to let them suffer, and just when and how to deliver them from it.]

He Can Find a Way

Sometimes very grievous trials come a Christian's way. It is natural for him to cast about for a way out, but there seems no way, the difficulties seem insurmountable. The situation may seem utterly hopeless with no ray of light, but the Lord knows. His knowledge far excels ours and He can find a way out. Nothing is impossible to Him, and nothing hid from Him; He can find a way and His way will prove to be the best way.

A GREAT DELIVERER

The Scriptures are full of cases wherein the Lord delivered His saints in unexpected ways. He delivered Joseph from prison in Egypt through Pharaoh's dreams. He caused Ahasuerus to have a sleepless night in order to deliver Mordecai from the gallows and all the Jews from being killed by wicked Haman. He caused the Red Sea to part in order to deliver the children of Israel out of the hands of Pharaoh. He stopped the mouths of lions and stayed the burning power of fire to deliver Daniel and his three friends. He caused the ravens to bring food to Elijah, and later caused the widow's pot of oil to diminish not, in order to deliver His servant from starvation. These are but a few of many cases we could add to Noah and Lot, whom Peter mentions.

NEW TESTAMENT EXAMPLES

The New Testament relates many examples, too. He delivered Peter from prison (Acts 12) and Paul from the awful storm at sea (Acts 27). When Christ and His disciples were terribly tossed by the winds and the waves, He rebuked the wind and the sea and there was a great calm. Even today storms may rage around us, but with a word He can send peace and calm. In order to accomplish this He can raise up friends, destroy enemies, change the course of events, alter men's hearts, or even do the miraculous.

MODERN EXAMPLES

We could give many modern examples of the Lord delivering the godly out of trial. Many stories have come out of the recent wars. The defense of Malta, as written by General Dobbie, is a thrilling narrative of the intervening hand of the Lord. Many accounts of super-human preservation and rescue of wrecked boat and plane crews have been published. All tell of the prayers and faith of one or more of these rescued. "The Lord knoweth how to deliver the godly out of trial."

He Delivers Us

The Lord not only delivers us from trial, but from this present evil world (Gal. 1:4), from evil (Mat. 6:13), the law (Rom. 7:6), the fear of death (Heb. 2:15), from the power of darkness (Col. 1:13) and the wrath to come (I Thess. 1:10). On our part, beloved, we should do our utmost to keep from entanglement in sin and the allurements of the world.

"The Godly"

The word here translated "godly" is a compound one literally translated "well-reverent." It could also be translated "pious" or "devout." It would indicate more than merely being saved; it would also suggest a consistent life for the Lord. A Christian who lives for himself and the world need not expect deliverance in time of trial. In fact, the Lord may purposely send trial in order to bring the careless closer to Himself. He may permit even the godly Christians to suffer certain things in order to teach them needed lessons. However, He will not permit His devout ones to suffer a needless trial. The Lord will never consider a man godly, who has not trusted Christ as his Savior.

"Reserve the Unjust"

The Revised Version translates the last part of our verse, "And to keep the unrighteous under punishment unto the day of judgment." This puts the punishment in the present tense and may indicate, that although the wicked ones may roam in this world at will, the Lord already has His hand upon them and is punishing them for their sins even now. At any rate, the Lord has them under surveillance, and they cannot escape unless they repent and trust Christ. "Reserved" tells of the certainty of the punishment of the wicked Christ-rejector. It would be easier for a murderer to get out of the death cell, than for one to escape the righteous judgment of the Lord. The judge cannot be fooled or bribed. No clever lawyers will be able to bring about an evasion of the issue, or even bring about a compromise.

No Annihilation

The word "reserved" also tells us that there is no such thing as annihilation. Every sinner who has ever lived in this scene is still in existence, either here on earth, or in hell and being reserved for judgment. Oh, that the unjust on earth would realize what lies ahead of them, and would flee to Christ for salvation.

"THE UNJUST"

The Bible is very plain in stating that all unsaved in the world are unjust. Rom. 3:10 says, "There is none righteous, no, not one." Just and righteous are the same words in the Greek. They are not "just" practically because they sin every day. They are not "just" legally because they break the law. Neither are they "just" by imputation, for they have not trusted Christ. All these unjust sinners, whether still in the world or already out of it, are "reserved under punishment unto the day of judgment."

"UNTO THE DAY OF JUDGMENT"

There is a day coming when every sinner will appear before the judgment bar of God. We do not know how soon this day will arrive, but its coming is certain. Whether it be near at hand, or some time away, it does not change matters much, because the sinner is already under punishment. Those who are dead are already suffering the pangs of God's judging hand. They are already in God's prison house awaiting the day of trial. Their punishment is even now severe, but after the judgment it may be even more terrible.

THE PUNISHMENT IS FOREVER

This final judgment will not only be severe, but it will be everlasting. The Word speaks of "eternal damnation" in Mark 3:29, and "eternal fire" in Jude 7. John 3:36 says, "He that believeth on the Son hath everlasting life; and he that believeth not the Son shall not see life; but the wrath of God abideth on him." Paul says to the unrepentant sinner in Rom. 2:5, "But after thy hardness and impenitent heart treasurest up unto thyself wrath against the day of wrath and revelation of the righteous judgment of God."

"TO BE PUNISHED"

We have seen how this is "under punishment" in the Revised Version and seems to indicate punishment in the present tense, as though the unjust were already being punished in this scene.

We know that sin brings its own punishment. A liar will suffer for his lying; a thief will eventually get caught; a drinker has his bad after effects; a sexual sinner is apt to be afflicted with venereal disease, etc. Besides this we believe most have mental anguish because of their sin. The Lord constantly puts stumbling blocks in their paths and reminders of the punishment which lies ahead. He constantly thrusts in arrows of conviction which spoil a sinner's happiness.

Examples of Present Torment

One prosperous farmer said he could be happy here, if it wasn't for the cemetery across the road. Another man said, "Those gospel signs along the highways are everywhere; they spoil a man's motoring trips." Still another said, "I used to drive a taxicab in Muskegon, Mich., and about once a week somebody would load me down with literature about Jesus Christ. Why can't He leave a fellow alone?" Many may seem outwardly happy and prosperous, but the Lord only knows about their mental punishment and anguish. Of course, this is all only a prelude to the real punishment in hell which they will suffer, unless they repent and believe. We trust that many will flee to Christ and escape that place, "Where their worm dieth not, and the fire is not quenched" (Mark 9:44).

2:10 "But chiefly them that walk after the flesh in the lust of uncleanness, and despise government. Presumptuous are they, self-willed, they are not afraid to speak evil of dignities."

In this verse Peter tells of the type of false teachers he is especially attacking. He condemns two things in them. First that they live in the ways of the flesh, that is in uncleanness; and second, they set aside all authority, claiming that this abuses their Christian liberty. We find in these false teachers presumption, pride, and shameless degradation.

"Walk After the Flesh"

The word here translated "flesh" has a variety of meanings in the Bible. Sometimes it only means the meat of an animal or human. Sometimes it is the body, as opposed to the spirit in man. Most often, as here, it speaks of the frailties and sinful passions of human nature. Every Christian lives in the flesh, but no Christian should walk after the flesh. "Though we walk in the flesh, we do not war after the flesh" (II Cor. 10:3). The flesh and the spirit are contrasted in Rom. 8:1-13. "That the righteousness of the law might be fulfilled in us, who walk not after the flesh, but after the spirit" (Rom. 8:4).

Pleasing the Flesh

The false teachers of our chapter were making the pleasing of the flesh their main object. They gave themselves license to do all manner of unclean things, and evidently misapplied Scripture in order to justify their evil. As we read further into the chapter, the two sins of which they were especially guilty were adultery and covetousness. We fear many professed Christians today do not hesitate to satisfy their carnal lusts.

"The Lust of Uncleanness"

The Scriptures everywhere condemn uncleanness. Many seem to think that because we are not saved by what we do, or how we live, that it does not matter much whether we live clean lives or not. This is a serious mistake. When we are saved, it is not by clean living, but we are saved in order to live cleanly. We are saved from sin and uncleanness to live a pure life for the Lord. Many think that salvation is merely being freed from the penalty of sin, but the Scripture everywhere attests that when one trusts Christ he is also saved from the power of sin.

Many Profess Who Are Not Saved

If this power to live a clean life is not manifest in one who professes salvation, the Scripture suggests that such a one is not saved at all. "For God hath not called us unto uncleanness, but unto holiness" (I Thess. 4:7). Rom. 1:24-27 tells of the uncleanness of the heathen of Paul's day. For those who profess Christianity and yet live in these sins, is for them to go back to heathenism. "For this ye know, that no whoremonger, nor unclean person, nor covetous man, who is an idolator, hath any inheritance in the kingdom of Christ and of God" (Eph. 5:5 also I Cor. 6:9, 10).

ILLUSTRATIONS

One man recently said to us, "I do not think the Lord is too much interested in whether a man lives a clean life or not, just so he is devoted to Christ." We know the man was utterly mistaken. Of course a devoted life is very important, but we question a man's devotion if his life is not clean. Another said to us, "I don't think God will hold it against a man if he goes on a little binge once in a while." Of course this man was utterly mistaken, too. The Lord will hold it against a man who drinks to excess. We are not teaching sinless perfection. A Christian may fall into sin, but he certainly will not and should not live in it.

"DESPISE GOVERNMENT"

"Government" is literally "dominion" as in the Revised Version. Some translate it "authority." This can be applied to any authority, whether it be of government officials, assembly elders, or the authority of God and His Word. These false teachers despised any authority which would put any restraint on their unbridled lusts. Perhaps, to mislead their followers, they said, like some today, "Oh, we are not under the law; it does not matter much what we do. We are living in New Testament times, and this is the dispensation of grace." So they mix truth with error. It is blessedly true that we are under grace and not under law, but it is despicably untrue to say, therefore we are not under authority, and we can live as we please.

CHRISTIAN LIBERTY IS NOT LICENSE

They may have also talked about Christian liberty, quoting "Stand fast therefore in the liberty wherewith Christ hath made us free" (Gal. 5:1). This refers especially to ceremonial law from which Christ has indeed freed us. He frees us from scores of other things, but He has not freed us to sin as we please. In fact sin is a slave master from which the Lord frees His own (John 8:34-36).

PARENTAL AUTHORITY

While parental authority is not in view in our verse, nevertheless we feel it necessary to stress it continually. It is the place where the foundation for respect of authority must be laid. If children are taught to obey their parents, it will not be hard for them to obey governmental authorities, nor the Lord and His Word. Not only the law says, "Honour thy father and thy mother," but we read in Col. 3:20, "Children, obey your parents in all things: for this is well-pleasing to the Lord" (also Eph. 6:1-3). The stubborn and rebellious son who would not obey his parents in Old Testament times was to be stoned to death (Deut. 21:18-21). We are happy to know that in our homes and also in our schools, there is more insistence upon obedience than there was a decade ago.

GOVERNMENTAL AUTHORITY

Respect for governmental authority seems to be at a very low ebb. Many deliberately set about to disobey the law. Every law from traffic ordinances to income tax payments are openly flaunted. They claim the government is beaten out of millions of income tax dollars every year. And then there are thousands who are seeking to overthrow our present form of government. There is very good counsel in Prov. 24:21, "My son, fear thou the Lord and the king: and meddle not with them that are given to change."

BE SUBJECT TO THE GOVERNMENT

Romans 13:1-7 tells how we as Christians should be subject to the powers that be, and how they are set in their places by the authority of the Lord (also I Pet. 2:13, 14). In time past, Christians have erred in that they have resisted the government and at times have even lorded over it. We know how Catholic popes have at times usurped authority over kings, and do so even today when they can.

THE AUTHORITY OF GOD

When the authority of God and His Word is cast aside, life is brought down to the level of the animals. This is Peter's conclusion in verse 12. With God's authority gone, all other soon goes, too. This is the position into which these false teachers had sunk, and into which they were leading their followers. They were virtually saying, "we will not have this man to reign over us" (Luke 19:14). They who propagate error will soon walk in sin;

and they who walk in sin will soon propagate error. Men love a religion which does not bind them too strongly morally. If they can be assured that this is not necessary, they will be ready to follow anyone. Let us have a tender conscience about obeying God's Word, and the Lord will bless us and reward us.

"Presumptuous Are They"

We have had folks say to us, "It is presumption for you to say you know you are saved." It is never presumption to tell the truth. If you have of a truth taken your place as an unworthy sinner before the Lord, and received Christ as your Savior, and been born again, it is doubt, not faith, to question your salvation. Of course, if you have not received this new birth from the Lord, then it is presumption to expect to go to heaven. Especially is this so, if you are, like these false teachers, living an unclean life besides. It is presumption for such to think that they will escape the judging hand of the Lord.

Daring

The word "presumptuous" is literally "darers." The Revised Version has "daring." Some translate it "audacious." And truly it is a daring thing to despise the authority of God. If sinners knew the awful judgment which lies ahead they would rather tremble.

"Selfwilled"

These false teachers were selfwilled. They wanted their own way about everything. They did not care what the Lord said, or anyone else; they intended to do as they wanted. This pampering of self is a dreadful thing. The selfish man injures himself and others as well. He is not happy, and makes others unhappy, too. How much better to live for others and the Lord. "We then that are strong ought to bear the infirmities of the weak, and not to please ourselves. Let every one of us please his neighbour for his good to edification. For even Christ pleased not himself" (Rom. 15:1-3).

His Will or Ours?

How much better to do the will of God, rather than our own. The great apostle Paul asked at his conversion, "Lord, what wilt thou have me to do?" From that day forth he sought to do the Lord's will. A self-willed man can ruin a work for God. We recently heard of a pastor of a large congregation who was causing the work to go down, not because his preaching was poor, but because he was determined to have his own way in everything.

"Are Not Afraid to Speak Evil of Dignities"

The Revised Version has for this last expression, "Tremble not to rail at dignities," and is a more exact translation. "Speak evil" is literally "blaspheme," and "dignities" is "glories." This may refer to glorious or honorable things or personages. Because of the next verse, we believe Peter had personages in mind. These arrogant men did not tremble when they openly blasphemed greater ones than themselves. They probably spoke in an evil way of church elders, as well as government officials. Perhaps some of these elders sought to check them in their licentious ways, and this caused them to rise up in anger and to rail at them.

The Tongue can be Awful

What an awful thing the tongue can be. We have noted how James, in his epistle, speaks of this wicked little member in scathing terms. Its capacity for evil is unlimited. How we need to put a watch on it at all times. It not only can injure the speaker and the one spoken of, but can also poison the mind of the hearers. Let us not be like Korah, Dathan and Abiram who spoke against the authority of Moses and soon suffered from the chastening hand of the Lord.

Respect Officials

Let us not speak evil of those set in authority over us in the government. Some otherwise fine Christians seem to do this without much thought. Paul quotes Ex. 22:28 when he says, "Thou shalt not speak evil of the ruler of thy people" (Acts 23:5). "Curse not the king, no not in thy thought" (Eccl. 10:20). Let us remember that to speak evil of rulers is to speak evil of God, who set them over us (Rom. 13:1-4).

XVIII

ANGELS AND BRUTE BEASTS

(II Peter 2:11, 12)

2:11. "Whereas angels, which are greater in power and might, bring not railing accusation against them before the Lord."

[Here angels are placed in bold contrast to the wicked false teachers of our chapter. These wicked men dared blaspheme dignities of a much higher order than they were themselves, while these unfallen angels would not dare to do the same of creatures of a far lower order than they were themselves.]

"Angels — Greater in Power and Might"

This is the second time Peter brings in angels in this chapter. However, in verse 4, he speaks of fallen angels, but these in our verse are those who have not fallen. Peter says these angels are "greater in power and might." They also exceed all humans in morality; certainly they exceed these false teachers in this respect. They have never sinned. They do His commandments, and hearken unto His voice (Ps. 103:20). They do His will perfectly. "Greater in power and might" could be translated "greater in forcefulness and miraculous power." These are similar words in the Greek, but the latter usually has the sense of miraculous attached to it. They "excel in strength" in their own right, but they have additional powers given to them by the Lord for special purposes. For instance, one angel was sent to be with Daniel in the lion's den, and he shut the mouths of these wild animals. They are often pictured as mighty creatures (Ps. 104:4, II Thess. 1:7). Angels also exceed humans in wisdom (II Sam. 14:20, etc.).

"Bring Not Railing Accusation"

"Railing accusation" is a good translation. The wicked men of our chapter were bringing blasphemous accusations against dignities, or authorities who were far greater than themselves. Angels would not dare do the same of authorities far inferior to themselves. No doubt, it is part of the angels work to make reports before the Lord, and they must tell the truth, and so must at times bring accusation against dignities who sin, but they would not do it with vile or abusive language. They speak only in a calm and serious manner even when accusing the worst sinners.

Let Us Not Be Railers

We have on rare occasions heard Christians lose their tempers and rail and accuse each other in an awful way. This is to be like the devil. He is the accuser of the brethren (Rev. 12:10). It is a terrible thing to curse a brother, or to rail at him, or to accuse him falsely. This brings great reproach and does great damage to the cause of Christ. It has scattered the flock and left excuse for the unsaved for not trusting Christ.

Vile Sinners

The language of many sinners in the world today is terrific. They rail and accuse not only earthly authorities, but God and Christ. Their audacity is surprising. They would not dare abuse the name of their worst earthly enemies the way they do the name of the Lord. They are worse than Shimei who cursed David (II Sam. 16:7, 8), or Korah, Dathan and Abiram who questioned the authority of Moses.

The Angels and the Devil

Jude, in using similar language, brings the angel's accusation of the devil. Michael the archangel disputed with the devil about the body of Moses. Michael did not bring a railing accusation against him but said, "The Lord rebuke thee" (Jude 9). No doubt he realized that Satan was a powerful being still. The Scriptures call Satan "the strong man armed," and "the prince of the power of the air," and "the God of this world." At one time he had a very high place in heaven, and the angels still recognize a measure of dignity because of this former high estate. We believe some Christians make a serious mistake when they lightly speak of this enemy of ours. Let us not go beyond what angels did.

"BEFORE THE LORD"

[The angels stand "before the Lord" and report to Him. This dignified presence would have a sobering effect on their behavior and speech. As they stand before His majesty they speak in tones of awe and caution. They state simple facts and leave the judgment of the matter to the Lord. Let us not forget we are ever in the Lord's presence too, even though we cannot see Him with the natural eye. May this sober us as it does the angels, and cause us to speak with caution. If we have accusations, let us, as they, present them before the Lord, not before men. Again, let us never use the language of the railer or blasphemer.]

2:12. "But these, as natural brute beasts, made to be taken and destroyed, speak evil of the things that they understand not; and shall utterly perish in their own corruption."

[In our last verse Peter shows how unlike angels these wicked men are. Now in our verse he shows how much like animals they are. They are like dangerous wild animals fit only to be destroyed, or other animals without sense only good for food. They speak evil of things concerning which they are ignorant. To be ignorant of a matter is bad enough, but to speak evil of it, is plain folly. For such only trouble lies ahead.]

"AS NATURAL BRUTE BEASTS"

What awful sinners we sometimes find in the circle of Christian fellowship. Peter likens these men to brute beasts. Ever since the time of Judas there have been those who profess to be Christians, yet all the time are unsaved and wicked men. That there are such today, no one with an enlightened mind will deny. There still are brutes who pose as leaders, and beasts who pass for teachers.

"NATURAL"

The Revised Version has "born mere animals." There was nothing spiritual about these men; they were wholly sensual like the animals. There was no evidence at all of a new life from the Lord, and so their appetites were wholly natural. Like the animals, they were directed solely by their natural reasonings and lusts. These men who professed to be spiritually enlightened were really on a common level with the animals. As the animals are unashamed in their evil ways, so these men also delighted to riot in the daytime, as our next verse indicates.

"BRUTE"

Men are likened to brutes often in the Word, especially in the Old Testament (Ps. 49:10, 92:6, Jer. 10:8, etc.). The Revised Version calls these men "creatures without reason." While some animals show some signs of being able to think, for the most part their passions rule over their lives. With these men, their passions ruled over their reasons too. Men in recent years have shown great reasoning powers in their multitude of inventions, and they glory in this. However in it all they have risen but a very little morally. In most of them their reasoning powers have not enabled them to control their passions. "They are wise to do evil, but to do good they have no knowledge" (Jer. 4:22). How sad to see otherwise smart men ensnared by the lust of the flesh. Christ in the heart alone is able to deliver such.

"BEASTS"

"Animals" would be better than "beasts." The Scripture often likens sinful man to some animal. The last verse of our chapter likens him to a dog and a swine. He is also likened to a horse, a mule, a fox, a wolf, a bear and a lion. Many of these terms are in use even today. Call a man a beast, or a dog, or a swine, and see what happens. We often hear the expression, "stubborn as a mule" and "wise as a fox." Many are called "wolves" today, too. May we rise above these animals without reason, and control our animal instincts, by the help of the Lord.

"MADE TO BE TAKEN AND DESTROYED"

Many animals are born just to be taken to the slaughterhouse to die, that they may be food for man. More than likely though, Peter has wild animals in mind, who, because of their destructiveness, are caught and killed. Some translators have "captured" or "caught and destroyed." We know how in Africa lions will kill stock and sometimes become man-eaters. Then great hunting parties are formed to capture and kill them. This is true of tigers and leopards at times in India too. Peter says these false teachers are no better than wild animals, who, because of their own destructiveness, should be taken and destroyed. If a man sinks to the level of the beasts he can only expect to be treated as such by the Lord.

"SPEAK EVIL"

The Scripture often condemns evil speaking. Evil speaking takes on many forms, but our verse suggests the worst form, that of railing (R.V.). All evil speaking results from a desire to be of greater importance in the eyes of others. The evil speaker has the thought that in dragging down others, he pushes himself up. However, it seldom has the desired effect. It may drag others down, but it usually drags the speaker down too, in the estimation of the hearers. It is a habit which does no one any good. Usually the speaker, the hearer, and the one spoken of, are all injured by it.

"THINGS THEY UNDERSTAND NOT"

The Revised Version has, "railing in matters whereof they are ignorant." It is bad to be ignorant, but worse when one speaks of evil of that concerning which he is ignorant. This is plain folly and recklessness. These men had no understanding of the right ways of the Lord, but professed to be of great understanding, and railed on those who tried to teach the right way. Ignorance is often back of evil speaking. If men really knew, they would never dare to speak evil of God and Christ. Because of ignorance great men of God have been bitterly criticised. Little mean men found fault with the great apostle Paul. Most all great men since then have had to bear similar attacks. Do not be dismayed when you find yourself the butt of some bitter attack by someone far inferior to you. This is especially hard to take from those who profess to belong to the Lord.

"SHALL UTTERLY PERISH"

The last phrase of this verse is literally, "shall be corrupted in their own corruption." The Revised Version has, "shall in their destroying surely be destroyed." It is just another way of saying, "Whatsoever a man soweth, that shall he also reap" (Gal. 6:7). If a man sows corruption he will reap corruption; if he sows destruction he will surely reap destruction.

THEIR JUDGMENT IS CERTAIN

The word "shall" tells of the certainty of the judgment which was to befall these wicked men. It may be delayed, but it will surely come. These men were not only useless to Christianity, but destructive of it, and they could not expect that their wicked actions would produce anything but their own destruction. "His mischief shall return upon his own head, and his violent dealing shall come down upon his own pate" (Ps. 7:16). This misery and destruction often comes already in this life, but certainly unless there is repentance and a true turning to Christ, it will come after death.

XIX

THE EVIL WAYS OF FALSE TEACHERS

(II Peter 2:13, 14)

2:13. "And shall receive the reward of unrighteousness, as they that count it pleasure to riot in the day time. Spots they are and blemishes, sporting themselves with their own deceivings while they feast with you."

After again telling of the judgment awaiting these unrighteous men, our verse goes on to tell more of their shameful actions. They cared not who saw and knew of their debased behavior, and openly carried on their riotous ways in the daytime. This naturally brought disgrace upon the Christian company; they were like spots and blemishes to the pure in the assembly. They seemed to take delight in the knowledge that they were able to deceive others of the Christians. All the while they were taking all the privileges of the Christian assembly and even took a place at the sacred feast, the Lord's supper.

"The Reward of Unrighteousness"

This second chapter of II Peter has many very unusual Greek words and consequently there are quite a variety of thoughts brought out by various translators. This first phrase of our verse would perhaps be best translated, "Shall carry off as their due the reward of unrighteousness." The Revised Version has "Suffering wrong as the hire of wrong doing." The implication is certain that these men would receive judgment from the hand of God according to their guilt.

The Sin Question or the Son Question?

Sometimes we hear one say, "It is no longer the sin question, but the Son question." We do not believe this will stand the test of Scripture. It is indeed the Son question, but it is also the sin question. Our verse plainly says that judgment will be according to their sin. It is like a disease and its remedy. Supposing a man has a serious disease, but there is a remedy for it. However, he does not take the remedy and dies. Why did he die? Well, you say, "He died because of his sickness." True enough, but another will say, "He died because he did not take the remedy." Again this is true. In the same way a man's sin will bring judgment, and the Scripture everywhere testifies that the worse the sin, the worse the punishment. At the same time a man's rejection of Christ as the remedy for his sin is also the cause of his condemnation. So we conclude it is both the sin question and the Son question.

Christ Saves From Sin

When Christ saves a sinner He does more than save him from the penalty of sin. He also saves him from the power of sin. Not that a saved person will never fall into sin, but he is given power so that sin need not rule over him. A true Christian may fall into sin, but he will not live in it. If we find one who seems to have no power over sin, then we immediately wonder whether he is saved, even though he may profess to be. "Thou shalt call his name Jesus: for he shall save his people from their sins" (Mat. 1:21).

"Pleasure To Riot in the Day Time"

Most sin is done in the dark or under cover so it cannot be seen. Thieves broke into our home one night. They also stole our car another night. Most drinking and carousing is at night. "They that be drunken are drunken in the night" (I Thess. 5:7). These men who professed to be Christian teachers were worse than the sinners in the world. They were so wicked and shameless in it that they delighted to riot in the daytime. What did they care who saw it, or what they thought of it. They are like those of whom Paul speaks, "Whose glory is in their shame" (Phil. 3:19). These sinners so loved this rioting that they could not get enough of it at night, but must practice it even in the daytime. Such shameless sinners certainly deserve judgment in this life and also in the next. Sin is always bad, but when it is so open and shameless it is terrible.

"Count It Pleasure"

These wicked men thought they were having a wonderful time. No doubt they had some pleasure in their rioting. In Heb. 11:25

we read, that Moses chose "rather to suffer affliction with the people of God, than to enjoy the pleasures of sin for a season." Sin may bring temporary pleasure, but brings no lasting joy. It does not follow that pleasure is always sinful. There are many things in the world which are clean and which a Christian may delight in, providing he does not abuse them by excess.

Ask Yourselves These Questions

Sometimes, especially young Christians ask, "Is it all right to go there or do this?" Ask yourself these questions. Is it clean? Does it have an unsavory reputation? Does it rob me of a chance to serve the Lord? Will it put a damper on my spirituality? Can I afford the time spent on it? "Let us walk honestly, as in the day; not in rioting and drunkenness, not in chambering and wantonness" (Rom. 13:13). "But let us, who are of the day, be sober" (I Thess. 5:8).

"Spots They Are"

These false teachers not only had spots and blemishes on them, but their very persons were spots and blemishes on the company of Christians. They were a scandal and a disgrace to Christ and Christianity. Out in the world they probably would not look so bad, but in the company of the pure Christians their sin looked serious, yea, filthy. Like a filthy dog let into the house will defile the house, so these filthy men would have a defiling effect on the whole assembly of Christians.

How Unlike Christ

How unlike Christ these sinners, who professed Christianity, were. They not only had, but they were spots and blemishes. We read of our Lord Jesus, that He was "a lamb without blemish and without spot" (I Pet. 1:19). They were more like the devil than like Christ. If Christ is in the heart, certainly this will in some measure produce Christ-likeness. If not, then we may well question whether Christ is within.

Cleansed by the Blood

All men are by nature spotted by sin. When they trust Christ as Savior they are cleansed not from the penalty of sin only, but from sin itself. "The blood of Jesus Christ his Son cleanseth us from all sin" (I John 1:7). Are we cleansed by His blood? If our lives are still filthy we may well question whether we are saved. "Who gave himself for us, that he might redeem us from all iniquity, and purify unto himself a peculiar people, zealous of good works" (Tit. 2:14). If one is living in iniquity and impurity what right has he to say he is redeemed? The result of redemption is not apparent.

Sinners Cleansed

The grace of God and faith in Christ has cleansed many vile sinners. We know a man who was often found in the gutter stupefied by drink, but now saved and cleansed. We know a man who was a terrible blasphemer, but now also saved and cleansed. So a gangster, an atheist, a thief, a communist, and many others. Faith in Christ does not give license to sin, or to live in filth, but cleanses from these things.

Present Us Spotless

Christ will eventually present every true Christian spotless and clean every whit. "That he might present it to himself a glorious church, not having spot or wrinkle, or any such thing; but that it should be holy and without blemish" (Eph. 5:27). This is the ultimate aim and purpose of redemption. If we do not even see the beginning of this now, we have no right to suppose that the end will ever be so. These false teachers were teaching that Christianity gave liberty to every form of licentiousness. How far they were from the truth.

"Sporting Themselves With Their Own Deceivings"

These men were deceivers and themselves deceived, and in it all they were "sporting themselves." They probably were boasting of their fine clothes, ease, and luxury. They may have even boasted about their evil ways. The Revised Version has "revelling in their deceivings." They may have even revelled in the fact that they were able to lead unstable souls into their way of believing and living. It is to be noted that error in belief is sure to lead to error in life. Uncleanness in thought is sure to lead to uncleanness in the body. He who thinks lightly of sin is surely on slippery ground. "Fools make a mock at sin" (Prov. 14:9). "It is sport to a fool to do mischief" (Prov. 10:23).

"DECEIVINGS"

What an awful thing it is to be a deceiver, especially when it comes to the things of the Lord. These men were deceiving people into believing that Christianity gave license to lust. This no doubt led some to profess to be Christians without ever being born again, and then perhaps, led some true Christians into sinful ways. To deceive is to be like the devil. He deceived Eve in the garden of Eden and he has been busy deceiving men ever since.

MANY DECEIVERS TODAY

There are many deceivers in the world today. Any who deny the deity of Christ, or the atoning value of His precious blood are deceivers. Many belittle the truth of the Word of God. Such are deceivers; as also are those who teach salvation by observing ritual or by church membership. Some try to teach that law keeping or moral living will assure a place in heaven. They make the cross of Christ of none affect and are deceivers. They who make light of sin are also deceivers, because they do away with the necessity of the cross. When one makes light of sin in a Christian, he is also a deceiver, because Christ died to put away sin, and to liberate from it. So deception takes on an infinite variety of forms. Let us ever be on guard that we neither be deceived, nor what is worse, a deceiver.

"WHILE THEY FEAST WITH YOU"

"While they feast with you" would indicate that these sinful men were right in the closest fellowship with the Christians. There has been some question as to just what this feast was. It is natural to suppose it refers to the Lord's supper, which is called a feast in I Cor. 5:8. Some have thought that this feast was a meal which the Christians had in between meetings. Some came from long distances and without suitable transportation it would be easier to bring their meals with them, than to try to go home and then come back again. Some have thought that they had a regular meal in connection with their remembrance feast.

FLAGRANT DISORDER

Certainly at some of these early church gatherings there was flagrant disorder, as we cannot help but know from I Cor. 11:20-22. "When ye come together into one place, this is not to eat the Lord's supper. For in eating every one taketh before other his own supper: and one is hungry, and another is drunken. What? have ye not houses to eat and drink in?" Evidently at these meals some poor, who had but little, went hungry, while some were gluttons and some even drunk. Perhaps Peter is referring to very similar things. These false leaders were actually changing these gatherings of the Christians into riotous lewd times. They were thereby bringing reproach and disgrace to the name of Christ and to His precious holy feast.

THE LORD'S SUPPER NOT FOR UNSAVED

We know that today some sit with the Lord's people at the Lord's supper while living in open sin. Some churches are very lax in this respect. We have heard of drunkards, adulterers, and other questionable characters actually encouraged to take this place. Some even teach that there is special blessing for a sinner who partakes of this supper, and that it helps in the forgiveness of sin. The Scripture teaches the reverse; that it will add to the judgment of such who partake of the Lord's supper (I Cor. 11). It is a remembrance feast for those who are saved, and who are not living in open sin. We do not believe that wicked people should ever be permitted to partake of this holy feast.

OPEN SINNERS SHOULD BE DENIED FELLOWSHIP

Of course this does not mean that one should be excommunicated for minor sin or failure, but when one, by his life, brings disgrace upon the name of Christ, and the company of Christians, he should be denied fellowship with the people of God, especially at the Lord's supper. "Therefore put away from among yourselves that wicked person" (I Cor. 5:13). Those early companies of Christians would have been better off without those wicked deceivers in their midst.

2:14. "Having eyes full of adultery, and that cannot cease from sin; beguiling unstable souls: an heart they have exercised with covetous practices; cursed children."

In this verse and following ones, Peter goes into the very depths of the sin of these wicked teachers. They are guilty of awful iniquity and entice weak souls into similar practices. Sinful pleasure and obtaining of wealth seems to be their sole ambition and Peter calls them children of the curse.

"EYES"

The eyes are often the start of sin. Eve "*saw* that the tree was good for food, and that it was pleasant to the eyes" (Gen. 3:6). That was the start of sin in the world. Achan says, "When I *saw* among the spoils a goodly Babylonish garment, and two hundred shekels of silver, and a wedge of gold of fifty shekels weight, then I coveted them, and took them" (Joshua 7:21). His seeing caused him to covet and to take, and so he brought great trouble to Israel, and death to himself. The eye is ever on the alert to see things, and Satan will use it to lead one into sin if he possibly can. Therefore we need to give heed as to what we see. What is seen at the movie or over the television is not always too clean. We fear for the moral effect television will have in some Christian homes.

"FULL OF ADULTERY"

The first part of this verse is literally, "Having eyes full as an adulteress." Their adulterous passions showed in the eyes of these wicked men, as their gaze shamelessly wandered from one female to another. The word "full" would suggest that they had eyes for almost nothing else. Their eyes were ever on the lookout for someone who would be easy prey for their enticements. We fear there are many today who seldom look at one of the opposite sex without having adultery in mind. "But I say unto you, That whosoever looketh on a woman to lust after her hath committed adultery with her already in his heart" (Mat. 5:28). Beautiful young women, who are special targets for these lustful sinners, need our sympathy and our prayers.

"ADULTERY"

Adultery has caused many a great one to fall. Amnon's sin against Tamar was a shameful thing (II Sam. 13). Many a modern great man has likewise been overcome by this sin.

Adultery, if not soon forsaken, often leads to other sin. In an attempt to conceal it there surely will be deceit. Everything up to murder has followed in its trail. Adultery often brings its own punishment in the form of veneral diseases. The Lord is very strong in His condemnation of adultery, even as He is very strong in His condemnation of murder. He hates sin in connection with that which produces new life, even as He hates sin in connection with taking life that already exists. A Christian should be very much on guard lest Satan trip him up by this snare. "Whoremongers and adulterers God will judge" (Heb. 13:4).

"Cannot Cease from Sin"

These men had become so debased and so ingrained in their sin that they had become powerless to stop it. Bad habits have a way of fixing themselves upon a person. They get to a point where only the Spirit of God can break them. These men were not saved and so, devoid of the Spirit, and since they were teaching false doctrine they were in almost a hopeless condition. "Can the Ethiopian change his skin, or the leopard his spots? then may ye also do good, that are accustomed to do evil" (Jer. 13:23). Beware lest some evil habit engulf us.

"Beguiling Unstable Souls"

There are always unstable souls who can be led astray. This is evident from the fact that almost any kind of crazy sect can start up and gain followers. Sometimes these unstable souls are merely unsaved professors of Christianity; sometimes they are saved ones, but weak in knowledge and unstable by nature. There are many today who "by good words and fair speeches deceive the hearts of the simple" (Rom. 16:18). How important it is to be firmly established in the truth of the Word.

Some Follow Their Ways

The word "beguiling" is literally "laying baits for." It is like a hunter setting a trap with some choice bait to catch some certain wild animal. That these men were able to ensnare some weak females into their traps is strongly suggested by the apostle. No doubt they were able to convince some that since they were not under the law and had Christian liberty, it was perfectly legitimate to indulge in sexual immorality. We have heard of similar things in modern times.

Covetous Hearts

These men had hearts "exercised with covetous practices." Instead of a desire to please the Lord, they had hearts that desired only sinful pleasure and wealth. "Their heart is trained in greed" (Montgomery translation). The heart is the source of lust. "From within, out of the heart of men, proceed evil thoughts, adulteries, fornications, murders," etc. (Mark 7:21-23). Perhaps they had ways of not only enticing these simple women into sin, but also causing them to willingly part with their money or property.

Not Free to Sin

These false teachers may have excused their covetousness too, by saying, "We are not under the law and so it is not wrong to covet." It is interesting to note that the sins brought to our attention in this verse, adultery and covetousness, are both strongly condemned in the ten commandments. The law demands punishment for infraction, and so we thank God we are not under the law, but this in no way gives a Christian the right to be a lawless one. When we trust Christ, we are freed from sin, but not free to sin.

Religious Rackets

One of the main purposes of these false leaders was to obtain wealth. It is not unusual today to find exactly the same conditions. Perhaps you did not know that the richest organization in the world is a so-called Christian church. And some of the methods they use to get money out of their parishoners' pockets certainly indicates that they have the obtaining of money as one of their principal aims. We fear that the whole story of purgatory with its indulgences for the dead is an invention of false teachers for the purpose of extortion. It is well to give to a known good cause, but watch out for the religious beggar. A real servant of the Lord will say with the apostle Paul, "I seek not your's, but you" (II Cor. 12:14).

"COVETOUS PRACTICES"

Watch out for covetousness. It is a snare which has robbed many of the reward they might have had in glory. They are so busy chasing wealth, they have no time to serve the Lord. Money brings no satisfaction; the more you have the more you want. Proportionately more rich commit suicide than poor. In the end it will mock you; at death you must leave it all behind. How much better to be rich in Christ and to have great reward laid up in glory.

"CURSED CHILDREN"

"Cursed children" is literally, "children of the curse." We read of the curse very soon in the Word. In the third chapter of Genesis we have the serpent (Satan) cursed because he deceived Eve. Eve is not cursed, but she is told, "I will greatly multiply thy sorrow," and the ground is cursed because of Adam's sin. In Gen. 4:11, we have Cain cursed because of the slaying of Abel. It is always sin which brings the curse and these men of our chapter were sinners exceedingly, so Peter rightly calls them "children of the curse." Their sin brought a curse not only on themselves, but on those who listened to their words and fell into their trap. They probably too, by their ways, caused outsiders to curse the assembly of Christians and Christianity generally. They deserved only the wrath of a sin-hating God. "Depart from me, ye cursed, into everlasting fire" (Mat. 25:41).

BLESS, AND CURSE NOT

True Christians desire to be blessed and to be a blessing. We often ask our children, five boys and three girls, "What do you want to be in this world, a curse or a blessing?" Of course they say they want to be a blessing. We then tell them that the only way to be a blessing is to let Christ come into their hearts, and then live for Him, and try to be like Him. Beloved child of God, are you a real blessing in this world? If you are, the Lord will bless you in time, and certainly, in eternity.

XX

THE WAY OF BALAAM

(II Peter 2:15, 16)

2:15. "Which have forsaken the right way, and are gone astray, following the way of Balaam the son of Bosor, who loved the wages of unrighteousness."

Peter, in continuing to speak of these false teachers, says here that they have forsaken the right way of the Lord and had gone in the way of Balaam. As we will notice, he could not have chosen a more fitting illustration of these sinful men in all the Old Testament. He has twice accused these teachers of covetousness (verses 3 and 14) and we know this was particularly the cause of the downfall of Balaam.

"Forsaken the Right Way"

These men knew the right way, but forsook it because of covetousness. There has been much controversy as to whether these were ever saved or not. Some insist that they were once saved, but fell away from their salvation. We believe rather that they never were saved at all, but like thousands today, they made an outward profession to Christianity without ever receiving a new life from the Lord. However it may be, Peter definitely pronounces eternal judgment upon them, and let no one presume that they can leave the path of decency and honesty, and yet escape the wrath of God.

Many Never Truly Trust Christ

Many know that they should trust Christ and follow Him, but because of the love of sin, or fame, or wealth, they never really commit themselves to Him, even though they may make an outward show of Christianity. It soon is evident that they are not true children by the way they turn back into sin and follow the ways of Satan.

A Deliberate Choice

To deliberately choose the wrong way when the right way is known, makes the sin of the offender all the worse. This is what

Balaam did and also the sinners of our chapter. No wonder Peter says in verse 17, "For whom the blackness of darkness has been reserved" (R.V.).

"THE WAY OF BALAAM"

Balaam is one of the puzzles of Scripture. In every way he seemed to be a true prophet of the Lord, yet his base actions for gain would indicate that he loved money far more than the will of the Lord. He was numbered amongst the prophets, as Judas was numbered amongst the apostles. The love of money proved to be the downfall of each.

GOD SPOKE TO BALAAM

Many nice things could be said of Balaam. First of all, he was a man who had dealings with and revelations from the Lord. After Balak's men come to him, God asks him, "What men are these with thee?" He tells Him they are men from Balak, who wanted him to curse Israel. The Lord then forbids him to go to curse Israel because He wanted them to be blessed (Num. 22:9-12). The Lord again speaks to him in Num. 22:32-35 by means of His angel, and then again in Num. 23:4, 5. In spite of all this hallowed association, how sad to see Balaam go absolutely contrary to the revealed will of the Lord. One would think that this personal acquaintance with the Lord would bind his heart to Him forever. Many today go contrary to what they know to be the Lord's mind as revealed in His Word, often too, because of covetousness.

HE TALKED LIKE A TRUE PROPHET

Balaam was not afraid to acknowledge the Lord before others. He said in Num. 22:38, "The word that God putteth in my mouth, that shall I speak." These were grand words for him to say. Evidently he meant them too, and when it came to openly cursing Israel, he did not do it. He said what the Lord told him to say, and instead of cursing Israel, he blessed them. A true servant of the Lord makes it his business to proclaim only the Word of the Lord.

GOD SPOKE DIRECTLY THROUGH HIM

The Lord put His own words directly into Balaam's mouth (Num. 23:5, 16). He really makes some glorious prophecies in

Num. 23:18-24, and also in Num. 24:3-9, and again in Num. 24:16-24. He even had a vision of the Almighty as we read in Num. 24:3, 4, and that the Spirit of the Lord came upon him in Num. 24:2. After all these things, we wonder that he could stoop into evil practices for paltry honor and gain, but he surely did. We have met some in our day who, like Balaam, could use lofty heights of speech, and yet sink into base actions. Let us beware lest our life come short of our profession.

The Counsel of the Ungodly

Balaam must have had a reputation as a prophet of the Lord, or Balak never would have called him to curse Israel. It is always dangerous to a servant of the Lord, when the world offers him some reward for serving them. Usually they ask things which are not to the glory of the Lord, or to the benefit of the Lord's people. "Blessed is the man that walketh not in the counsel of the ungodly" (Ps. 1:1). Let us seek to go only by the Word of God.

Not a Fable

Because of the miraculous actions and speech of Balaam's beast of burden, many have sought to discredit the whole story of Balaam. They say it is the invention of some storyteller. One thing is sure, no Jew would ever invent a story in which such sublime words are put into the mouth of a Gentile. If it was not a true story, we do not believe Moses would have ever included it in his book of Numbers.

These Teachers Like Balaam in Other Ways

While our verse especially likens the teachers of our chapter to Balaam in his love for money, there are other striking parallels. First, note that Balaam and these teachers were professed religious leaders. There is nothing more terrible than to have those who are supposed to be lighthouses on the road to heaven, lead men down the way of death and hell. Peter calls these teachers, "children of the curse" in verse 14. Balaam dared not directly curse Israel, but his wicked counsel to Balak proved a curse to them. Finally, these wicked teachers induced the unstable to fall into sin, even as Balaam, by his counsel to Balak, induced the children of Israel to sin grievously.

His Covetousness

In Num. 22:7, we find the elders of Moab and Midian come to Balaam with the rewards of divination in their hands. How he would have liked to have had that money, but the Lord told him not to go. The men go back to Balak, but he sends other princes more noble than the first and promises more money to Balaam and honor besides, in fact, anything that he might desire. He did so want to go, so instead of saying "no" at once he again takes it to the Lord, and asks that he be allowed to go. Then the Lord tells him he may go, but warns him to say nothing except what the Lord told him to say.

Covetousness Leads On

So Balaam goes, thinking that there might be further relenting on God's part, and that he might yet be allowed to curse Israel and so gain the reward. The incident of his own beast of burden speaking to him and the angel in the way could not stop his avarice. He was determined to go on, and get this reward if there was any way to do it. He had a wicked desire to do what Balak wanted him to do, even though he knew it was all wrong to curse Israel. Like Simon Magnus in Acts 8:19, he wanted to turn the gift of God into worldly gain. Like Judas himself, he was ready to betray the Lord for a few pieces of silver. The Lord Jesus says, "Ye cannot serve God and Mammon," but Balaam was determined to try.

Covetousness a Bad Sin

Some think covetousness not a bad sin, but the Lord calls it idolatry (Eph. 5:5). With many the love of money vies with the love of God. Some will stoop to almost anything in order to gain wealth. "The love of money is the root of all evil" (I Tim. 6:10). A servant of the Lord need not be covetous, since the Lord has promised to meet all his needs. We have served Him now for seventeen years without any human guarantee of any kind, and we must say we have lacked no good thing. Let us learn to be content with such things as we have. Let us never like Balaam prostitute our high office for mere paltry gain.

"THE WAGES OF UNRIGHTEOUSNESS"

If you would earn the wages of unrighteousness you must do unrighteously. Balaam received the rewards of unrighteousness, with the full knowledge of his wrong doing. He said, "Let me die the death of the righteous, and let my last end be like his!" (Num. 23:10). While he wanted to die the death of the righteous, sad to say, he did not seem to want to live the life of the righteous. We read in Num. 31:8 of his untimely end in the midst of the enemies of the Lord's people.

BALAAM'S WICKED COUNSEL

As we read over Num. 22 to 24, we might conclude that what Balaam did was not so bad. He certainly blessed Israel rather than cursed her. Now just what did he do that was so wrong, and which caused Balak to give him the reward after all? In Num. 25 we read how the men of Israel committed whoredom with the daughters of Moab, and how they were enticed to worship the Moabitish gods. This angered the Lord and many of the Israelites died by the sword and of a plague. Balaam had told Balak that he could not curse Israel, but advised him that if he would send his young women in amongst the children of Israel and allure them into fornication, that they would bring the curse of God upon themselves (Num. 31:16). This wicked counsel brought the money to Balaam, but terrible trouble to Israel.

THESE TEACHERS WERE LIKE BALAAM

The false teachers of Peter's day were very much like Balaam. They posed as true brethren and taught license in the name of freedom, and that principally for the sake of money. They talked in Biblical language in order to lead their followers into as wicked a life as Balaam suggested to Balak. False teachers today have led the church into an unholy alliance with the world. This has beguiled many and greatly weakened the testimony of the Lord, something which open persecution has never been able to do.

2:16. "But was rebuked for his iniquity: the dumb ass speaking with man's voice forbad the madness of the prophet."

This verse brings in Balaam's beast of burden, through whom the Lord miraculously spoke in order to warn and stay the prophet in his folly. But so set was Balaam in his determination to do all in his power to gain this coveted reward, that even this did not stop him. Our verse almost suggests that Balaam was out of his mind, because of his avarice.

"Rebuked for His Iniquity"

Balaam's iniquity was so great that the Lord felt it necessary to rebuke him in a very special way. Because of his covetousness, he set out to curse the people of God, who had done him no wrong, and had done nothing to deserve his curse. Certainly a servant of the Lord should never curse anyone, or be a curse to anyone. Like the Lord Jesus, he should ever seek to bless and to be a blessing. This should be true of all the Lord's people. May we each ask ourselves the question, "Am I a blessing to the world or a curse?"

Rebukes of the Lord

We believe the Lord often rebukes sinners, sometimes in a startling way. It may be by accident or narrow escape, or by sudden death of a friend. We read a supposedly true story of a man who dreamed he was escorted through hell by the devil. What a dread place it was. Finally the devil said, "You may go now, but you will be back here within a year." The man awoke with a cold sweat on his brow and was quite a changed man for a time. But slowly he slipped back into his sinful ways and forgot about his dream. About the end of a year he had a fall from his horse and was quickly ushered into eternity. Sometimes these uncommon rebukes will cause one to trust in Christ, but often it sobers them only for a time, and soon they are back into their old sinful ways.

"The Dumb Ass Speaking"

This part of our verse could be literally translated, "the voiceless beast of burden speaking with man's voice." Some have belittled the thought of this miracle. "How could a voiceless animal speak?" Wasn't there an angel of the Lord right on the path? We have seen men by ventriloquism put words into the mouth of a puppet or an animal. It is ridiculous to think that an angel could not do as much. Certainly Balaam's folly deserved a shock of this nature, and it was not a difficult thing for the Lord to do.

His Covetousness Brought This Rebuke

It is well to remember that Balaam's covetousness brought on this rebuke. Let us beware of this sin. In Balaam's time most people were poor and could not afford a beast of burden. The fact that he had one would indicate that Balaam was not poor, and he need not have coveted this money.

The Story

We read this story of Balaam and his beast of burden in Num. 22. Although strongly disapproving his going, the Lord gave Balaam permission to go. As the prophet journeyed, an angel stood in the path with a drawn sword in his hand. He was hidden from the eyes of Balaam, but the animal saw him and turned off the road into a field. Balaam then beat the poor animal to get him back on the road. Then the angel stood in the road in a place between two walls, and the beast in an attempt to get by crushed Balaam's foot against the wall. They managed to get by the angel, but the poor animal received his second beating. The third time the angel stood in a place where they could not get by him, and the beast fell down to the ground under Balaam. Then Balaam really got angry and beat the animal with a staff.

The Miraculous Speech

It was then that the Lord put words into the mouth of the ass saying, "What have I done unto thee that thou hast smitten me these three times?" Balaam answered, "Because thou hast mocked me: I would there were a sword in mine hand, for now would I kill thee." Then the Lord opened Balaam's eyes and he saw the angel with the sword in his hand, and Balaam was afraid and fell on his face. He said, "I have sinned," and also that if his way displeased the Lord, he would return. Again the Lord gives him permission to go, but warns him to say only that which He told him to say. Instead of turning back, he goes on, still hoping, no doubt, that there would be someway to get that reward.

Balaam and His Beast of Burden

In many ways Balaam's beast was better than Balaam. In the first place she saw things that Balaam did not see. When the angel appeared, she turned out of the way, but Balaam persisted in his perverse way. This unclean animal was cleaner than the prophet; she did no wrong; he was obstinately disobedient. His actions were more asinine than those of his ass. How awful it is to think that the Lord used an unclean animal to rebuke his oft inspired prophet.

The Lord and His Creatures

The Lord can use any of His creatures as He sees fit. One has said, "Peter had a cock to tell of his cowardice, Balaam an ass to tell of his avarice." The Lord used a great fish to give Jonah a submarine ride and so return him to the path of obedience. He used the ravens to feed His prophet Elijah. We recently heard of a man who was brought to know the Lord through the actions of his mule. Someway the Lord said to him, "You are worse than your mule. Every night he bows to his Creator, but you do not." Thereafter he watched his mule, and sure enough, before lying down for the night, the mule would get down on his knees and stay there for a few moments. This showed the man his folly and he turned to Christ for salvation.

"Forbad the Madness of the Prophet"

The word translated "forbad" would be better "hindered" or "stayed" as in the Revised Version. The warning voice of the beast of burden hindered Balaam only in his method. His wicked counsel brought a curse upon Israel and eventually his own death (Num. 31:8). Our verse calls Balaam's sin "madness." His avarice caused him to act in a senseless manner, almost like a madman. Once having started on his headstrong course, nothing could stop him. Many today act almost like madmen in their rush to obtain the things of this world, only to be mocked thereby in the end. Judas obtained his thirty pieces of silver, but what did it get him? In remorse he went out and hanged himself.

"The Prophet"

There has been much controversy as to whether Balaam was a saved man or not. Some of his statements are so sublime and so evidently inspired of the Lord, that we wonder how he could stoop so low, because of his covetousness. It is to be noticed that at the very end of his statements about Balaam, Peter calls him "the prophet." He may have been a child of God after all in spite of his sin.

Judas and Balaam

As we study the life of Judas, we must conclude that, in spite of the fact that he was numbered with the apostles, he never really was a child of God. One has said, "Judas kissed the door of heaven, then turned around and went to hell." Similarly Balaam may have been so close as to be numbered with the prophets, and say inspired things directly from the mouth of God, and yet not be saved. Beloved, let us be sure we are more than close, but really inside the fold.

XXI

WELLS WITHOUT WATER

(II Peter 2:17, 18)

2:17. "These are wells without water, clouds that are carried with a tempest; to whom the mist of darkness is reserved for ever."

In this verse Peter likens these false teachers to wells without water, and clouds driven with a tempest, so bringing no rain. They are as empty and useless to humanity as a dry pit in a hot barren desert. He also pronounces their eternal doom in the blackness of darkness.

"Wells Without Water"

"Wells" would be better translated "springs" (R.V.), or "fountains." Wells were dug by man, but fountains and springs were natural sources of water. These were a great blessing to the land of Palestine. The climate for the most part was hot and dry and the people depended on springs for their water supply. Picture a tired traveler, thirsty and hot, coming to a well or a spring, only to find it utterly dry. Instead of helping him, it would but aggravate his troubles.

The Boon of Water

We in this favored Western land little appreciate the great boon of water. We have such an abundant supply and such wonderful systems of distribution, that we hardly give it a thought. When we are thirsty, all we need do is turn on a spigot and we hardly need think of conservation. Recently however, some sections of our great land have suffered from water shortage. If we lived in Eastern lands we would soon come to highly appreciate a fountain of water.

Wells Type of Blessing

Wells and springs of water in the Bible are always emblematic of blessing and refreshment. In Isaiah 55:1 we read, "Ho, every one that thirsteth, come ye to the waters." "With joy shall ye draw water out of the wells of salvation" (Isa. 12:3). "The well-spring of wisdom as a flowing brook" (Prov. 18:4). The mouth of a righteous man is a well of life" (Prov. 10:11). At Jacob's well the Lord Jesus says to the Samaritan woman "Whosoever drinketh of this water shall thirst again: but whosoever drinketh of the water that I shall give him shall never thirst" (John 4:13, 14).

The World is Full of Empty Wells

Spiritually this world is a desert place. There is nothing in it to satisfy the human heart. Wealth, fame, pleasure, all turn out to be wells without water. Many slave a lifetime to fulfill an aim or ambition only to find upon realization that it does not satisfy the cravings of the human heart.

Empty Religious Leaders

What a sad thing to find one turning to religion for satisfaction, only to find that those who dispense it are also wells without water. Many today, like those whom Peter condemns in our chapter, profess to have just what a thirsty soul needs, but dispense only things which leave one empty and dry. Instead of dispensing the Word of God, with Christ as their main theme, they spread man's notions and even plain falsehoods.

False Cults

There are many cults today which teach unscriptural and even unholy theories, which bring only sorrow and disappointment to those who are enmeshed in their ways. Nothing short of Christ in the soul can give peace and victory over sin. How sad to think that many will find themselves outside at last, dupes of wicked men, fit only for the judgment of God. How severe will be the judgment of those who profess to be guides and teachers, who should dispense blessing and refreshment, but who belie their character and bring only disappointment and death. How thankful we should be, who have been led to know that Christ is the dispenser of the water of life, and have come to Him for salvation and blessing. Let those of us who seek to serve Him in any capacity be sure that we are wells well-filled with the pure water of life.

"CLOUDS — CARRIED WITH A TEMPEST"

"Clouds that are carried with a tempest" further tell us of the utter emptiness and uselessness of these false teachers. These Eastern lands often need rain badly. Clouds on the horizon fill hearts with hope. How sad then when a strong wind arises and blows these clouds over and the land remains dry and parched. Sometimes these tempests not only drive away the clouds, but damage the crops and even blow down buildings. How sad when those who should dispense salvation and blessing, bring nothing but dearth and damage. May we, who profess to be the servants of the Lord, spread the blessed gospel into dry places.

TOSSED TO AND FRO

These men were as clouds driven before a storm. They had no settled position or principles, driven first this way and then that, as their own lust and covetousness might drive them. Sorry to say, there were those ready to be driven by them. "That we henceforth be no more children, tossed to and fro, and carried about with every wind of doctrine, by the sleight of men, and cunning craftiness, whereby they lie in wait to deceive" (Eph. 4:14).

"MIST OF DARKNESS"

"Mist of darkness" is literally, "thick gloom of darkness." Jude calls it "the blackness of darkness" (Jude 13). It is no doubt the same pit of darkness reserved for the fallen angels (II Peter 2:4), in which these false teachers will at last find themselves. The word "reserved" tells us that this place of outer darkness is held in readiness to receive these wicked men. This great and terrible prison house was originally built for the devil and his angels (Mat. 25:41), but will eventually house all who in disobedience refuse the Lord's mercy through Christ. This blackness of darkness is surely a place to be avoided at all costs.

"FOREVER"

The words "for ever" at the end of the verse put the clinching argument to the awfulness of this place. Those who find themselves there will be utterly hopeless in the awfulness of their position. The sinner in this scene may yet find mercy by fleeing to Christ. Only those will find themselves in this awful place who persist in their rebellion and rejection of Christ. Just as surely as there is an eternal heaven for those who trust Christ, there is an eternal hell for those who persist in their sin and refusal of Him.

2:18. "For when they speak great swelling words of vanity, they allure through the lusts of the flesh, through much wantonness, those that were clean escaped from them who live in error."

Here we are told of some poor souls who had been led out of the evil practices and idolatry of heathenism, or the errors of ceremonial Judaism, only to be ensnared into the false teaching of a perverted Christianity. False teachers misled them by wonderful oratory, and a promise of unrestrained liberty in immoral living.

"GREAT SWELLING WORDS OF VANITY"

These false teachers used "great swelling words of vanity." This reminds us of a balloon filled only with hot air. What wonderful diction these men had, and how positively they spoke, and what a pretense to great learning and wisdom. They made great claims for themselves, like Simon the sorcerer (Acts 8:9). They boasted of their superior knowledge and great accomplishments, like Nebuchadnezzar (Dan. 4:30). They could talk of nothing else but their perverted beliefs, as though they were the only things of any importance. Truth does not need long sermons to substantiate it; but error, in order to deceive, must have many and noisy words. At Ephesus the idolatrous people cried out for about two hours, "Great is Diana of the Ephesians" (Acts 19:34).

"WORDS OF VANITY"

One has said, "Error is like a rotten house which needs the most props to hold it up." The false teachers made plenty of noise, but their words lacked sense and were empty. This is true of much preaching today. We recently heard a man over the radio; an excellent orator with pleasing voice. He used plausible arguments, which at bottom were utterly false and deceiving.

More Sound than Sense

We have heard some speakers who were fundamentally sound, yet it seemed their speech was more sound than sense. We once heard just such a speaker. He had a tremendous vocabulary, and could produce the most beautiful sounding sentences, yet when he was done, we wondered what he had been trying to say. After just such an oratorical display, an aged brother got up and said, none too kindly, "Words, words, bushels of them, and not an ounce of sense in the lot of them."

"They Allure"

If it were only a matter of empty or vain words it would be bad enough, but these were words designed to allure the weak and unlearned into ways of sin. These men were like hunters setting definite traps to catch the unwary. Their words were not words of ignorance, but deliberately deceitful in order to bring advantage to self at the expense of others. Some men develop great skill in promoting error, and are unspeakably dangerous to young and not firmly grounded believers. False cults are ever on the lookout for those who only make a profession to Christianity, whom they may lead astray.

"Through the Lusts of the Flesh"

The appeal of these false teachers to the weak and unstable was that it was consistent with Christian liberty to sin to their hearts' content. This license suits exactly the natural man, and so they had great success, especially with those who knew nothing of the new life in Christ. The natural man likes an easy religion which puts no check on morals, and there are such today as there were then.

"Wantonness"

These men not only taught that it was not wrong to live in lust, but they practiced it themselves. No doubt with fair speeches and perverted religious arguments, they betrayed and seduced some fine young women. This they did to satisfy their own corrupt passions, and at the same time to gain money and followers. (See Verse 14).

NOT LICENSE, BUT RESTRAINT OF LUST

True Christianity does not give license to immoral living, but rather brings the animal nature into subjection. Paul says, "I keep under my body, and bring it into subjection" (I Cor. 9:27). Again, "For the grace of God that bringeth salvation hath appeared to all men, teaching us that, denying ungodliness, and worldly lusts, we should live soberly, righteously, and godly, in this present world" (Titus 2:11, 12). "Let us walk honestly, as is the day; not in rioting and drunkenness, not in chambering and wantonness, not in strife and envying. But put ye on the Lord Jesus Christ, and make not provision for the flesh, to fulfil the lusts thereof" (Rom. 13:13, 14). Be very much on guard against any professed teacher, who makes light of sin. A true servant of Christ will surely preach self-denial, and the restraining of lust.

"CLEAN ESCAPED"

"Clean escaped" has been variously translated. The Revised Version gives it, "just escaping." Some make it "about escaped." "Really escaped," we believe would be the most exact translation. What had these ensnared ones previously escaped? As we noticed, in connection with I Pet. 1:1 etc., many of those to whom Peter was writing were brought out of heathen sin and darkness. Perhaps some too had escaped from Jewish ritualism. They heard the gospel and saw that their heathen idolatry was all wrong. Before they were really brought to know Christ as Savior, or at least before they were firmly established in the truth, wicked perverts got hold of them, and led them into corruption almost equally serious as that from which they had escaped; perhaps even into worse sin than that in which they had ever indulged. They fled into a home from a lion in the streets, where they thought they were safe, only there to be bitten by a serpent lurking in the shadows.

REFORMED FOR A TIME

Many today become concerned about their sinful condition. They look for some help from some religious system or cult. They are ready to do any manner of penance, or go through any required ceremony. As time goes on, they discover that there is no power in their religion, and perhaps the leaders do not even live clean lives themselves. Soon the poor men are back into their life of sin and maybe into worse sin than ever.

Christianity Is More than a System

It is one thing to accept Christianity as a system, and quite another to really receive Christ as Savior. Those who only have a form of Christianity are quickly and easily led astray into some other system, or even back into sin. How sad to think that there were and are religious leaders who not only deceive people with false doctrine, but actually encourage by lip and practice a life of sin. Such deserve the severe punishment our chapter indicates will be their lot.

XXII

NOT LIBERTY, BUT BONDAGE

(II Peter 2:19, 20)

2:19. "While they promise them liberty, they themselves are the servants of corruption: for of whom a man is overcome, of the same is he brought in bondage."

We have already noted that the bait these false teachers used to lead unstable souls into error and sin was the promise of liberty. Of course they defined liberty wrongly, saying that liberty meant license to sin as they pleased. They did not explain that lust itself became a master and one who followed in its ways became a slave of corruption.

"They Promise"

Satan has always been liberal with his promises, and these servants of his were the same. Already in the garden of Eden he promised Eve, "For God doth know that in the day ye eat thereof, then your eyes shall be opened, and ye shall be as gods, knowing good and evil" (Gen. 3:5). He did not tell them that when once they knew evil they would not be able to refrain from it, and so would be like himself. He even made promises to Christ at the time of His temptation saying, "All these things will I give thee, if thou wilt fall down and worship me" (Mat. 4:9). He still whispers promises into the ears of the unsaved, saying, "Follow me and I will give you riches, or fame, or happiness." He will ever warp Scripture to gain a victory, even as he did with Christ at the time of His temptation.

False Promises

These false teachers were making promises too. They said, "We will give you liberty, and you will be free to do as you please. No need to curb your passions; did not Jesus say, 'If the Son therefore shall make you free, ye shall be free indeed' " (Jno. 8:36). They did not add what the Lord Jesus said in Jno. 8:34, "Whosoever committeth sin is the servant (slave) of sin."

PAUL AND LIBERTY

Perhaps they quoted what Paul said in Gal. 5:1, "Stand fast therefore in the liberty wherewith Christ hath made us free, and be not entangled again with the yoke of bondage." They did not explain that this was liberty from the ceremonial law, and they certainly did not quote Gal. 5:13, "For, brethren, ye have been called unto liberty; only use not liberty for an occasion to the flesh, but by love serve one another." Their promises sounded logical and good, but they were false and did not bring gain, but only great loss.

MANY PROMISES ARE BROKEN

Promises are easy to make, but not always so easy to keep. Ofttimes people make promises, but when the time comes they cannot keep them. Sometimes they could keep them, but they do not want to keep them. Many promises are made without any intention of keeping them. This is a plain deceit. Watch out for the man who makes many promises. The more he makes the more likely he is a deceiver.

LET US KEEP OUR PROMISES

Let us, who know the Lord, be very cautious with our promises, and when we do promise, let us do our utmost to fulfill them. To promise and not to do, is to be like the devil himself. A Christian should be very cautious in promises especially in money matters. Let us never buy anything, if there is danger that we will not be able to pay. The Scripture says, "Owe no man anything" (Rom. 13:8). To have a reputation for not paying our bills is to bring reproach on the name of Christ.

"PROMISE THEM LIBERTY"

These men promised liberty, but not the type the Scripture promises to the Christian. The Word pictures the unsaved as in bondage to sin, the lusts of the flesh, to the world, to Satan, to fear of death and hell. It is from these things that one who trusts Christ is liberated. These wicked teachers sought to lead their followers into the very things from which Christ sought to liberate them.

Christ Does Not Enslave

All down the ages there have been those who derided Christianity as a religion which brought one into bondage. They are like the devil who told Eve in the garden that God was putting needless restraint on them. The main cry of the communists today is that it puts people in bondage. However, they are all wrong. While a true Christian will lead a restrained life, it is not because he is in bondage. He lives this kind of a life because he realizes that sin brings bondage, and that the more he lives for Christ the greater freedom he has. We are freed from sin, not free to sin.

No Absolute Liberty

Liberty is defined as "freedom from restraint," but there is no such thing as absolute freedom in a civilized country. One cannot do just as he might like. Mrs. Nieboer's mother came to this country from England as a young girl. Her father told her that this was a free country. Soon after, while passing through a market, she picked up an orange and began to eat it. Her father asked her, "Where did you get that?" "I took it off the counter over there." He said, "Why you can't do that, I will have to pay for it." Then she said, "I thought you said this was a free country?" We have no liberty to steal even in this free country. If we think we have, we will soon find ourselves behind bars with all our liberty gone.

We Cannot Do As We Please

One might thing he has liberty to curse or abuse his neighbor at will, but if he is not careful he is apt to find himself in plenty of trouble. Another might think he has liberty to practice adultery as he pleases, but he is likely to find that he has liberty of an unwanted kind. His wife may divorce him and his children leave him. There must be a measure of restraint, or none would be safe on our streets after dark. Every country needs its policemen, its courts, and its jails.

Restraint Is Part of Civilization

Half of a mother's life is restraining her children. From infancy they must constantly be told that they cannot do as they please. It is the same in school, and later as one is employed he must heed the bell or the whistle. Then as a citizen of a country, one must be law abiding in order to guarantee more liberty to others. There is only true liberty in any country in the measure that the animal nature of its citizens is restrained. The more they are held in check on the bottom, the more they will spread out into true liberty on the top. One who loves liberty, will not only think of his own freedom, but that of his neighbor. He will restrain himself the moment he sees that his actions deprive another of some aspect of liberty.

CHRISTIAN RESTRAINT IS NOT BONDAGE

A young man in the Service Men's Center in Chicago once said, "You do not smoke, you do not drink, you do not gamble, you do not go to shows; what in the world do you do for a good time?" We tried to tell him of the joys we had in Christ, but of course, he could not understand. To the writer, and to any true Christian, to refrain from these things is not bondage. A Christian receives a new nature upon trusting Christ, and has no desire to indulge in these things. It is not bondage when one does not do the things he does not desire to do. For the writer to drink, or to smoke, or to gamble, or to do other vile things would be torture, not liberty.

WE SERVE GLADLY

It is not bondage for a parent to serve the family he or she loves, and it is not bondage for a Christian to serve the Lord whom he loves. In fact, the more one denies himself and serves the Lord, the greater he realizes his liberty in Christ. He realizes that it is a priceless freedom to be free from the bondage of sin, Satan, and the fear of death and hell, and he gladly obeys the Lord.

"SERVANTS OF CORRUPTION"

Peter says that these teachers, who were promising liberty to their followers were themselves "servants (slaves) of corruption." Montgomery translates this "slaves of rottenness." How awful it is when professed Christian leaders live rotten lives, slaves of their own rotten passions. When one is a slave to some form of sin, he is in the worst form of bondage. Instead of having liberty, he is a miserable vassal. These men had so sunk into sin that they were slaves of their own lust. They "cannot cease from sin" (vs. 14). Especially were they slaves to adultery and covetousness.

SLAVES TO HABIT

The latter part of our verse says, "Of whom (or what) a man is overcome, of the same is he brought in bondage." Many are virtual slaves of habit; of liquor, of tobacco, or of sensual living. We know of some who have quit smoking or chewing for a time, only to return to it more enslaved than ever. A slave of chewing tobacco told us that he had quit for three years once, but that there never had been a day in that time when he did not want a chew.

A SLAVE TO DRINK

Before salvation a friend of ours was a slave to drink. Between stealing to buy liquor and his drunkenness, he was in and out of jail continually. He tried to break this habit by taking the Keeley cure, but it only helped him for a very little while. His parents put him on a farm, but he remained sober only as long as he could not get drink. One day as he stepped out of jail, he walked into a mission and said to those in the office, "In a few days I will be back in jail unless you can help me." They told him that they could not help him, but that the Lord Jesus could. Before he left that place he was gloriously saved, never to get drunk again, and went into jail only to preach the liberating gospel to the prisoners. Thank God for our Lord Jesus; He can break every fetter.

HABIT GROWS

Many who are slaves to habit never meant to be. When a man takes his first drink, he never means to become a drunkard. The habit slowly grows until finally the man finds himself a slave. "His own iniquities shall take the wicked himself, and he shall be holden with the cords of his sins" (Prov. 5:22). We have demonstrated this to children by putting a boy on a chair. We would first tie one strand of fine cord about him and to the chair. This he could easily break. Then we would wind three strands around him. This he could also break, but with more difficulty. It would only take about ten strands to completely tie him up. Just so, a sinner is "holden with the cords of his sins."

SLAVES TO MANY THINGS

Many things in the world bring sinful men into bondage. Misers are slaves to money, and many rich men too. Some are slaves to the opinion of others, or to the world's fashions. During the bobbed hair craze many women had their hair cut, even though they knew it was a shame according to the Word of God (I Cor. 11:6). Many would never dare wear clothes a bit out of date. Some are slaves to their own fears, their consciences constantly keeping them in torment. It may be that some are in direct bondage to the devil himself, almost like the demon possessed in the Bible (Mat. 8:28-34). "And that they may recover themselves out of the snare of the devil, who are taken captive by him at his will" (II Tim. 2:26). Many have no moral strength to resist evil, and they know they are in bondage to Satan.

SIN WILL OUT

We recently read of a doctor who was found guilty of murdering a woman. She had been one of his patients, and lured him into sin with her. From then on he was virtually her slave. She held him in sin, and extorted large sums of money from him. He tried to break from her, but she threatened to expose him to his wife, and so break up his happy home. Finally in desperation he killed her, but the crime was detected and he received just punishment. "Be sure your sin will find you out" (Num. 32:33).

CHRISTIANS BEWARE

Let us be very much on guard lest Satan get us into bondage to any sin. "Let not sin therefore reign in your mortal body, that ye should obey it in the lusts thereof" (Rom. 6:12). "For sin shall not have dominion over you" (Rom. 6:14). To serve sin or Satan is real bondage, but to serve Christ and righteousness is true liberty.

2:20. "For if after they have escaped the pollutions of the world through the knowledge of the Lord and Saviour Jesus Christ, they are again entangled therein, and overcome, the latter end is worse with them than the beginning."

At first glance this verse seems to teach that even the truly saved may be entangled in sin, removed from Christ, and finally lost. Yet, we think this hardly possible in the light of scores of Scriptures which teach the eternal salvation of those who have been born again by putting their trust in Christ. We believe it speaks of those, who through hearing of Christ, abandoned their heathen lives and idolatry, but did not have their natures changed by a new birth. For such it is easy to sink back into sinful ways. They have escaped from their old lives, but have not escaped to Christ, the Savior of sinners. The last verse of this chapter would indicate that there had been no change of nature in these men.

"Escaped the Pollutions"

We believe Christendom today is full of those who know much of Christ, and profess to be Christians, yet have never been truly saved. In fact, Christianity has put a measure of restraint on our whole nation, but that does not mean that all are Christians. Many believe that the mere fact that they are born in this so-called Christian land automatically makes them Christians. When you question their salvation they say, "What do you think I am, a heathen?" Some know enough of Christianity to know that they should not live in sinful ways, but still they are not saved.

Morally Clean, Yet Entangled

Some are raised in Christian homes, educated in Christianity from infancy, know the way of salvation, live a comparatively moral life, but do not get saved, and then later fall into sin. The writer was saved only a short time, when he was drafted into the army during World War I. By the grace of God, and the help of Christ, we were able to withstand the fierce temptations and onslaughts of Satan. One fine young man, a preacher's son, guarded and taught all his life, but evidently not saved, was soon swept off his feet. The temptation was too strong for him; he soon was drinking and committing all manner of evil with the boys.

Reformed but Not Transformed

It is possible to be reformed, yet not transformed. Some come under the sound of the Word, hear about Christ, learn the way of salvation, live better lives for a time, only to later sink back into sin. It is possible for one to have the light of the gospel and to be morally helped, and yet not to have the life of Christ in the soul. One has said, "A religious education has restrained many whom the grace of God has not renewed."

"THE POLLUTIONS OF THE WORLD"

"The pollutions of the world" are like a filthy cesspool. Many Christians, especially preachers, do not often get a sight of this filth. We recently unexpectedly, and almost unwittingly, sat down at a banqueting table with a group of about 50 men and a few women, employees of a company in one of our large cities. I was completely unknown excepting to the Christian who brought me. Perhaps if they had known a preacher was in their midst, they would have restrained their filthy talk, and drunken revelry. My friend who brought me to this banquet, took no part in this revelry, but he thought some who did take part were Christians, although not strong. We did not stay to see the worst of it all. If you are a child of God, who has in a measure slipped back into some of this cesspool of filth, escape again quickly to Christ.

"THROUGH THE KNOWLEDGE OF THE LORD"

Some have claimed that the expression "through the knowledge of the Lord and Saviour Jesus Christ," proves positively that these were genuinely saved, but then lost. Young's Literal Translation gives this as, "through the acknowledging of the Lord," rather than "knowledge of the Lord" and this is better. It would indicate their profession of Christ rather than a personal knowledge of Him. One might know much about Christ and yet not really know Him in a personal way as Savior. Many know the way of salvation without receiving the new birth, just as many may know how to get to a distant city, yet never go there.

"AGAIN ENTANGLED THEREIN"

The word "entangled" is literally "braid in" and is variously translated as "enmeshed" or "caught," as in a net. Peter pictures these deceived souls as birds or fish caught in a net. These false teachers came along, used plausible arguments, and taught that it was not necessary to restrain lust, and those unstable were quickly swept away. If one is not born again, he always has the craving to satisfy the lusts of the flesh. How sad that within the gates are enemies, who instead of leading souls to Christ, lead into sin.

Good Men Fall

Sometimes even good men, children of God, fall into sin. Think of David's sin with Bathsheba, and Peter's denial of Christ. You will notice though that both of these showed real penitence for their sin. This is always manifest in a true child of God, but not so with one who merely professes to be a Christian. The Christian has fierce enemies in Satan, the world and the flesh, and they would drag him down, but thank the Lord, Christ stands ready to go into the battle with him. The unsaved are overcome by these enemies, but the Lord stands ready to break the net and so release His own.

"The Latter End Is Worse"

For those who are "overcome, the latter end is worse with them than the beginning." How often this is true. They lived badly before they professed Christianity, but when they sank again into the filthy cesspools, they were worse than ever. It reminds us of the story the Lord tells of the man out of whom the demon departed. The house is empty, swept, and garnished, but sad to say, remains empty. The man was rid of the demon, but he did not let Christ in to fill the empty place. The demon comes back with seven other demons. Truly with that man his latter end is worse than his beginning (Mat. 12:43-45).

Great Enemies of the Truth

The greatest enemies of true Christianity are those who once professed to be saved, but then under the guise of religion, were led into some false thing, or manner of life. They will battle fiercely for their error. They are like Satan himself, who fell from his high estate, and now seeks to mar the testimony and the lives of those who belong to Christ.

His Wrath Will Wax Hot

When Christ was here He was very hard on the pharisees, who professed to be religious leaders and teachers, but lived in and taught error. He said, "Ye shall receive the greater damnation"

(Mat. 23:14). His language in the whole chapter is most scathing. We believe He is no different today. He hates sin, and certainly His wrath will wax hot against those who, under the pretense of being Christian teachers, lead others into sin. It would be better to be a Hottentot in Africa than to stand in the shoes of such false teachers.

XXIII

THE DOG AND HIS VOMIT

(II Peter 2:21, 22)

2:21. "For it had been better for them not to have known the way of righteousness, than after they have known it, to turn from the holy commandment delivered unto them."

This verse is an enlargement of the thought expressed in the last part of verse 20, "the latter end is worse with them than the beginning." One might be excused for not walking in the right way, when he does not know it, but when he knows it, there is no excuse for not walking in it. Ignorance can be a very bad thing, but disobedience is always worse.

"It Had Been Better"

Peter is writing about those who had been raised in heathen darkness and sin, or perhaps ceremonial Judaism. These, because of hearing the gospel, had left their errors, and had embraced Christianity as their system of religion, but now had turned aside to believe error, and to live licentious lives. He said it would have been better for them never to have heard the truth at all, than to so turn away from it. In the first place, their knowing the truth made their responsibility the greater, and so their judgment the more severe. Secondly, when a worldling lives a sinful life no one notices or cares, but the moment one makes a profession to Christianity, be it ever so faulty, it brings reproach on the name of Christ and His people.

The Testimony of Christ

The Lord Jesus testifies everywhere to this same truth. He says, "If I had not come and spoken unto them, they had not had sin, but now have they no cloke for their sin" (John 15:22). "And that servant, which knew his lord's will, and prepared not himself, neither did according to his will, shall be beaten with many stripes. But he that knew not, and did commit things worthy of stripes, shall be beaten with few stripes" (Luke 12:47, 48).

In Mat. 11:20-24 the Lord pronounces woes on Chorazin, Bethsaida and Capernaum, because He had there done many of His mighty works, but they repented not. He said it would be more tolerable for the wicked cities of Sodom and Gomorrah in the day of judgment than for them. How terrible will the judgment be for those who know the way, and profess to be on the way, and yet believe in unrestrained wickedness.

"The Way of Righteousness"

"The way of righteousness" is the way of Christ. He said, "I am the way, the truth, and the life" (John 14:6). From then on Christianity is often called "the way;" nine times we have it in the book of Acts (9:2 etc.). Paul says, "I persecuted this way unto death" (Acts 22:4). Peter uses it three times in this chapter. In 2:2 he calls it "the way of truth," in 2:15 "the right way," and in our verse "the way of righteousness." These false teachers of our chapter were making Christianity the way of lust, revelry, and covetousness, but Peter calls it "the way of righteousness." These men knew (rather acknowledged) "the way of righteousness," but they did not love it and did not walk in it. "In the way of righteousness is life" (Prov. 12:28), but not in "the way of unrighteousness."

"Turn from the Holy Commandment"

There is something dreadfully wrong when one turns from the right way to walk in the ways of sin. When one turns away from the Lord, he thereby leaves the impression that there is something wrong or weak about Christianity, and so brings reproach on the name of the Lord. This is truly a serious thing. "But the soul that doeth ought presumptuously, — the same reproacheth the Lord; and that soul shall be cut off from among his people" (Num. 15:30). "Therefore to him that knoweth to do good, and doeth it not, to him it is sin" (James 4:17).

"Holy Commandment"

When Peter uses the expression "holy commandment" we believe he is giving a terse description of Christianity. Some seem to think that every time the Scriptures speak of law or commandment, it refers to the ten commandments. Of course this is not so. Paul speaks of seven different laws in the book of Romans. Anything the Lord demands of us can be spoken of as a commandment.

A HOLY COMMANDMENT DEMANDS A HOLY LIFE

We believe the "holy commandment" spoken of here speaks of trusting Christ and, as a result, living for Him. We believe the Lord is highly displeased with those who show disrespect for His gospel, and refuse to walk in ways of obedience to Him. Peter calls this commandment a "holy commandment," but these false teachers acted as though Christianity was an unholy commandment. Both the expressions, "the way of righteousness," and the "holy commandment" condemn the unrighteous and unholy ways of these men. They were neither righteous, nor holy, nor obedient as the word "commandment" demands. We trust that we not only trust Him for salvation, but as a consequence, live righteous, clean, and obedient lives to His glory and praise.

2:22. "But it is happened unto them according to the true proverb, The dog is turned to his own vomit again; and the sow that was washed to her wallowing in the mire."

In this verse Peter brings in a couple of Proverbs to drive home his point. He likens these sinful leaders to dogs and swine. Either of these terms would be very insulting to a Jew. He makes it even more insulting by likening them to dogs returning to their vomit, and sows washed turning to their wallowing in the mire.

"THE TRUE PROVERB"

Peter quotes two proverbs, one taken from the book of Proverbs and the other from the speech of his day. A proverb is a short pithy statement packed full of truth. Both of these proverbs fit this description graphically. The first one is found in Prov. 26:11, "As a dog returneth to his vomit, so a fool returneth to his folly." Peter quotes from the book of Proverbs often, showing that he was very well acquainted with the Old Testament (I Pet. 1:7; 2:17; 4:8; 4:18). Both of these proverbs picture a greed for filth, which was so true of these false teachers.

"THE DOG"

In the Orient dogs are not often tamed or brought into the home as pets. Most run wild and are considered vile and unclean. When tamed and properly cared for, dogs prove to be fine, friendly, and loyal animals, but in the East they are mostly fierce and greedy. With them it is a fight for existence. The Israelite was not allowed to bring the price of a dog into the house of the Lord, because a dog was an abomination to the Lord (Deut. 23:18). Goliath says to David, "Am I a dog, that thou comest to me with staves?" (I Sam. 17:43). When one called himself a dog, he was taking the lowest of the low places. Mephibosheth took that place before David (II Sam. 9:8) and the Syrophenician woman, before Christ(Mat. 15:27). To be called a dog by another was considered highly insulting. Both of these proverbs of our verse must have stung these false teachers to the quick.

"TURNED TO HIS OWN VOMIT AGAIN"

The sight of a dog devouring his own vomit is not as prevalent here as in the Orient, but the writer has seen dogs do it. In the Orient they are not well cared for, and they are often hungry. They live mostly on garbage . Occasionally the time comes when they can get an abundance of food. Then they are apt to be greedy and to eat too much, which may incite vomiting. It is then that they, in their greed, will devour their own vomit.

THEY RETURNED TO THEIR EVIL LUSTS

In what way does this picture the men condemned in our chapter? They had disgorged the vile things of heathenism, but now under the guise of Christian liberty, they were returning to their old sinful lusts. Peter says, this is as disgusting as a dog returning again to his own vomit.

A CHRISTIAN IS NOT A DOG

The Christian is often likened to a sheep in the Word, but never to a dog or a sow. These are unclean animals, but a true Christian has been cleansed by the precious blood of Christ (I John 1:7). These referred to in our verse were dogs to begin with, they continued so to be, and ended up as such. There is no indication that their natures were changed at all. They had left their heathenism and seemed changed for a time, but the very fact that they soon returned to sin just as vile as formerly, proved that they never had been changed into new creatures by the power of Christ. We see some today who for a time seem reformed, but the fact that they soon slip back into sin proves that they never were really transformed. We do not believe our verse can be used to prove that one genuinely saved may be lost again forever.

"The Sow that was Washed"

The sow was an unclean animal to the Jew. He utterly detested the animal and he would never eat its flesh. When the Lord would picture one who had fallen to the very basest condition, he pictures him as tending swine, and so destitute that he was ready to eat the swine's food (Luke 15:15, 16). Hogs not only are unclean and love the mud, but they too are greedy. Did you ever see a herd of them at the feeding trough, and hear how they squeal and see how they fight for the greatest share of the food? Call a man a hog today and everyone knows what you mean. How appropriate to call these covetous teachers sows. Another thing, a hog is always rooting in the ground. How like a covetous man whose whole ambition is earthly.

"To Her Wallowing in the Mire"

The washing of a hog is entirely external and does in no way change her nature. She is just as much a sow after washing as before. Unless her nature is changed there is nothing to keep her from returning to the mud just as soon as she has the opportunity. It is a sinner's nature to sin and he may for a time reform, but unless he receives a new nature by trusting Christ, he will again quickly return to his sin. Some believe that to reform a bit and then to join a church will guarantee them a place in heaven. This is a fatal mistake; one must receive a new life from the Lord and be changed to a saint before he is fit for heaven.

Sows or Sheep?

"For ye were as sheep going astray; but are now returned unto the Shepherd and Bishop of your souls" (I Peter 2:25). The sow returns to the mire, but the sheep to the shepherd. The reformed sinner often returns to his sin, but those who are saved, but backslidden, return to the Savior. If these men had been born again and had received the nature of sheep, they never would have returned to their mire. "My sheep hear my voice, and I know them, and they follow me: and I give unto them eternal life; and they shall never perish" (John 10:27, 28). Sometimes the sheep may wander a bit, but He will bring them back.

XXIV

BY WAY OF REMEMBRANCE

(II Peter 3:1, 2)

3:1. "This second epistle, beloved, I now write unto you; in both which I stir up your pure minds by way of remembrance."

In this chapter Peter turns from speaking scathingly of false licentious teachers, to warning the Christians of those who scorn and ridicule the Christian truths, especially the coming of the Lord and the judgments which were to follow. It deals not with ecclesiastical error, but with the mocking of the unbeliever.

Verse Summary

The first verse of this third chapter brings to our attention that this is Peter's second letter, and indicates that he wrote them both to the same Christians. He also tells of the purpose of both of his epistles, namely, to stir them up in the ways of the Lord. He did not necessarily mean to bring new truth to their attention, but to impress them with the importance of the truths which they already knew.

"This Second Epistle"

Peter's first epistle was written principally to encourage and exhort the Christians of Asia Minor in time of great suffering and persecution. There was danger of them becoming disheartened, and to question whether they were in the right path. Perhaps the messenger who delivered Peter's first epistle brought back a report which caused him to write this second one. He may have reported that discouragement was not their only danger, but that they were also in danger from within by false teachers, who were drawing the Christians into loose living. Then there was also the danger from those who mocked at the thought of the coming again of our Lord Jesus. There are always enemies of the Lord's people near at hand, and we must be much on guard.

"BELOVED"

This third chapter is so much different from the second that one might almost think that a different man wrote it. In the second chapter, Peter almost thunders denunciations against the false teachers; in this chapter, in writing to the loyal and the true, he uses many terms of endearment. Four times he calls them "beloved." He knew when to be severe and sharp and when to be kind and tender. Would that all Christians knew when to be the one and when the other. The servants of the Lord must be serious and straightforward in their dealings with sin, but kind and tender in their dealings with the saints. In our verse, it is "beloved" be mindful; in verse 8, be not ignorant; in verse 14, be diligent; in verse 17, beware.

"I NOW WRITE UNTO YOU"

The word "now" in our verse seems to indicate that Peter hurried to write this second epistle, and that it was written soon after the first. It has the sense of the word "already." When he heard that other dangers beset these Christians besides suffering and persecution, he hurried to write them, that he might also be a help to them in these matters. Would that we too were in a hurry to help those who are in trouble or danger.

"I STIR UP"

It was Peter's purpose in both of his epistles to stir up the Christians. When trials or difficulties come it is easy to become despondent, and consequently, inactive. He would arouse the Christians to vigilance and diligence. We believe this is necessary today too. There are multitudes of Christians despondent, inactive, or asleep. Pray that somehow, someway, they may be stirred to new life. Here and there we hear of a stirring, an awakening, a revival, if you please. May the Lord be praised.

"YOUR PURE MINDS"

"Sincere minds" as in the Revised Version is better than "pure minds." It was nice that Peter could testify to the sincerity of their minds. If he were here today, could he say the same of us? They were open-minded and earnest as to their convictions, and were ready to receive the truth. However, with such people there is always the danger of being deceived and led astray by arguments which are false, but made to seem plausible. We believe the Lord esteems very highly, godly sincerity in mind and heart. There is much of half-hearted lukewarmness, which we read the Lord is about to spue out of His mouth. (Rev. 3:16). "That ye may be *sincere* and without offense till the day of Christ" (Phil. 1:10). "Let us keep the feast — with the unleavened bread of *sincerity* and truth" (I Cor. 5:8).

"By Way of Remembrance"

As in 1:12, 13, Peter is explaining that he is not trying to bring new thought, but trying to impress upon his readers truths which they already knew. Some are always looking for new things to bring to the people, and in it all they forget to stress the all important fundamental truths. It is always to be remembered that young converts rising up need the milk of the Word, as well as that the older ones need the meat. Peter desired especially to remind his readers of the things which were coming in the last days, concerning which he speaks in this chapter. We wrote some on the wonders of the memory in connection with 1:12, 13. One has said, "Memory is like a golden thread upon which are hung varied facts and experiences like pearls, which link youth with old age."

3:2. "That ye may be mindful of the words which were spoken before by the holy prophets, and of the commandment of us the apostles of the Lord and Saviour."

The purpose of this verse is to show that the words of both the apostles and the prophets were of equal authority, and that they were equally inspired of the Lord. Also that the words of the apostles were the very words commanded by the Lord Jesus Himself.

"Be Mindful of the Words"

In Peter's day there would be a tendency, especially by Jewish believers, to think very highly of the word of the prophets, and to believe in their inspiration, but in our day we are likely to think more highly of the word of the apostles. Peter puts both on the same plane and would not have us neglect either. We should cultivate the habit of meditation on both the Old and New Testaments. Of course, for a young believer, the New Testament should come first, but after he once has a fairly good understanding of that, he should study the Old Testament in the light of the New.

"THE WORDS — SPOKEN — BY THE HOLY PROPHETS"

Some might ask, "Is there anything in the words spoken by the prophets which have an application to us of our time? Were they not written for the people of their time?" Many of their words did indeed have a special message for the people of their time, but they certainly often went far beyond that. A great deal of their work was to exhort and warn their own generation, but much of it is applicable to all times.

THEIR PROPHECIES

The prophets prophesied a great deal of the Lord's first coming into this world. All of this is now literally fulfilled. To truly know and to grasp this, gives us great confidence in the truth of their prophecies. They prophesied of His birth (Isa. 7:14, Mic. 5:2); they prophesied of His life (Isa. 42:1-7, Isa. 50:4); they spoke of His suffering and death (Ps. 22; Isa. 53); they spoke of His resurrection (Ps. 16:9-11; Ps. 40:1, 2). Perhaps more often than any of these they spoke of His coming again, His reign on earth, and the judgments which are to precede it and also follow it. That the Lord Jesus Himself understood all these things is evident from Luke 24:25-27. "Then he said unto them, O fools, and slow of heart to believe all that the prophets have spoken: Ought not Christ to have suffered these things, and to enter into his glory? And beginning at Moses and all the prophets, he expounded unto them in all the scriptures the things concerning himself" (also Luke 24:44, 45; Luke 1:70; Acts 3:18, 24-26; I Pet. 1:10-12).

PROPHECIES CONCERNING HIS COMING AGAIN

In verse 4 Peter brings in the coming again of the Lord, and in verse 10, the day of the Lord, and no doubt it is especially in connection with these events that Peter would have his readers heed the voice of the prophets. Zechariah 14 tells of His coming again and also His reign on earth. His coming and His reign are beautifully pictured in Psalm 72. Isaiah over and over speaks of His reign (Isaiah 11 etc.). The day of the Lord especially speaks of the Lord's judgment, both at the beginning of His reign and also in connection with the very end (Joel 2:11; Isa. 13:6; Jer. 46:10 etc.).

"THE HOLY PROPHETS"

In chapter 2, Peter speaks of false prophets and teachers; here it is of true prophets and teachers. He calls them holy prophets, not only because they were clean men, but because they were set apart by the Lord to reveal His will to His people. They were commissioned of the Lord, and spoke with authority. In the first chapter Peter says, "Holy men of God spake as they were moved of the Holy Spirit" (II Pet. 1:21).

"THE COMMANDMENT"

In the Revised Version the last part of this verse reads, "and the commandment of the Lord and Saviour through your apostles." Thus Peter is speaking of the commandments of Christ as given through the apostles. Neither the apostles nor the prophets spoke in their own name. The prophets continually said, "Thus saith the Lord." The apostles continually come "in the name of the Lord." We are not told that Peter had any special command of the Lord in mind. While the word is in the singular, he no doubt meant that everything the apostles spoke were the commandments of the Lord. Let us remember that commandments are given to be obeyed. Let us be "doers of the word, and not hearers only" (James 1:22).

"THE APOSTLES"

Here as in 1:16-21, Peter links the prophets and apostles together. Paul does the same thing in Eph. 2:20; "Ye - - are built upon the foundation of the apostles and prophets, Jesus Christ himself being the chief corner stone." By linking them together, Peter is advocating the same inspired authority for each. Both spoke out the commandments of the Lord. As Peter was the leading apostle, he is hereby indicating that his letters were inspired by the Spirit of God. We have noticed how the Revised Version says "your apostles." Since Paul was the one most used in connection with the Christians of Asia Minor to whom Peter is writing, Peter is hereby also acknowledging the apostleship of Paul. Because Paul was not numbered with the twelve while Christ was on earth, some questioned his apostleship, but Peter did not seem to. (See verse 15.) These are what marked out one as an apostle: he must have seen the Lord Jesus and been personally commissioned by Him (I Cor. 9:1). Both of these things happened to Paul on the Damascus road (Acts 9).

"Lord and Saviour"

"Lord and Saviour" seems to be Peter's favorite title for our Lord in this second epistle. Besides our verse, we have it in 1:11, 2:20 and 3:18. If we are happy to have Christ as our Savior, we also should be happy to have Him as our Lord. "Lord, what wilt thou have me to do" (Acts 9:6).

XXV

SCOFFERS

(II Peter 3:3, 4)

3:3. "Knowing this first, that there shall come in the last days scoffers, walking after their own lusts."

The apostle would warn his readers and also those of us who live in these last days, that we may expect scoffers. Not all will accept the gospel; some will turn away with a sneer. The reason for this is that they are not ready to give up their life of lust. As an excuse for their sin they belittle and ridicule Christianity.

"Knowing This First"

Peter did not want his readers to live under the false impression that they would have an easy time without opposition and ridicule. The expression, "knowing this first" indicates that he thought it very important that they be warned of these things. They say, "To be forewarned is to be forearmed." One man was brought out of a life of sin to know Christ. He thought that immediately all his friends and relatives would be saved. He was bitterly disappointed when most of them laughed and sneered at him. We are glad to say that a few were brought to know Christ through his efforts.

"In the Last Days"

Sometimes the expression "the last days" refers to this whole dispensation from the cross to the coming again of Christ. This is apparently so in Acts 2:17 and Heb. 1:2. We believe at other times it refers to the very end of this age. We surely believe this is true in II Tim. 3:1-5; "In the last days perilous times shall come. For men shall be lovers of their own selves, covetous, boasters, proud" etc. We believe Peter too had the very end of this age in mind. He speaks of the coming of Christ in the next verse, and of judgments of God which are to come much later than that even. At the same time, it is true that there have been scoffers in every age from Christ's time down to the present day.

Peter's knowledge of conditions in the last days and the judgments to follow indicate clearly that he was inspired of the Lord in his writings.

"SCOFFERS"

The Revised Version reads, "mockers shall come with mockery." Weymouth's suggests that these mockers mocked at everything. Our next verse indicates that they mocked especially at the promise of the coming again of our Lord Jesus. There were mockers even in Old Testament times (Psa. 1:1; Psa. 12:4; Prov. 1:22; Isa. 28:14).

WHY DO THE SCOFFERS SCOFF?

Because of their sin many hate the gospel. They want to live without any restraint, so some ridicule the very thought that God exists. They certainly do not want to believe that He will bring them into judgment, so they ridicule anything which suggests that He might. Having no sound logic to refute it, they turn to ridicule and scoffing.

SCOFFING TODAY

Scoffing has always been prevalent, but we believe it is worse than ever in recent times. We have often had the scorner heap his scorn upon us. We have had him do this as we passed out tracts, or spoke personally to him. Especially have we had it in connection with open air work. One time while speaking at such a meeting, a woman used vile and bitter language against us. We could not hear all she said because of our speaking, but the others said it was unprintable. So vile it was that some in the audience took hold of her and tried to quiet her, and finally pushed her down the street. We have wondered whether she was not actually possessed by Satan himself. It is not unusual to hear scoffing today in theaters, at parties, banquets, etc. Some publications are also guilty of this heinous sin. We are happy to say though, we do not believe this mockery is quite as brazen as it was fifteen or even ten years ago. We see signs today of a revival of true Christianity. We hope it will end in a wave of blessing.

THE EFFECT OF SCORN

The scorn of the mocker has often had serious effects. We believe it has caused some to fall away from the faith in these last days. Some weak ones cannot withstand the profane witticisms of these mockers, and they surrender. Others dread trusting Christ because they realize that they will be targets for some of these scorners. If a Christian fails, he is immediately made the butt of the mocker's ridicule, so let us all beware and walk closely with our Lord, lest we give them occasion to mock.

The Seriousness of Scorn

To deride Christ and His coming again is a most serious offense. To deride a Christian for his faith is not only rude, but it is cruel and inhuman. Such are enemies of righteousness and the welfare of humanity. They are the chief instruments in the hands of the wicked one. The Word calls them fools. "Fools make a mock at sin" (Prov. 14:9). Since they have served Satan so well, these mockers need expect nothing better than to share his judgment. When down in hell there will be no saints on whom to heap their scorn. One has said, "Not one flash of wit will for a moment relieve the darkness of eternal night."

"Walking After their Own Lusts"

Those who scorn the things of God usually are the ones who walk "after their own lusts." Scoffing and evil living go together. In fact, it is because the gospel condemns their evil living that they deride and scoff at it. This is the main reason why men hate Christ, the Bible, and Christians. These mockers say, "We will say what we please, we will mock if we want to; no one will stop us, and we will sneer at the thought of Christ coming to punish us." "Our lips are our own: who is Lord over us" (Psa. 12:4). "We will live as we please too, and will tolerate no interference."

3:4. "And saying, Where is the promise of his coming? for since the fathers fell asleep, all things continue as they were from the beginning of the creation."

This verse tells us that the special point of attack of the scoffers will be the coming again of Christ. As a proof for their arguments they use the unchangeableness of nature. They say, "There have been no changes in things since we can remember and since the time our fathers can remember, and we do not believe there will be any changes in the near future."

"WHERE IS THE PROMISE OF HIS COMING?"

Peter wrote his epistle some 30 years after the ascension of Christ. The early Christians believed that Christ would come back again very soon, and told everyone what they believed. No doubt they told too of the judgments which were to follow this coming. Perhaps some who heard them said, "That is all you talk about; Christ is coming back again. If He is coming back again, why doesn't He come? We do not believe He is coming at all." Now it is 1900 years later, and still He has not come. We hear exactly the same kind of scoffing today. One man said to us not long ago, "The coming again of Christ is all I have heard since I was a boy and still he has not come." We told him that his very statement made us believe that Christ would soon come, because Peter says, "There shall come in the last days scoffers — saying where is the promise of his coming?"

PROPHETIC STATEMENTS ALWAYS RIDICULED

Even in Old Testament times many ridiculed the prophetic statements of the servants of the Lord. "Behold they say unto me, Where is the word of the Lord? let it come now" (Jer. 17:15). "That say, Let him make speed, and hasten his work, that we may see it, and let the counsel of the Holy One of Israel draw nigh and come, that we may know it!" (Isa. 5:19). "Son of man, behold, they of the house of Israel say, The vision that he seeth is for many days to come, and he prophesieth of the times that are afar off" (Ez. 12:27). No doubt when Noah built the ark many laughed and ridiculed saying, "Noah you had a nightmare, the flood will never come"; but it came. Even so, mockers are saying today, "Christ will never come," but He will.

HE CAME ONCE — HE WILL COME AGAIN

One of the greatest events to ever happen in the history of this world, was when a baby was born in Bethlehem in a stable. This was the Creator of heaven and earth paying us a visit. "The dayspring from on high hath visited us" (Luke 1:78). The Lord came, but sorry to say, men despised and rejected Him, and nailed Him to an accursed cross. He came in humility with His glory veiled so that He might by dying be made an atonement for our sins. He is coming back again, but this next time it will be different. He will come in great power and glory. He will come to be the judge and ruler of the whole earth, and none will be able to resist Him.

HIS COMING IS CERTAIN

The coming again of our Lord Jesus is certain. The New Testament abounds with references to this fact. He says Himself in John 14:2, 3, "I go to prepare a place for you. And if I go and prepare a place for you, I will come again, and receive you unto myself; that where I am, there ye may be also." Then again in Acts 1:11, immediately after His ascension, angels tell the disciples, "Ye men of Galilee, why stand ye gazing up into heaven? this same Jesus, which is taken up from you into heaven, shall so come in like manner as ye have seen him go into heaven." The very last promise of the New Testament is, "Surely I come quickly" (Rev. 22:20). He will keep His word.

TWO ASPECTS OF HIS COMING

As far as we can understand the Scriptures, there are two aspects to this coming of our Lord Jesus. There seems to be a coming for His bride the church, and then, a coming with the church. I Thess. 4:13-18 certainly seems like an altogether different event than Mat. 25:31-46 or Rev. 19:11-16.

THE RAPTURE

Let us briefly note some things concerning the first aspect of His coming, generally called the rapture of the church. Notice John 14:1-3, where the Lord speaks of going to heaven. He tells how He will there prepare a place for His own, and then come again to take them to heaven to be with Himself. More is told of this rapture in I Thess. 4:16, 17, where it says that the Lord Himself shall descend from heaven, the dead in Christ shall rise from their graves, and the living saints shall be caught up together with them to meet the Lord, not on the earth, but in the air. Apparently at this time all dead and living saints will be caught up to heaven to be with the Lord. We believe the parable of the ten virgins in Mat. 25:1-13 teaches the same thing. There we find the five wise virgins at His coming taken into the marriage supper with the bridegroom. We read more of this marriage supper in Rev. 19:7-10, where the church is united to Christ in a special way.

His Coming in Power and Glory

Immediately following the account in Rev. 19 of the marriage supper, we read of the Lord's coming in power and glory to judge and to rule the nations. This aspect of His coming is the one most often referred to in the New Testament. In Rev. 19:11-16, we see Him riding on a white horse and the armies of heaven following Him. These armies we believe to be the same saints who were at the marriage supper of the Lamb. Rev. 19:8 especially emphasizes that "the fine linen is the righteousness of saints." Both the bride of Rev. 19:8 and the armies of Rev. 19:14 are arrayed in this fine linen. Zech. 14:5 tells us that when He comes He will have all His saints with Him. Notice Mat. 25:31, 32, where it tells of His coming in glory and how He shall sit on the throne of His glory, and how all the nations shall be called before Him to be judged of Him. After this judgment we believe He will establish His kingdom on earth as we read in Rev. 20 and so many places in the Old Testament. This kingdom period is often called the Millennium because of the 1,000 years mentioned in Rev. 20. Perhaps not all of our readers will fully agree with our understanding of these coming events, but we believe they are correct and Scriptural.

These Promises Not Believed

Many in Peter's day did not believe these promises concerning Christ's coming. Many in our day also disbelieve them. They reason, He is not coming because He has not come, as though a delay in a promise means it will not be kept. The main trouble was, they did not want to believe, and in order to bolster their unbelief and to shake the true Christians too, they mocked the thought of the promise of His coming. Sorry to say, many in pulpits today, do not believe these promises either. Some say with the wicked servant of Mat. 24:48, "My Lord delayeth His coming."

The Signs of the Times

There are many evidences that the coming of the Lord draweth nigh. This too, is a very large subject and we will be able to make only a few suggestive remarks. Study the condition of the world as the Word pictures it just before the coming of the Lord, and you will find our age fits it perfectly (Mat. 24:4-12; Dan. 12:4 etc.). At Christ's coming the Jews will be back in the land, as we find them today (Isa. 27:12, 13; Isa. 11:10-16). The church is certainly in a lukewarm state as we have it pictured in the Laodicean Church in Rev. 3:14-19. This we believe is a picture of the last condition of the church before Christ's coming. "When the Son of man cometh, shall he find faith on the earth?" (Luke 18:8).

His Coming a Time of Joy to Some, But Sorrow to Others

The coming of the Lord is not something to be dreaded by the true Christian. For one who loves the Lord and walks with Him, it will be a time of great blessing and reward. It is pictured as the hope of the church. However, for the unsaved it will be a time of judgment. We should warn the unsaved to flee to Christ before He rises from His seat and shuts the door (Luke 13:25). For those outside it will be a time of "weeping and gnashing of teeth" (Luke 13:28). Remember, His coming will be sudden, as a thief in the night.

"Since the Fathers Fell Asleep"

These scoffers, when speaking of "the fathers" may have been thinking of the Old Testament prophets who prophesied concerning the day of the Lord. They may have said, "The prophets who spoke of the coming of the Lord have been dead a long time, but the day is still not here; we do not believe it will come at all." It is a question whether these scoffers were Jewish, and so rather than thinking of the Old Testament fathers, they may have meant the apostles and other Christian workers who had died. Then they may have been referring to their own immediate ancestors. "Ever since grandfather can remember and his parents could remember, there has been no great changes in the world, and we do not believe the Lord is coming to bring about any great changes."

"Fell Asleep"

"Sleep" was a common way of picturing death in New Testament times. The Lord says, "Our friend Lazarus sleepeth" (John

11:11). We have it also in I Cor. 11:30 and I Thess. 4:13, 14, etc. "Sleep" speaks only of the body, never of the spirit. Paul says, "Absent from the body,—present with Lord" (II Cor. 5:8, also Phil. 1:21-23).

"All Things Continue as they Were"

There seems to be no change in natural things. Day follows night with exact precision. So we have with the seasons too. Spring follows winter, and summer follows spring. It is a good thing that this is so, or we would not be able to plan. The farmer would not know when to plow and when to plant. If some days were longer than others, some 26 and then some 22 hours, what a time we would have keeping our clocks right. Even a change of 5 minutes a day would quickly upset our civilization. We believe the Lord purposely keeps all things in this exact relationship. The scoffers of our chapter were using this unchangeableness of nature as an excuse for their unbelief. They were arguing, "Nothing unusual has happened down the years, so nothing unusual will happen."

Materialists

Materialists abound today. We hear them talk of the fixed and settled laws of nature. We read a statement by a so-called scientist in which he said there had been no change in the magnetism of the world for 1,500,000 years. He said the rocks proved it. Of course he was insinuating, like our scoffers, that no change was likely to happen soon, if ever. If there is a God at all, they say, He only works along the lines of natural law. He could not intercede in a special way in His own world, according to them.

Scientific Research

In recent years men have tried very hard to prove by scientific research that many of the Bible statements are not true. Darwin's writings have made many think that to believe the Bible was unscholarly and manifested ignorance. We are thankful to say that in very recent years, the Bible has been winning the argument. More and more, scientific research is proving the Bible to be true, rather than untrue.

Miracles

In spite of the many miraculous things in nature, many today do not believe in the miracles of the Bible. One man said to us not long ago, "I don't believe in those miracles we read of in the Bible." We told him that that was strange, because the world was filled with miracles, and then looking him straight in the face, we said, "I am looking at a miracle right now." He said, "Do you mean me? I am no miracle; once I was an egg, and now I am a man." We replied, "Now isn't that a miracle?" He thought there must be something wrong with my head, but no doubt, you will agree that the human body is one of the miracles in the world.

Miracles Above the Natural

We generally think though, that things are only miraculous when they are above the realm of the natural. Some think that if there ever was anything super-natural, it has now been done away with forever. They argue that since there are no miracles today, that there will be none in the future. We believe that for this age God has purposely eliminated to a great extent the supernatural, because He desires that we live by faith, not by sight. That does not mean that in future ages He will not again resort to the miraculous.

God's Judgments

No doubt the early Christians preached judgment in connection with the coming again of our Lord Jesus, and there will surely be judgments meted out to His enemies at that time. To prophesy judgment is especially distastful to the unsaved. When Lot came to his sons-in-law they scoffed at his statement that Sodom was to be destroyed (Gen. 19:14). No doubt Noah's hearers did the same upon his predictions of the flood. When you warn sinners today the result is often the same. They say, "Judgment has not come, and it will not come." They wilfully forget what happened to Nineveh, and Babylon, and Sodom, and Gomorrah. God has brought judgments in the past and He will in the future.

There have been Great Geological Changes

There is no excuse for modern man to say that there have been no changes in nature since creation. There are evidences all about us that there have been many and great geological changes in the world. Geologists claim that at one time Lake Erie was a river, and that its course is easily discernible in the lake bottom. This river entered Lake Ontario near where Hamilton, Ont. now is. Some mighty upheaval caused this river to be dammed, and so Lake Erie was formed. The water kept rising until it started spilling over near what is now Lewistown, N. Y. This upheaval may have been caused by the flood. The Niagara River could have easily carved out its gorge since the time of the flood.

ANOTHER GEOLOGICAL CHANGE

They also say that Lake Chatauqua in New York state was once a river which flowed toward Lake Erie. Now it is a lake which gives rise to a river which flows into the Allegheny, thus to the Ohio, then the Mississippi, and finally to the Gulf of Mexico. The flood may be responsible for this too. We certainly cannot say that all things have continued "as they were from the beginning of the creation."

OTHER CHANGES

It has long been a mystery why the mammoth elephants, now extinct, could be found so well preserved in North Eastern Siberia. They are found frozen by the thousands up in this country. They must have frozen very quickly and never thawed out again to be so perfectly preserved for perhaps thousands of years. Scientists have cut steaks from them, and found them still edible. They have found undigested food in their stomachs, which shows that they lived on grasses now far removed from that climate. There is only one explanation, there must have been a sudden and great change from a mild to an extremely cold climate.

THE ICE AGE

From our school days we have heard how at one time the northeastern section of the U.S.A. was covered with ice the year around. They call it the ice age. They say the same was true of northwestern Europe. They claim that at one time the British Isles were completely icebound, along with a great deal of the continent. Here too, there must have been some great, and no doubt, sudden climatic change. We recently heard that in Alaska they have discovered fossils of some of the most delicate ferns, which only grow in comparatively warm climates.

A CHANGE IN POLES

What brought about these great changes. A recent scientist has stated that more than likely at one time the north pole was situated some 20 degrees off its present location, perhaps on the eastern edge of Greenland. If this change happened suddenly it certainly would account for the frozen elephants in northeastern Siberia as well as the fern fossils in Alaska. It would also account for the ice age in northeastern North America and northwestern Europe. We have been wondering whether the Lord might not have used something of the nature of a change in polar location to bring on the mighty flood mentioned in our next verse. There have been great changes since creation, and we need not question the Word when it says there will be more.

"FROM THE BEGINNING OF THE CREATION"

These scoffers were saying, "all things continue as they were from the beginning of the creation." We must give them credit for believing in creation, and so of course, in a Creator. While they admit that there is a God, yet they do not believe in the God of the Bible. Some today do not seem to believe in a creation at all. We recently saw a telecast reproduction of what was a trial of some of the leaders of the Euthanasia Society. The president of the society, a Doctor Potter, a protestant clergyman, was asked twice by the opposing attorney, "Who created the world?" His astounding reply was, "I cannot tell, I do not know." He did not believe the first verse of the Bible, "In the beginning God created the heaven and the earth." No doubt the terrible falsehood of evolution is to blame for much folly amongst those who profess to be servants of the Lord. Thank God, that awful lie is on the way out.

XXVI

WORLD CHANGES BY WATER AND FIRE

(II Peter 3:5-7)

3:5. "For this they willingly are ignorant of, that by the word of God the heavens were of old, and the earth standing out of the water and in the water."

Peter now starts his refutation of their statement that there had been no changes since the creation. He first of all brings to mind the fact that there were already changes in connection with the creation. At one time all was one fluid mass called "waters," and the earth came out of these. He speaks also of their wilful forgetfulness (R.V.) concerning these changes.

"They Willingly are Ignorant"

It is very difficult to convince men of truth when they do not want to believe. They immediately look for some reason to bolster their unbelief, and they try to forget or sidetrack any reasons which may be advanced to make them believe. These men were wilfully forgetting the fact that at one time during creation things were altogether different than they are now, and so it would not be impossible for them to be different again. In our last verse these scoffers professed to believe in creation. "All right," says Peter, "the story of creation itself proves your reasoning unsound. There were radical changes at that time. Does that not prove that it is possible for further changes to happen?" Our next verse tells how they were wilfully forgetting that there were great changes in connection with the flood.

Watch Our Wills

The scoffers wanted to forget these things in order to excuse their sin. "And this is the condemnation, that light is come into the world, and men loved darkness rather than light, because their deeds were evil" (John 3:19). Remember, wilful ignorance or forgetfulness will be no excuse when the sinner stands before the Lord. Even Christians can let their wills interfere with what they know to be the Word of God. One brother told us very frankly that he did not believe a certain Scripture which we brought to his attention. It was because he did not want to believe it. Sometimes others are in exactly the same position, but rather than admit it, they seek to twist the Word, or find some excuse for not applying it to themselves.

"BY THE WORD OF GOD"

Creation was not an accident, not a fortunate gathering together of atoms which developed and formed until we have this world and all things on it. It was all by the Word of God. He commanded and it was brought into existence. Nine verses in Gen. 1 start with the words, "And God said." "By the word of the Lord were the heavens made; and all the host of them by the breath of his mouth" (Psalm 33:6). "Through faith we understand that the worlds were framed by the word of God" (Heb. 11:3). He spoke and it was done. Great geological changes have happened since creation; these too, were by the Word of the Lord. Again by the Word of the Lord other severe judgments will yet happen to this scene.

"THE HEAVENS WERE OF OLD"

Peter without question is here referring to Gen. 1:2-10. There we read not only of the creation of the world, but also of the sun, moon, and the stars. We read of the firmament in the midst of the waters, and how the waters above were divided from the waters below, showing forth the heavens. There has been a great deal of discussion as to whether the heavens were actually created at that time or just manifested. It matters not, they were all brought into being by the Word of the Lord. "And he is before all things, and by him all things consist" (Col. 1:17).

"THE EARTH STANDING OUT OF THE WATER"

The last part of this verse speaks of the appearance of dry land on the earth, as we have it recorded in Gen. 1:9, 10. At one time this world was without form and void, and evidently completely covered with water. The Revised Version says, "and an earth compacted out of water," as though the earth was actually made out of the water.

A MOLTEN MASS

Some have thought, and that not without reason, that when it speaks of "waters" in Gen. 1:2, it does not mean water in our accepted sense today, but rather means "liquid," and that the earth at that time was a molten mass. Scientists claim that at some time in the distant past this was actually the condition of the earth. Out of this molten mass the Lord caused the dry land to appear, and of course the water as we know it today as well. This all may be mere supposition, but to us it appears to have logic in it. This would mean that we must take the days of creation, not as 24 hours, but long periods of time. We do not believe this foreign to the thought of Scripture. Oftentimes "day" is used in the Word in this way. Notice verse 8 of our chapter, "that one day is with the Lord as a thousand years."

"AND IN THE WATER"

Instead of "in the water" the Revised Version has "amidst the water." The earth's surface is now three-quarters covered with water, and the dry land is now literally standing in the midst of the water. Truly this water is a great blessing. The Lord's method of lifting it up from the earth into clouds and then sending it down to nourish plant, animal, and human life, is truly wonderful. This same water, which is such a blessing to man, at one time was used to cause their destruction, as our next verse relates.

3:6. "Whereby the world that then was, being overflowed with water, perished."

Some apply this verse to a judgment which happened to the world before the creation of man. We believe it more logical to apply it to the flood of Noah's time. Peter has already made reference to this deluge in 2:5. This flood was one of the things the scoffers of our chapter were forgetting. They were forgetting the great changes which came in connection with creation itself, and they were also forgetting the great geological upsets in connection with the flood. If they would stop to think of the terrible flood which destroyed nearly all of mankind, they would not question but that the Lord might interfere with the course of events of this scene in some other way.

"THE WORLD THAT THEN WAS"

The people in the world before the flood were exceedingly wicked. "And God saw that the wickedness of man was great in the earth, and that every imagination of the thoughts of his heart was only evil continually" (Gen. 6:5). It was because of these sins that God brought on the judgment of the flood. He had a quarrel with man and this was His method of removing these sinners from this scene. No doubt men scoffed and sneered about Noah's ark and the promised flood, but it came in spite of their unbelief.

HEEDLESS OF THE WARNING

That the sinners of Noah's day were utterly heedless of the warning is evident from Mat. 24:38, 39, "For as in the days that were before the flood they were eating and drinking, marrying and giving in marriage, until the day that Noe entered into the ark, and knew not until the flood came, and took them all away: so shall also the coming of the Son of man be." Peter likens the time before the flood to the time before the coming of the Lord, just as our Lord Jesus did.

"OVERFLOWED WITH WATER"

No conscientious Bible student can question that there one time was a great flood on this earth. Both Old and New Testaments everywhere attest to this fact. If there was no flood then the Bible cannot be trusted. Even the words of Christ Himself are not trustworthy, because He mentions it on more than one occasion. Some seem to think that rain only brought on the flood, but the Scripture is very plain in stating that the "fountains of the great deep were broken up, and the windows of heaven were opened" (Gen. 7:11). Evidently great tides swept up from the oceans and overflowed the land.

HOW WAS THIS BROUGHT ABOUT?

We believe the Lord could bring on the flood by just a Word from His mouth, but He probably used means of one kind or another. One scientist suggested that this world may have been formerly surrounded by a giant ice ring some miles up in the atmosphere, and that the breaking up of this ring brought on the flood. It is interesting to note that we never read a word about rain before the time of the flood. We do read in Gen. 2:6, that the earth was watered by a mist.

OTHER SUGGESTED METHODS

We have already suggested that the Lord may have brought on the flood by a change in location of the earth's poles. Then He could have brought it on by the gravitational influence of some mighty comet which He permitted to get close to this earth's orbit. We know how the moon's gravitation brings on the tides. A giant comet near this earth could multiply this many times.

EVIDENCES OF THE FLOOD

There are many evidences on the earth that there at one time was a mighty flood. They say that coal is formed by tremendous pressure being applied to vegetable matter. It would appear that immense forests have been suddenly leveled and then buried under tons and tons of earth, thus forming these giant coal deposits. A mighty surging flood could easily be the reason for this. Fish fossils have been found miles and miles away from any body of water, some on high ground. Huge tidal waves may have swept fish far inland and then buried them under tons and tons of earth. Human skeletons have been found deep down in the ground far lower than any would normally be buried. These and many other things give indication that there once was a great water catastrophe in the history of the world.

GOD AND THE FLOOD

The flood was no accident of nature. While the Lord may have used some means to bring it on, yet it came at His direct command. Creation came by the Word of the Lord, and the flood did the same. He at one time divided the waters (Gen. 1:6-8). At the time of the flood He ordered them back into an heap to destroy man and beast. This all shows His great power, but also His fierce anger against the sin of man. If scoffers today could be made to realize that at one time God swept away a whole world of sinful men, they would not question that future judgments might follow, but would quickly flee to Christ for salvation. Only eight souls entered the ark and were saved from God's wrath. Sorry to say, only a few today have fled to Christ for refuge and are safe from the wrath to come.

NOT ANOTHER FLOOD BUT FIRE

The Lord has promised that there never again will be a world wide flood (Gen. 9:8-11). Whatever He used to bring it on, He will not use it again, at least not for the same purpose. But that does not mean that He cannot, as He sees fit, use other agencies to bring on universal destruction. He has said that someday He will use fire for this purpose. Perhaps some said to Noah, "This world has been going on for 1500 years since Adam; nature has been stedfast; it will continue so to be." Many are saying similar things today. They say the laws of nature have been fixed and unchanged for thousands of years, and there is no reason to believe that there will be any change in the near future. You remind them of the flood and they will not believe that there ever was one. They are very apt to be caught by the judgment of the Lord, even as the antediluvians were caught by the flood. Remember, the world was destroyed by water; it can and it will be destroyed by fire.

WATER AND FIRE

Water and fire are both great blessings to us. We could not do without either for a single day. They are great friends of man, and we use them for thousands of purposes. Yet water was used to destroy the old world and fire will be used to destroy the present world. These great friends become enemies because of man's sin.

"PERISHED"

The old world perished by water. Since the old world was not completely annihilated, the word does not necessarily mean annihilation. Some have even tried to make "perish" mean this in John 3:16. While the old world perished, yet a new one grew up out of the old. Animal and human life came out of the ark to repopulate the earth. Life in the seas as well as plant life survived the flood. Let no man say that the man who dies in his sins will be annihilated; he will die, but his spirit will live in hell forevermore.

3:7. "But the heavens and the earth, which are now, by the same word are kept in store, reserved unto fire against the day of judgment and perdition of ungodly men."

Here Peter tells us that some day this present world will be destroyed by fire. He seems to imply that the earth is stored with fire waiting for the day when the Lord will call it forth to do its appointed work. He says that this judgment, like the flood, will be because of the ungodliness of men.

"The Heavens"

In that great and terrible day which lies ahead, even the heavens will be affected. Peter says in verse 10, "In the which the heavens shall pass away with a great noise." "For the heavens shall vanish away like smoke, and the earth shall wax old like a garment" (Isa. 51:6). The Lord Jesus says, "Heaven and earth shall pass away, but my words shall not pass away" (Mat. 24:35) (also Psa. 102:26, Isa. 34:4, Heb. 1:10-12). Just what this implies is hard to say. Certainly it cannot include the abode of the Lord. Perhaps it means our solar system, the sun, the moon, and our sun's planets, and maybe even more.

What Will Happen?

It may be that the Lord will use some heavenly orb, such as a great comet to upset our world in its routine circuit and cause it thereby to melt with fervent heat. This could easily affect our whole solar system, and cause great confusion in the skies. A Doctor Velikovsky has recently written a book entitled "Worlds in Collision." In it he claims that a large heavenly body whizzed around in our solar system for centuries before it was finally trapped by our sun and became the planet now called Venus. He further claims that it was this comet which caused the sun and the moon to stand still in Joshua's day, and also was the reason for many another miraculous event of Old Testament times. While we are not in a position to say that the doctor's conclusions are all correct, we believe this book convincingly proves that strange things have happened in the heavens in the past, and that it is not at all impossible for more and yet stranger ones to happen in the future. Because the laws of our solar system seem stable and fixed now, is no indication that they will always remain so.

Without doubt, in that great day of judgment there will be great changes in the heavens.

"The Earth"

We believe the earth will be the chief target for attack on this terrible day of judgment, and that it will again become a molten mass (see vs. 10, 12). Our verse gives the purpose of this, that once for all the Lord would rid this world of all sinful men. Out of this molten mass He will produce a new heaven and a new earth, from which sin will be completely eliminated, and wherein righteousness will dwell (verse 12). "And I saw a new heaven and new earth: for the first heaven and the first earth were passed away; and there was no more sea" (Rev. 21:1).

"By the Same Word"

The expression "by the same word" refers back to verse 5. There we have "by the word of God the heavens were of old." Creation came about by the word or command of God. Peter is here saying that by the same command they will be destroyed by fire. Men think our world exists because of the laws of nature. They are only the method by which the Lord works; they all act according to His will. As He desires He can change them, or even suspend them. A single word from Him, even as our Lord Jesus spoke to the raging sea, can change everything.

"Kept in Store"

Instead of "kept in store," the Revised Version has "stored up for fire." The margin reads, "stored with fire." A literal translation could read, "are treasured up with fire." Peter's thought seems to be, the heavens and the earth are stored up with fire awaiting the day of judgment. Everyone knows that there is great heat in the bowels of the earth. Volcanoes and earthquakes prove this to be so. That there is great heat in the heavens is evident from our sun. Every star visible to the naked eye, apart from the few which are planets of our solar system, are bodies stored up with great heat. The heavens certainly are stored up with fire.

"Reserved Unto Fire"

Our verse indicates that both the heavens and the earth are being kept in readiness for this great judgment of fire. The fire is only waiting God's time and God's word. Scoffers are hereby warned that, although God may delay His judgments, it is not because He cannot immediately execute them. It is not yet the time when He wills to do so. His means are ready at hand to be used whenever He sees fit.

"FIRE"

The people of the world are beginning to realize that complete destruction by fire is not at all impossible. Two small atom bombs practically wiped off the map two large Japanese cities. They say the heat generated by one of these things is great enough to melt the rocks and fuse the sand. They are now working on a hydrogen bomb, which they claim will be far more destructive than the atom bomb. Some are fearing that these bombs may actually some day wipe all life from off the earth. If man can create such powerful weapons of fire, certainly it will not be difficult for the Lord to do so. They claim that these terrible bombs are the discovery of God's secret of power. The heavens are stored with this same kind of power awaiting God's word to be used in awful judgment on the earth.

UNCONTROLLED FIRE IS TERRIBLE

What an awful thing uncontrolled fire can be. So often we hear of whole families being burnt to death, and we shudder at the thought. How much more terrible to think of a whole world being destroyed in this way. The flood must have been terrible, but it seems to us that fire will be worse. Our world is a ready tinder box. It is stored with immense quantities of coal and oil. We need fear no coal shortage, except by miner's strikes, for hundreds of years to come. We were reading lately that in Saudi Arabia there is a pool that contains more oil than the United States has consumed in its whole history. When we think that the Lord has atomic power which is able to melt the rocks, these things will but add to the general conflagration.

FIRE IS GOD'S MODE OF PUNISHMENT

Judgment by fire is God's threat hanging over every unrepentant sinner today. The Lord Jesus says, "Depart from me, ye cursed into everlasting fire, prepared for the devil and his angels" (Mat.

25:41). "Therefore the tares are gathered and burned in the fire" (Mat. 13:40). "For our God is a consuming fire" (Heb. 12:29). "And death and hell were cast into the lake of fire" (Rev. 20:14). (Also II Thess. 1:8, Heb. 10:27, Rev. 21:8).

"THE DAY OF JUDGMENT"

Peter calls this terrible day, "the day of judgment." We have this same expression often in the Word (Mat. 10:15, 11:22, 12:36). We believe it usually refers to the great white throne judgment concerning which we read in Rev. 20:11-15. This is the judgment of the wicked dead. We read that the graves and the sea shall give up their dead to be judged according to their works. We believe this judgment of the great white throne will be very closely linked with the destruction by fire. We have fire coming down from heaven in Rev. 20:9, and in Rev. 21:1 we have the new heaven and the new earth. We do not believe though that the expression, "the day of judgment" always refers to the great white throne judgment, for it evidently refers to the judgment seat of Christ in I John 4:17. There, in speaking to Christians, he says. "That we may have boldness in the day of judgment."

"PERDITION"

In the Revised Version "perdition" is translated "destruction." It could also be translated "ruin" or "loss." It does not necessarily mean annihilation. To be found an ungodly man in that day, will certainly bring great loss. It will mean to suffer the same fate as the man of sin, "the son of perdition" (II Thess. 2:3), and the beast of Rev. 17:11, who "goeth into perdition." How wise is the man who, ere it is too late, flees to the Lord Jesus for safety. How much better to be ready for glory than to end in perdition.

"UNGODLY MEN"

As the flood was the result of ungodliness in man, so this final judgment will be also. It will not only entail the burning of the earth, but it will be a sweeping off of this earth all wickedness and all wicked men. This is not only to punish evil doers, but to prepare this earth for a time when only righteousness will dwell upon it. What a wonderful place this will be when not a sin will longer mar its beauty.

WHEN WILL THIS JUDGMENT COME?

Some today are momentarily looking for the end of the world. Peter does seem to link this judgment with the coming of Christ, and yet we believe it is far removed from it. The scoffers of Peter's day were saying in connection with the coming of Christ, "all things continue as they were from the beginning of creation." Peter first reminds them of the great changes in connection with creation itself, then reminds them of the great changes in connection with the flood, and now reminds them of the great change still to come with the judgment of fire. He is not necessarily linking this up with the coming of Christ. We believe many things, some stupendous, must happen before the world is actually purged with fire.

ORDER OF EVENTS GIVEN IN REVELATION

Some may not fully agree with us, but we believe the book of Revelation gives the order of events as they will happen. First we have the rapture of the church at the end of chapter 3, because we find the church in heaven in chapter 4. We have the details of the rapture given in I Cor. 15:51-57, I Thes. 4:13-18 and in John 14:1-3. Then we have the great tribulation spoken of in Rev. chapter 6 through chapter 18, also Mat. 24:15-26, etc. After that we have Christ coming, first to judge the nations, and then to rule and to reign over them (Rev. 19:11 to Rev. 20:6 and Mat. 25:27-31). According to Rev. 20:4, this reign will last for 1,000 years. At the end of this time Satan will be let out of the bottomless pit, and he will bring insurrection against the Lord once more. Then comes the judgment of the great white throne (Rev. 20:11-15), followed closely by the destruction with fire. In Rev. 21:1 to Rev. 22:7, we have the new heavens and the new earth in which will dwell righteousness. Some might not agree with the order of events as we give them here, but certainly, they must agree that all still must happen. We believe personally, that John, in Revelation, gives the correct order, while Peter gives some of the high-lights.

XXVII

THE LORD IS NOT SLACK

(II Peter 3:8, 9)

3:8. "But, beloved, be not ignorant of this one thing, that one day is with the Lord as a thousand years; and a thousand years as one day."

In verses 3-7, Peter has been lashing and refuting scoffers who were questioning the coming again of Christ. Now he turns to the saints of God to encourage them in the promises of the Lord. Perhaps some of the Lord's own were saying, "These scoffers seem to have an argument, the Lord did promise to come back soon, and He has not come." Peter would assure them that this apparent delay was no delay at all in the reckoning of God, but that rather, as our next verse indicates, it showed His long-suffering. To the scoffers, in our previous verses, he promises judgment, but to the Christians, he manifests love. He calls them "beloved."

"Be Not Ignorant"

Peter does not want the Christians to be ignorant or to forget, as it reads in the Revised Version. They must not be like the scoffers of whom we read in verse 5, "they willingly are ignorant." Either ignorance or forgetfulness can seriously hinder one in their Christian pathway. If we read and meditate on the Word of God, we will not be ignorant. If we really make it our constant companion, we will not forget His precepts. It was especially the character and purposes of the Lord which he did not want them to forget.

Psalm 90

The language of our verses seems to be borrowed from Psalm 90:4; "For a thousand years in thy sight are but as yesterday when it is past, and as a watch in the night." It is interesting to see how Moses, in this Psalm, contrasts the eternal existence of God with the fewness of the days of man. Of God, in verse 2, he says, "From everlasting to everlasting thou art God." In verse 9, speaking of man, he says, "We spend our years as a tale that is told." Verse 10 is well-known; "The days of our years are three-score years and ten; and if by reason of strength they be fourscore years, yet is their strength, labour and sorrow; for it is soon cut off, and we fly away."

"ONE DAY"

In the latter part of our verse, Peter gives the thought of Psalm 90:4, but in the first part he reverses it. He says, "One day with the Lord is as a thousand years." One day to us may be very short, or very long, according to circumstances. To children one day seems long, but to older people, who are trying to accomplish something, it goes by all too quickly. To one who is not well and cannot sleep, how long the nights seem, and the days roll at a very slow pace for such too. But to an active man, who is very busy, the days are all too short. "My days are swifter than a weaver's shuttle" (Job 7:6). Because our days are short and few, let us waste none of them, but let us be busy serving our Christ and living for Him. "Redeeming the time, because the days are evil" (Eph. 5:16).

"ONE DAY WITH THE LORD"

No doubt there have been great days in our history, such as the day when we were born, or the day when we were married. It was a greater day when we were brought to know Christ as our Savior. In magnitude of importance, a thousand years of our days could not begin to compare with one day of the Lord's Think of the vast importance of the day when our Lord Jesus was born into this world. Of even greater importance was the day of His death. Then think of the day He arose, and the day He ascended, and the day when He will come back again. What a great day Pentecost was, and so perhaps every day in the history of the world, has in one way or another, been a great day in the annals of the Lord.

LITTLE IS MUCH WHEN GOD IS IN IT

Oftentimes the Lord makes very much of what appears to be but very little in our sight. At a street meeting a passer-by sought to give the writer a dime. We refused to accept it. He threw it down at our feet, but we refused to pick it up. He said to himself, "That is a funny bunch, they surely are not in this for the money." This led to increased interest and eventually, his conversion. This man is now an active Christian worker who speaks in a gospel tent in his old home town almost every summer.

Other Examples

In a Sunday School which we conducted, once a year at a New Year's treat, we gave the children oranges and candy. A grandmother of one of the children said, "That is a funny place, they take no collections from the children, yet they give them candy and oranges." Out of curiosity she paid us a visit which eventually led to her salvation. A little boy said to me, "My sister has a nickel and I haven't got any." We told him that that could easily be fixed, and we gave him a nickel. We believe this little act of kindness touched his father's heart. He started coming to the meetings, was brought to know Christ, and now is the leading brother in a company of Christians which he, by the help of the Lord, brought into existence. Truly, "Little is much when God is in it."

"A Thousand Years"

A thousand years seems like a very long time to us. Just think, one thousand years ago it was the year 950. How distant and remote it seems; how little we know of it. But to the eternal God that day is but as yesterday. We, who are children of a day, cannot begin to figure time as He reckons it. One hundred dollars to a very rich man may be like a penny to one who is very poor. God has an eternity behind Him and an eternity ahead of Him; He is rich in time. What matters a few thousand years, He has an abundance of time in which to accomplish His purposes. We, like a boatman on a river, see only our immediate surroundings, but God, like a man on a mountain, sees the river of time from its source to its mouth. Scientists say this world has been a long time in its formation. They may be right; a God of eternity need be in no hurry. To the infinite God, time means nothing.

"A Thousand Years as One Day"

The scorners used the delay of Christ's coming as an excuse for their unbelief. No doubt the Christians were troubled by the delay too. By this verse, Peter would refute the arguments of the scorners, and encourage the hearts of the believers. They thought the thirty odd years since His ascension a long time. Peter says in God's reckoning it is only a very short time. In fact, a thousand years is only like a day in His sight. It is now over 1900 years since Christ left this scene, but in God's estimation it is not even two days. God knows no delay. At the appointed time He will come. The wicked scoffers thought that because His promise was delayed, that His purposes were abandoned, and they would not be judged. If the Lord desires to accomplish something in a short time, He is able; if He wishes to spread it over many years, He may.

Time Does Not Change the Lord

Remember, time does not change the Lord; He knows no weariness or weakness. He never slumbers or sleeps (Psalm 121). He never will grow old, His hand will never shake, His voice will never falter, His hair will never grow grey. His purposes do not change with changing years; there is no outside influence which can cause Him to change His plans. If He said, "I will come again," we may depend upon it, He will come. If He said, "I will judge the wicked," make sure, He will do it. His work shall be completed, His enemies will be conquered. The wicked servant may say, "My Lord delayeth His coming," and the sincere child may cry out, "How long O, Lord?", but His reply is "Surely, I come quickly."

He Acts as He Will

To God the future is entirely clear, but we must wait for it to be unrolled before us. The Lord knows when the appointed time will arrive, but we must wait, we know not how long. His apparent delays are not due to changeableness or lack of ability. His eternity demands no haste, and man's impatience will not in the least hurry Him. His almighty power could bring things to pass quickly, but if He wills, He can spread it over many years. If we would accomplish anything in our short span of life we must not delay, but the Lord has all eternity to work. "Whatsoever the Lord pleased, that did he in heaven, and in earth, in the seas, and all deep places" (Psalm 135:6). If He has not come, it is because He has not willed to do so.

Fifty Years

An average day seems to make very little change in a man. However, take 50 years and there is an immense difference. This is a very large portion of a man's life, but in the history of a nation it is considered only a small period of time. Our nation is considered very young, but it is 174 years old. Fifty years with the eternal, immortal God is next to nothing. He lives in an eternal day.

This is Our God

This wonderful unchanging God is our God, and although so mighty and majestic, He sent His beloved Son to die for us so that we might be forgiven and saved. How important that our lives be wholly for His glory. Bolstered with this knowledge of Him, we are undisturbed by mockers, and we fight on in the good fight of faith until our Lord Jesus comes, be the time long or be it short.

3:9. "The Lord is not slack concerning his promise, as some men count slackness; but is longsuffering to us-ward, not willing that any should perish, but that all should come to repentance."

The scoffers had said, "The Lord will not come because He has not come as He promised," and now perhaps even the Christians thought Him slow to keep His promises. Peter here gives the reason for this apparent slowness; He is longsuffering, and does not desire to punish sinners, but wishes to give them time to repent of their sins and trust Christ for salvation.

"The Lord is not Slack"

The word "slack" here has the sense of slow, late or delayed. "The Lord does not delay His promises" is a good translation. The Lord is never ahead nor behind time. Everything He does is right on time. He delivered the children of Israel out of Egypt at exactly the appointed time (Ex. 12:41). Christ was born into this world at exactly the time the Lord had set. "When the fulness of the time was come, God sent forth his Son, made of a woman, made under the law" (Gal. 4:4). At the time appointed, He will come again, as also will the fierce judgments recorded in our chapter.

"NOT SLACK CONCERNING HIS PROMISE"

Men judge the Lord by themselves. For various reasons men make promises but never keep them. Some never intend to keep them. They make them to gain temporary advantage, which having gained, they make no effort to keep the promises. The Lord has nothing to gain by promising things to man, so He cannot be charged with failure on this count. Some make promises, but very soon forget that they ever made them. To charge God with forgetfulness is practically to take His godhead from Him. "For God is not unrighteous to forget" (Heb. 6:10). Some are utterly indifferent to the promises they make, but certainly the Lord is not like this. "Hath he spoken and shall he not make it good?" (Num. 23:19). Men are fickle; they may have good intentions, but something comes along and they change their minds, and they do not keep their promises.

HE CHANGES NOT

Our God, like our Savior, is "the same yesterday, and today, and forever" (Heb. 13:8). "He changes not." Accidents happen to man, even death comes, and he cannot fulfill his promises, but nothing like this ever happens to our eternal God. No power can make our omnipotent God unable to do that which He has promised. Has He promised to come again? He will surely come. "For yet a little while, and he that shall come will come, and will not tarry" (Heb. 10:37). "Shall not God avenge his own elect — I tell you that he will avenge them speedily" (Luke 18:7, 8).

IS GOD SLOW?

Is our God slow? In some respects, yes. The Word says, "He is slow to anger," as we read in Neh. 9:17, Psalm 103:8 and four other places. It is a good thing that He is, or who would be able to stand before Him? Sometimes He may seem slow in answering our prayers, too, but He will send the right answer at the right time. One dear sister and her husband labored long and hard for the Lord in a Northern Michigan community. The desired results seemed very slow in coming. The sister said to us, "The Lord is certainly in no hurry." So it sometimes seems, but remember He is eternal and He need not hurry. May we with patience wait upon Him.

"Longsuffering"

Peter says the reason the Lord has not yet come is because He is longsuffering, and desires to see souls brought to repentance. He is extending the day of grace so that many may trust in Him. Longsuffering is part of His very character. As far as we know, there is nothing hindering His coming at once, except that He does not yet wish to do so.

He Always was Lonsuffering

The Lord always has been longsuffering. Peter already suggested this in connection with those who lived before the flood, "When once the longsuffering of God waited in the days of Noah" (I Peter 3:20). He was longsuffering with them for a long 120 years while Noah was building the ark. How longsuffering He was with the children of Israel during those 40 years as they journeyed from Egypt to Canaan. He also was longsuffering with the sinners standing around the cross. How He could stand idly by and see them condemn, and abuse, and then crucify His Son, is hard for us to understand. We marvel at our Lord Jesus too, as He prays to His Father, saying, "Father forgive them for they know not what they do." How much more human it would seem if He had cried out, "Father take all these wicked sinners and thrust them quickly into hell." This day of grace is now nearly 2,000 years old. Only His longsuffering compassion keeps our Lord from coming. He is very slow in meting out the judgments which this wicked world so justly deserves.

He is Longsuffering Still

Every day vile deeds are done in this world. Men steal, abuse, rape, murder their fellows. Not only that, but they curse the name of God and Christ, and do all but spit in His face. Would you stand idly by while some monster abuses and injures a dear friend if it was in your power to resist? Supposing it was directed against yourself, how long could you take it before you did what you could to punish the culprit? The Lord could immediately mete out stern judgment, but He does not, hoping that there will be repentance. We believe this longsuffering of the Lord demonstrates His greatness and power more than almost anything else. It takes a strong man to keep from striking out when greatly provoked.

Slow to Anger. Illustrations

Everyday sinners greatly grieve and provoke the Lord and tempt Him too, but He holds back His wrath. It is said that one atheistic lecturer would often pull out his watch and say, "If there is a God, I will give Him five minutes to strike me dead," but nothing ever happened. God might have quickly taken up the challenge, but He did not. Another man, so we are told, was even worse. He got up on the top of a hill and thrust a sword up into the air and defied God to come down and fight with him. While his blasphemous mouth was still open a bug flew into it, lodged in his throat and choked him to death. Only seldom does He answer in this way.

"Longsuffering to Us-ward"

The Revised Version has to "you-ward" rather than to "us-ward." It matters little which is right. No doubt Peter has humanity in mind. In spite of man's sin the Lord is longsuffering toward him. "But God commendeth his love toward us, in that, while we were yet sinners, Christ died for us" (Rom. 5:8). "Christ Jesus came into the world to save sinners" (I Tim. 1:15). The Word is full of expressions such as "any man," "whosoever," etc. The message of the gospel is to any man, anywhere, anytime. Any who are ready to confess their need and willing to receive Christ as Savior will be accepted of Him. Color or race does not matter, nor does degree of education, nor social standing, nor age. We have sometimes marveled that He is even ready to receive one in old age, after a whole life has been wasted on self and the things of the world. His longsuffering is so great that He will receive any who come to Him no matter what the time or circumstances. "But thou, O Lord, art a God full of compassion, and gracious, longsuffering, and plenteous in mercy and truth" (Psalm 86:15). Truly, "God is love" (I John 4:8).

"Not Willing"

"Not wishing," as it is in the Revised Version, is better than "not willing." "As I live saith the Lord God, I have no pleasure in the death of the wicked; but that the wicked turn from his way and live" (Ez. 33:11). "For this is good and acceptable in the sight of God our Saviour; Who will have all men to be saved, and to come unto the knowledge of the truth" (I Tim. 2:3, 4). The Lord delights in salvation, but not in judgment. To send sinners to hell brings Him no pleasure. "There is joy in the presence of the angels of God over one sinner that repenteth" (Luke 15:10).

Unrepentant Sinners Will Not Escape

Of course, this does not mean that an unrepentant, Christ rejecting sinner will escape. Although the Lord has no delight in it, the Scriptures are full of evidence that He will certainly mete out judgment to those who reject His mercy. A parent has no pleasure in punishing his children, but if he is wise, he certainly will do it when they deserve it. A monarch may hate to punish his lawless subjects, but if he is wise, he will have jails, and perhaps even a gallows for serious offenders. That God will punish sin is very evident from the fact that He already permits suffering and death to enter this scene. The fact that Christ died on the cross to be made an atonement for our sins is evidence that the Lord has no pleasure in the death of the sinner, but that He desires his salvation. By the same token, if sin is so serious that Christ had to die before even one sin could be forgiven, the sinner need not hope to go unpunished, if his sins are not put away by putting faith in Christ. Sin is odious to God, and He will punish for it, but He longs to forgive.

"Not Willing that Any Should Perish"

"Perish"; what an awful word it is. It evidently means far more than physical death. It means "eternal death," perhaps rather "eternal punishment." There would be no point to the verse at all if it meant only physical death, since the saved die as well as the unrepentant. We believe our verse means that the Lord, does not wish that any of His creatures suffer the pangs of hell or the lake of fire. He longs for sinners to repent and to be saved and so escape these judgments. Christ says to all, "Come unto me" (Mat. 11:28) and in Isa. 45:22, "Look unto me and be ye saved, all the ends of the earth." God is not obliged to spare, but He delights in mercy. Judgment is called His strange work; He would far rather save. However, He can only save on a righteous basis, which is faith in the atoning work of Christ.

Many Have Perished

Peter has already indicated that the old world perished in the flood (3:6). Sodom and Gomorrah perished (2:6). Sinning angels perished (2:4). Who are in danger of perishing now? "Behold, ye despisers, and wonder, and perish" (Acts 13:41). "The wicked shall be turned into hell" (Psalm 9:17). "Except ye repent, ye shall all likewise perish" (Luke 13:5). "He that believeth not shall be damned" (Mark 16:16). There is only safety in trusting Christ.

"That All Should Come to Repentance"

Nothing delights the heart of the Lord more than to hear a sinner say, "I have sinned," and to come to His feet in true repentance. What a joy it brought to the father's heart in Luke 15:21, when the prodigal son said, "Father, I have sinned against heaven and in thy sight, and am no more worthy to be called thy son." Peter says in our verse that the Lord would have *all* come to this place. How quickly the Lord spoke peace to the thief on the cross who said, "We receive the due reward of our deeds" (Luke 23:41). How ready the Lord was to spare Nineveh when its king and all his subjects put on sack cloth, and cried mightily unto God (Jonah 3:4-10).

Repentance Necessary

Let no sinner expect though that he can get by without repentance. "And the times of this ignorance God winked at, but now commandeth *all* men *everywhere* to repent" (Acts 17:30). "But shewed first unto them in Damascus, and at Jerusalem, and throughout all the coasts of Judea, and then to the Gentiles, that they should repent and turn to God, and do works meet for repentance" (Acts 26:20).

WHAT IS REPENTANCE?

Many think of repentance as sorrow for sin. It may include that, but it certainly is more. It means to have a change of mind. When one repents, he has first of all a different thought of sin. He sees that sin is a very serious thing in God's sight. He also has different thoughts of himself. Most unsaved believe that they are not so bad, and that God should not be too hard on them. They are self-righteous, like one man who said to us, "I treat my help and my family well, and I do not injure or owe anyone: if God is not satisfied with that, He better send me to hell." When true repentance comes over a man, he sees himself a guilty, vile, and good for nothing sinner in God's sight. He then also sees that God should righteously confine him to eternal punishment, but he quickly flees to Christ for salvation.

WHY THE DELAY?

Now here is the reason for the Lord's apparent delay in coming again; He desires to manifest longsuffering and to give the sinner ample time to repent of his sin. No one will be able to say, "I had no time to repent, judgment came so quickly." He will refuse none who come to Him in true repentance. "Him that cometh to me I will in no wise cast out" (John 6:37). Any who are lost will have no one to blame but themselves; God gave them time and opportunity to repent, but they would not. His patient longsuffering will at last be ended and the stroke of judgment will fall suddenly.

LESSONS FOR THE CHRISTIAN

The Lord is longsuffering to the Christians too, but let us be very careful not to provoke or grieve Him by sin. May each of us be very diligent in warning the sinner of the seriousness of his sin, the certainty of judgment; but also tell of the love and tender mercy of the Lord to the repentant sinner who is ready to trust Christ.

XXVIII

THE DAY OF THE LORD

(II Peter 3:10-12)

3:10. "But the day of the Lord will come as a thief in the night; in the which the heavens shall pass away with a great noise, and the elements shall melt with a fervent heat, the earth also and the works that are therein shall be burnt up."

Here Peter returns to the subject brought up in verse 7, namely the burning of this present scene with fire. He begins by saying the day of the Lord, always a day of judgment in the Word, will come silently and unexpectedly like a thief in the night.

Days

In the New Testament, besides "the day of the Lord," we have "the day of the Lord Jesus," "the day of Christ," and "the day of God"; and many times, "the day of judgment." All these days are judgment days. "The day of the Lord Jesus" and "the day of Christ" refer to the day when the Lord Jesus will sit on His throne to judge the Lord's people in connection with their rewards (I Cor. 1:8, 5:5, etc.). The Revised Version gives "the day of the Lord" instead of "day of Christ" in II Thess. 2:2. "The day of God" is only mentioned once in the Word in the 12th verse of our chapter, and is linked with the destruction of the world by fire. We also have " that great day of God Almighty" in Rev. 16:14, where it seems to be linked with the battle of Armageddon.

"The Day of the Lord"

"The day of the Lord" is always a day of fierce judgment against those who know not our Lord Jesus. The first reference to this is in Isa. 2:12, where we read, "For the day of the Lord of hosts shall be upon everyone that is proud and lofty, and upon everyone that is lifted up; and he shall be brought low." "Alas for the day! for the day of the Lord is at hand, and as a destruction from the Almighty shall it come" (Joel 1:15). Joel speaks of it five times and most of the prophets mention it. "The day of the Lord is darkness, and not light" (Amos 5:18).

NEW TESTAMENT REFERENCES

The only two references to "the day of the Lord" besides our verse, are I Thess. 5:2 and II Thess. 2:2 (R.V.). Both of these speak of the judgment accompanying the coming again of our Lord Jesus, which would be before the millennium. Our verse seems to link up "the day of the Lord" with the final judgment by fire. It may be that "the day of the Lord" refers to the time when our Lord Jesus will be victor over all His enemies. If so, it would refer not only to the judgment at His coming, but to the whole millennium time, and also be the judgment of fire before the ushering in of the new heavens and the new earth. This would mean that our verse covers a long period of time, but this is not incompatible with verse 8; "A thousand years is as one day." There are other portions of Scripture which cover a long period of time such as Isa. 61:1, 2.

LET US BE READY FOR HIS COMING

If the order of events as related in Revelation is correct, and we believe it is, we should not be looking for the destruction of the world now, but for the coming of the Lord. As we read prophetic statements, which abound in the Word, we know that many things must happen before the end comes. However, we also discover that nothing, as far as we can see, needs to happen before the Lord can come for His church. It is for this event that we who are Christians should look. Our blessed Lord may come for us anytime. What a happy event that will be for those who are His own.

"WILL COME AS A THIEF"

Peter is emphatic in stating that "the day of the Lord" will come. Every promise will be kept. The coming of the Lord is as sure as the Word of God. In spite of mockers and apparent delay, "He will come." The last promise of the Bible is "Surely, I come quickly" (Rev. 22:20). When He does come, it will be suddenly and unexpectedly, like "a thief in the night." This expression "as a thief," makes many believe that this first part of our verse is speaking of the revelation of our Lord, or in other words, His coming in glory. However, we believe all important future events will overtake most of humanity as a thief in the night. Certainly His coming for the church will be a sudden event and a great surprise to many. To the church of Sardis the Lord says, "If therefore thou shalt not watch, I will come on thee as a thief, and thou shalt not know what hour I will come upon thee" (Rev. 3:3). We believe this has reference to the rapture of the church, as has also Mat. 24:42-44, and Luke 12:39, although some have taught that these speak of His revelation in glory. "Watch therefore: for ye know not what hour your Lord doth come. But know this, that if the good man of the house had known in what watch the thief would come, he would have watched" (Mat. 24:42, 43). We also have the likeness of a thief in I Thess. 5:2 and in Rev. 16:15, where, without doubt, it refers to His coming in glory. As both of these important events will come unexpectedly, no doubt, the last one, where the earth will be destroyed by fire, will also come as a complete surprise to nearly all.

Be Prepared

It is wise to be prepared for unexpected events. They happen everyday. Many are not prepared for sudden sickness, or accident, or death. Nations are often not prepared for war. Many are not prepared for the coming of the Lord. They go on in their sinful ways expecting to get saved someday, but suddenly something strikes; death comes, or perhaps the coming of the Lord. Every day some start out perfectly well, but before night they are in a morgue.

Terrible Times Ahead

As we read Revelation and other portions of the Word, we know that terrible times lie ahead for this world, and nothing can stop them. A thief may be resisted or foiled even though he comes unexpectedly, but nothing can stay the hand of God from bringing these dread events to pass. How wonderful it will be to be at home with Christ, and to be kept "from the hour of temptation (trial R.V.) which shall come upon all the world, to try them that dwell upon the earth" (Rev. 3:10).

Most Are Sleeping

As we read the story of the ten virgins in Mat. 25:1-13, we notice that all, the real and the professed, were asleep. We believe this would teach us that up to the time of His imminent coming, practically all professed Christians will be in a state of sleep and not expecting His coming. Have you heard the cry, "Behold the bridegroom cometh"? Be sure you are awake and have oil in your lamp.

"The Heavens Shall Pass Away"

Already in verse 7 Peter suggested this destruction of both heaven and earth with fire. Without question many changes will come to pass in the heavens. Perhaps our whole solar system and more will be completely disrupted by fire. If so, it would appear from this world as though the whole of the heavens were disintegrating. As we suggested in connection with verse 7, this could not include the abode of the Lord. Astronomers claim that as many as thirteen fixed stars have disappeared from the heavens within historic times. What has happened to them may happen to our sun, in which case our whole solar system would go. "The heavens are the works of thine hands: They shall perish; but thou remainest" (Heb. 1:10, 11).

"With a Great Noise"

Peter says "the heavens shall pass away with a great noise." Moffett says with "a crackling noise," and Montgomery, "with a crash." Perhaps the nearest to the original would be, "with a whiz," thus indicating a rushing roar. They say it is just such a rushing roar which accompanies an atomic blast. Knowing the roar of an immense fire we can well believe this would be so. Imagine not only the noise of burning forests, toppling cities, and boiling oceans, but even the heavens themselves ablaze.

"The Elements Shall Melt"

Some have thought that the word "elements" here referred to the stars. The word means "orderly in arrangement." We believe Peter means to say that this whole order of things shall someday be dissolved, as we have in the next verse. "The hills melted like wax at the presence of the Lord" (Psalm 97:5). (Also Ps. 46:6, Amos 9:5, Nah. 1:5). Scientists claim that at one time this earth was one molten mass. Our verse indicates that someday it will again be so.

"THE EARTH ALSO"

Peter certainly insists that at sometime in the future this old world will be destroyed by fire. He plainly states the fact in the 7th, 10th, 11th, and 12th verses of our chapter. This world which fascinates so many will one day be only a funeral pyre. As we suggested in connection with verse 7, we believe the Lord may bring this about through some heavenly orb. However, the world itself is very ready for it. Three hundred volcanoes have erupted molten matter from the earth's interior within historic times. Scientists claim that the outer crust of the world is probably not over 100 miles thick. If so we have a vast cavern of molten matter 7,800 miles in diameter under our feet.

OTHER FORCES

Besides these internal fires there are the forces of magnetism and electricity, and the Lord could turn these loose to accomplish His purposes. The compass, always pointing to the north, tells us that this world is kept in its position by powerful magnetic forces. The fierce electric storms which sometimes strike us tell us that the atmosphere is charged with power. One has pictured this world as a vast pile of wood with God's torch bearers waiting to start the giant conflagration.

FIRE WORSE THAN WATER

Water on the rampage can be an awful destructive force, as we have noticed in connection with the flood. However, you can touch water without pain, you can swim in it, or build a boat to ride upon it, and many forms of life can live in it, but no life can withstand fire. Noah with his ark full of animals survived the flood. Fish survived, and also all forms of plant life, but when this great fire comes, all will go. No ark will float over this fiery flood.

"AND THE WORKS THAT ARE THEREIN"

We presume Peter is here thinking of the works of man. Everything which man has developed and made will go up in flames at that time. Everything in which he has boasted, and gloried, and upon which he set his hopes, will be gone forever. The most beautiful estates, the most gorgeous cathedrals, the most wonderful government buildings, all will be turned t... only things which will survive are those which hav... the glory of the Lord.

ALL MUST BE CHANGED

Fire does not annihilate; it but changes the form of things. All matter which was in existence when the world began is still with us. The Lord hates sin, and by this fire He will once and forever rid this scene of it. All earthly corruption must go in order that this world may be "a new earth wherein dwelleth righteousness" (verse 13). Those of us who know Christ will see it and be glad.

3:11. "Seeing then that all these things shall be dissolved, what manner of persons ought ye to be in all holy conversation and godliness."

Here we have the practical application to this whole portion. Seeing that all these things, the present heavens and earth, shall melt away, what effect should this have on our lives? Should not the very thought of this cause us to live cleaner, more devoted, Christ-like lives in this world?

"ALL THESE THINGS"

"Things" have an awful hold on the heart of man. Even Christians are in danger of being swallowed up by the love of earthly things. How wise to hold loosely to these things which shall all pass away, and cling closely to the eternal things. This is not our abiding home. Some well-nigh worship nature. As we look at the gorgeous mountains and beautiful lakes, at the wonders of plant and animal life, it should cause us to glorify the Creator, not the creation. At all times remember all these things are but transitory, but the human spirit is eternal. Let us put less value on things, and more on the eternal spirit. Things do not satisfy a heart which needs the Lord.

"SHALL BE DISSOLVED"

The word "dissolved" means to melt away. It is put in the present tense in the original, as though already being dissolved. Perhaps the apostle would thereby impress us with the certainty of this dissolution. The passing of this whole scene surely preaches the vanity of man, his works, his pleasures, and his ambitions.

"What Manner of Persons"

Peter here brings in the practical application. Seeing all these wonderful things about us are soon to pass away, what sort of persons should we be? He suggests both our holy manner of life toward men and our pious attitude toward the Lord, but he does not answer the question. He leaves it to the readers to decide this for themselves. In the light of a sure and awful judgment which lies ahead, men certainly should flee to the Lord Jesus for salvation. Then we who are saved should realize that we are but strangers and pilgrims in this world, and should be ready to depart at any time. "Let your loins be girded about, and your lights burning; and ye yourselves like unto men that wait for their Lord" (Luke 12:35, 36). How watchful and prayerful we should be. How busy we should be too, in trying to reach others with the gospel. How anxious this should make us to lay up treasurers in heaven rather than on the earth.

"Holy Conversation"

The word "conversation" is usually translated "manner of life" in the Revised Version, but here it is translated as "holy living." As we noted before, "conversation" is an old English word which formerly meant one's whole manner of life, but has degenerated into meaning only "talk." We realize that all in this scene will soon be gone, so we should keep clean of all its contamination. The sinner says, "All things continue as they were from the beginning of the creation," and he continues on in his sin. The Christian says, "Not so, we are living in a changing scene, momentous events lie ahead," and he lives a holy life for the Lord.

Man's Sin

Man's sin has caused every bit of trouble which has ever been in this world. It has brought disease and death to plant and animal life as well as to man. He is to blame for the waste of nature, the deserts and the great ice caps at the poles. His sin wonderful government buildings, all will be turned to ashes. The only things which will survive are those which have been done to the glory of the Lord.

ALL MUST BE CHANGED

Fire does not annihilate; it but changes the form of things. All matter which was in existence when the world began is still with us. The Lord hates sin, and by this fire He will once and forever rid this scene of it. All earthly corruption must go in order that this world may be "a new earth wherein dwelleth righteousness" (verse 13). Those of us who know Christ will see it and be glad.

3:11. "Seeing then that all these things shall be dissolved, what manner of persons ought ye to be in all holy conversation and godliness."

Here we have the practical application to this whole portion. Seeing that all these things, the present heavens and earth, shall melt away, what effect should this have on our lives? Should not the very thought of this cause us to live cleaner, more devoted, Christ-like lives in this world?

"ALL THESE THINGS"

"Things" have an awful hold on the heart of man. Even Christians are in danger of being swallowed up by the love of earthly things. How wise to hold loosely to these things which shall all pass away, and cling closely to the eternal things. This is not our abiding home. Some well-nigh worship nature. As we look at the gorgeous mountains and beautiful lakes, at the wonders of plant and animal life, it should cause us to glorify the Creator, not the creation. At all times remember all these things are but transitory, but the human spirit is eternal. Let us put less value on things, and more on the eternal spirit. Things do not satisfy a heart which needs the Lord.

"SHALL BE DISSOLVED"

The word "dissolved" means to melt away. It is put in the present tense in the original, as though already being dissolved. Perhaps the apostle would thereby impress us with the certainty of this dissolution. The passing of this whole scene surely preaches the vanity of man, his works, his pleasures, and his ambitions.

"What Manner of Persons"

Peter here brings in the practical application. Seeing all these wonderful things about us are soon to pass away, what sort of persons should we be? He suggests both our holy manner of life toward men and our pious attitude toward the Lord, but he does not answer the question. He leaves it to the readers to decide this for themselves. In the light of a sure and awful judgment which lies ahead, men certainly should flee to the Lord Jesus for salvation. Then we who are saved should realize that we are but strangers and pilgrims in this world, and should be ready to depart at any time. "Let your loins be girded about, and your lights burning; and ye yourselves like unto men that wait for their Lord" (Luke 12:35, 36). How watchful and prayerful we should be. How busy we should be too, in trying to reach others with the gospel. How anxious this should make us to lay up treasurers in heaven rather than on the earth.

"Holy Conversation"

The word "conversation" is usually translated "manner of life" in the Revised Version, but here it is translated as "holy living." As we noted before, "conversation" is an old English word which formerly meant one's whole manner of life, but has degenerated into meaning only "talk." We realize that all in this scene will soon be gone, so we should keep clean of all its contamination. The sinner says, "All things continue as they were from the beginning of the creation," and he continues on in his sin. The Christian says, "Not so, we are living in a changing scene, momentous events lie ahead," and he lives a holy life for the Lord.

Man's Sin

Man's sin has caused every bit of trouble which has ever been in this world. It has brought disease and death to plant and animal life as well as to man. He is to blame for the waste of nature, the deserts and the great ice caps at the poles. His sin is that which will make it necessary for the Lord to someday purge this world with fire. How this should cause us to hate sin.

PURITY OF LIFE

What an incentive it is to purity of life when we think, that to restore this scene to its former purity and beauty, it will be necessary for the Lord to bring on its dissolution. We should be pure in every department of life. "Pure religion and undefiled before God and the Father is this, To visit the fatherless and widows in their affliction, and to keep himself unspotted from the world" (James 1:27).

"GODLINESS"

While "conversation" speaks of our outward life, "godliness" speaks of our attitude toward the Lord. It is interesting to note that both of these words are in the plural in the original, and so make them refer to everything of both a moral and spiritual nature. Many are moral to a degree, but seem to have little regard for the Lord. Others are the reverse; they do seem to love the Lord and the people of God, and the services of the Christians, but their lives are far from what they should be. We should manifest both. To have the one and not the other is to be like a one-legged man. Our lives must be clean, and also devoted to the service of the Lord. Our godly life should tell all men that we love the Lord. (see 1:6, 7).

3:12. "Looking for and hasting unto the coming of the day of God, wherein the heavens being on fire shall be dissolved, and the elements shall melt with fervent heat?"

This is the third time in a few verses that Peter mentions the dissolution of this scene by fire. He suggests that we should be looking forward to and earnestly desiring the coming of this day of God. Many fear and dread the coming of this day, but a true Christian longs for it, because he realizes it will be the end of all sin in this scene, and the introduction of eternal righteousness.

"LOOKING FOR"

When our verse says, "Looking for — the day of God," we do not believe it would suggest that we should be momentarily expecting it to come. It is right and proper to be momentarily expecting the coming of Christ for His own. At anytime we may hear that glad shout and be called away to be with Him. This will be a blessed day for the Lord's people, but a sad one for those who are left behind. "Looking for that blessed hope, and the glorious appearing of the great God and our Saviour Jesus Christ" (Tit. 2:13). As we read Revelation and other Scripture references, we believe there is the whole millennium time of Christ's reign here on earth, before the final burning of fire as our portion teaches.

How Do We Look for the Day of God?

In what way then are we to look for the day of God? We believe we should be looking forward to it, with the realization that then and only then will Christ have the complete victory over sin. We realize the victory was won by Christ on the cross, but the full effects of this victory will not be fully accomplished until this scene is purged with fire. A true Christian realizes that in this great conflagration he will be safe with Christ, and we will share the great victory with Him. He has no dread of this time but longs for its coming. He realizes that it is a day which will usher in the grand time wherein sin will be gone and righteousness will dwell forever and ever.

"Hasting Unto the Coming"

The expression "hasting unto" is translated "earnestly desiring" in the Revised Version. Some have thought that this teaches that we can in some way or other hasten this coming of the day of God. They say if we live in all holy behavior and godliness as suggested in verse 11, that we thereby hasten the coming of this day. This we do not believe is the meaning, even though the Greek word means literally "to speed" or "to urge on." Perhaps a good translation would be "to await eagerly" with the hope that it will soon come. If it is possible to hasten the coming of the day as our verse seems to suggest, it could only be by earnest prayer and witnessing for Christ by word of mouth and a consecrated manner of life. However, we believe God has His appointed times for all these future events, and it is right and proper that we earnestly anticipate their coming. We trust each of us can truthfully say with the apostle John, "Even so, come, Lord Jesus" (Rev. 22:21).

"THE DAY OF GOD"

This is the only place in the Word where we read this expression "the day of God." The day of the Lord is often mentioned in both the Old and the New Testaments (see vs. 10). This day of God is linked up with the dissolution of this scene with fire. Some have wondered about the expression "the day of the Lord" in verse 10, where it also is linked up with the burning of this scene. It may be that "the day of the Lord" commences at the time of the appearing of our Lord Jesus and ends with the coming of "the day of God." In other words, the coming of the day of God is the wind-up of the day of the Lord. The sooner the Lord Jesus comes, the sooner will come the day of God.

THE DAY OF THE FATHER'S GLORY

The millennium time is the time when the Lord Jesus will be especially honored. Perhaps the time after the purging of this scene with fire and the establishing of the new heavens and the new earth, will be the time when the Father will be especially honored. This may be the time when the Lord Jesus "shall have delivered up the kingdom to God, even the Father" (I Cor. 15:24-28). This will be the day when Christ shall have gained the victory over all His enemies, and when sin will be wholly eradicated from the heavens and the earth, and the honor of God vindicated to the full. In many ways today is man's day, but when the day of God has come, man's day will be gone forever. This day of God will be one of unending glory. We who have trusted Christ will share this glory eternally.

"WHEREIN THE HEAVENS BEING ON FIRE"

The latter part of this verse brings no new thought above what we have in verses 7 and 10. Some confuse this portion with what we read in Mat. 24:29. "Immediately after the tribulation of those days shall the sun be darkened, and the moon shall not give her light, and the stars shall fall from heaven, and the powers of the heavens shall be shaken." In this verse we have a darkening and a shaking of things, but no fire or melting. This accompanies the great tribulation time before the coming of the Lord in glory. Our verse in Peter evidently is much later and much more severe, even to the melting of the elements. We believe the millennium time separates these two periods of severe judgment. This would surely seem so from the order of events as they are recorded in Revelation.

We are not Alarmed

The true Christian reads of the melting of the elements without alarm. He realizes that he is perfectly safe with Christ. As Shadrach, Meshach, and Abednego were not harmed by Nebuchadnezzar's fiery furnace, so we who are Christ's will be unharmed by the fires of God's judgments.

XXIX

THE NEW HEAVENS AND THE NEW EARTH

(II Peter 3:13, 14)

3:13. "Nevertheless we, according to his promise, look for new heavens and a new earth, wherein dwelleth righteousness."

Here Peter assures us that, although someday fire will consume everything in this scene and actually cause the heavens and the earth to melt, yet that does not mean the consumation of all things. Out of the ruins will arise new heavens and a new earth, and in this new scene there will be no more sin, but righteousness will dwell.

"According to His Promise"

When Peter says "we according to his promise" he must be thinking of the promises in Isaiah concerning the new heavens and the new earth. In Isa. 65:17 we read, "For behold, I create new heavens and a new earth; and the former shall not be remembered, nor come into mind." Then again in Isaiah 66:22, "For as the new heavens and new earth, which I will make, shall remain before me, saith the Lord, so shall your seed and your name remain." How we thank God for His promises in the Word. We can absolutely depend on them. "He is faithful that promised" (Heb. 10:23). Has He said there will be new heavens and a new earth? It will surely come to pass.

Not Annihilation

Scientists have proved that matter can change its form, but it is not annihilated. A solid may change into a liquid, or a gas, but it is not gone. As we read the foregoing verses we conclude that this world will return to a molten state at the time of the future judgment of fire. After this it will again be solidified and renovated and refitted for human dwelling. The only thing which will be completely gone will be sin and its effects.

The Effects of Sin Will be Removed

In many respects this world is a marvelous place made by a great designer to be a fit place for all forms of life to dwell. We have exactly the right amount of atmosphere, moisture, and heat. As a consequence we have the air, land and water all teeming with life. Sin has in a great measure ruined the beauty of all this. The one creature, man, whom the Lord placed in dominion over it all, has brought trouble to the whole scene. We believe the Lord means to restore this world to its Edenic beauty and purity, and have it so He can again have full fellowship with His creatures, even as He did with Adam and Eve in the garden. What Satan has ruined God will fully restore. All this the Lord can do, because Christ made an atonement for sin by dying on the cross. Where sin abounded, God's glory will someday super-abound.

This Present Evil World

Our verse says that in the new heavens and the new earth righteousness shall dwell. Our present scene is indwelt by unrighteousness. The whole history of this world has been one of sin, corruption and carnage. Worst of all, it has been a history of enmity and rebellion against the Lord. The righteous have been the target of ridicule and abuse. The only absolutely righteous one who ever lived in this scene was crucified.

No Unrighteousness There

Our verse says but little concerning this new heaven and new earth; only that in it will dwell righteousness. Rev. 21 and 22 tell more concerning it, but much of that is only an enlargement on the thought of our verse. It will be wonderful to be in a place where right will no longer be under the foot of might. All which now blights and mars will be removed. No drunks will stagger down the alleys, and no rapists will be lurking in dark corners. Nature too will be cured. If there are any lions then, there ferocity will be gone; if there are any serpents their poisonous sting will be removed. Pests and enemies of plant life will be no more. He will silence the moan of a dying creation. "Because the creature itself also shall be delivered from the bondage of corruption into the glorious liberty of the children of God" (Rom. 8:21). "And God shall wipe away all tears from their eyes; and there shall be no more death, neither sorrow, nor crying, neither shall there be any more pain: for the former things are passed away" (Rev. 21:4). "And there shall in no wise enter into it anything that defileth, neither whatsoever worketh abomination, or maketh a lie: but they that are written in the Lamb's book of life" (Rev. 21:27).

"Wherein Dwelleth Righteousness"

Rev. 21 and 22 tell of a number of things which will be in the new heaven and the new earth. Rev. 21:3 is a lovely verse; "Behold the tabernacle of God is with men, and he will dwell with them, and they shall be his people, and God himself shall be with them, and be their God." The new Jerusalem will be there (Rev. 21:9-21) and a new temple not of wood and stone; "For the Lord God Almighty and the Lamb are the temple of it" (Rev. 21:22). No need for a sun or a moon, "For the glory of God did lighten it, and the Lamb is the light thereof" (Rev. 21:23). The river of life and the tree of life will be there (Rev. 22:1, 2). "And there shall be no more curse; but the throne of God and of the Lamb shall be in it; and his servants shall serve him" (Rev. 22:3). What a great pleasure it will be to be able to serve him without any struggle. All who are there will be holy in the absolute sense, just as our Lord is holy. What a blessed prospect, like Him and with Him forever more. We will have health without any danger of pain, joy without any thought of grief, love without any peril of parting, life without any threat of death, and Himself forever more. How we long for its coming. While waiting, may we serve Him with our whole being.

3:14. "Wherefore, beloved, seeing that ye look for such things, be diligent that ye may be found of him in peace, without spot, and blameless."

In the remaining verses of our chapter, Peter makes the final practical application to his readers. He has told them of the judgment of fire which is coming upon this world and also of the new heavens and the new earth which are to follow. Seeing his readers were looking for such things, how were they to conduct themselves? They should be alert, active, zealous in the things of the Lord, so that they would not be ashamed nor afraid at His coming. Neither should there be found in them anything unclean, nor anything for which they could be blamed.

"BELOVED"

This whole chapter runs over with Christian affection. Four times over (vs. 1, 8, 14, 17) Peter calls them "beloved." Then in our next verse, speaking of Paul, he says "our beloved brother Paul." In spite of severe trials and persecutions Peter wanted them to know that they were beloved of himself and also of the Lord. They should also love one another.

"YE LOOK FOR SUCH THINGS"

What are these things for which the Christians are looking? We believe Peter is thinking especially of those things mentioned in our chapter; namely the coming of our Lord Jesus, first for His church and then to rule and to reign over this world. Then they are looking for the dissolution of this world by fire, and lastly, the making of the new heavens and the new earth. At this time, we should be momentarily looking for Christ to come to take His own to glory. "So Christ was once offered to bear the sins of many; and unto them that *look for him* shall he appear the second time without sin unto salvation" (Heb. 9:28).

OUR ATTITUDE

How do we look for Him? Perhaps some with utter indifference, some with real dread, and some with great joy. If we really believe, it cannot be with indifference. If we are His and walking close to Him, it need not be with dread, but should be with great joy. These future events all hold great promise for the sincere believer in our Lord Jesus.

THIS LIFE IS ONLY PREPARATORY

If you planned to move to Australia or some other distant land, you would seek to learn all you could about the necessary journey and the land itself. We certainly will make a journey soon, either by death or at the coming of the Lord. It is only the part of wisdom to do all in our power to be prepared for that journey. Let us have a long range vision and not look only on things near at hand. Our life in this scene is but a prelude to tremendous things to come. Let us remember we are but strangers and pilgrims here, and the most important thing for us is to live a life for Him and like Him.

"Be Diligent"

This is the third time in this epistle that Peter urges his readers to diligence. In 1:5 it is to be diligent in developing Christian character; in 1:10, to be diligent in making our calling and election sure. In our verse we are exhorted to be diligent in our preparation in view of future events, that we may be found of Him in peace. Diligence speaks of hard, honest, persevering effort. Certainly if Christ is worth anything, He is worth a life of diligent service on our part. We represent Him in this world; we have a great work to do and little time to do it. Our verse especially urges us to be diligent in connection with our meeting our Lord in peace and without spot and blameless. In other words, we should make every effort to live a clean and upright life, so as to be able to face Him without shame or fear.

"Found of Him"

None can escape standing before the Lord. To the unsaved sinner we would quote Num. 32:23, "Be sure your sin will find you out." A man may get away with a great deal in this world. Much of his sin may be completely hidden, but when he stands before the Lord, all will be brought to the light. It is wonderful to find Christ in this life, or perhaps we should say, to be found of Him. Some are found by Him in the assembly or church, some on a sick bed, or in the closet. The author was found by Him beside the casket of a dear friend. Our verse refers to the time when we as Christians will stand before His judgment seat. How will we be found of Him then? Will we be found of Him in peace? Will we be found spotless and blameless? What the world thought of us will not matter then. Whether we were popular, honored, and feted, or esteemed of little account will be of no importance. The great question then will be, what does He think of us? Let us carefully examine our state and act accordingly.

"Found of Him in Peace"

Man by nature is at enmity with God. Our Lord Jesus "made peace through the blood of his cross" (Col. 1:20). Man is the guilty party in this warfare, but the Lord has made a way by which he may be reconciled. Now the moment even the vilest sinner confesses his guilt and asks for pardon he is fully forgiven on the ground of the cross work of our Lord Jesus Christ. "Therefore being justified by faith, we have peace with God through our Lord Jesus Christ" (Rom. 5:1). As a result of this peace with God and the knowledge that all is well between us and Him, we have the "peace of God" in our hearts. The closer we live to Him and the more we live for Him, the more this peace will abound in our hearts (Col. 3:15). As a result of this peace in our hearts we are sure to be peaceable with our neighbors, too. (Rom. 12:18).

Found in Peace at His Coming

Our verse does not speak primarily of peace with God because reconciled through Christ, nor peace in our hearts because of an assurance of this forgiveness, but a peace in our hearts at the time when we meet Christ face to face. Does the thought of His coming trouble us? Will we be fearful or ashamed as we stand before Him? We should not, and will not, if we are living for Him now as we should. If a teller of a bank has been perfectly honest, and has not been guilty of trickery or embezzelment, he will not fear the arrival of the bank examiners. If he is guilty he will tremble in his shoes. In like manner, if we have been good stewards of the manifold grace of God, we will be able to stand before Him without shame or fear at His coming. If we do not live for Him as we should, even though safe because saved, we will be disturbed at His coming.

"Without Spot and Blameless"

It is the desire of the Lord to find us "without spot and blameless" at His coming. We believe that "without spot" speaks of purity of heart and life, while "blameless" speaks of a life of righteousness lived before the world. Of course as to our standing in Christ, we are already before God without spot, but we believe the apostle is thinking of our practical everyday life. We are already looked at as "clean every whit" (John 13:10) in Christ, but as a result of this cleansing, we should live a pure life for Him. A true hope in the coming of Christ is sure to have a purifying affect. "And every man that hath this hope in him purifieth himself, even as he is pure" (I John 3:3).

IMPURE SPEECH

Not all Christians are pure in their speech or in their behavior. We recently spoke in a place on "Grieving the Spirit" (Eph. 4:30). We said that we believed things mentioned before this verse and also things following it were some of the things which would grieve the Spirit. We spoke some on "Let no corrupt communication proceed out of your mouth" (Eph. 4:29). We had no idea that one of the men in the meeting was a foul-mouthed man, although a professed Christian. He said nothing to us personally, but accused us to others of being a legalist and a holiness preacher, and would not come to any more of our meetings. Later some suggested that we be invited back for further meetings, but this brother (if he was such) made such a fuss that they did not dare have us back. Not long after this same man was the ringleader in other trouble and he left the assembly with other Christians. The Christians then felt free to invite us back, and only then did we learn of the trouble. If our speech is not pure, we will be ashamed at His coming.

PURE IN ACTION

Some are not only impure in their speech, but in their actions as well. They are like the false teachers we read of in chapter 2, who were "spots and blemishes" upon the companies of Christians with whom they were in fellowship (2:13). "Having eyes full of adultery, and that cannot cease from sin" (2:14). Let us rather be like our Lord Jesus of whom we read, "as of a lamb without blemish and without spot" (I Pet. 1:19). Surely, if we love Him, we will desire to be like Him. Let us keep close to Him and separate from every form of evil. Sin is such a serious thing that Christ had to die on the cross to make atonement for it, and surely, knowing this, we should hate it and be clean, healthy Christians.

"BLAMELESS"

In Christ we are blameless in God's sight, yet the devil accuses the brethren before the Lord (Rev. 12:10). And the world accuses the Christians constantly for all things with which they can find the least fault. We should seek to live purely for Christ so that neither man nor demon can bring a righteous charge against us. This means that all our dealings with the men of the world must be in absolute honesty and righteousness. Can they depend on our bare word more than on the bond of the unsaved? Would they dare trust us in their homes, or give us free access to their vaults? Certainly, if we are longing for a world in which righteousness dwells, we should live a righteous life now.

"BLAMELESS IN HIS SIGHT" (R.V.)

Perhaps Peter is not thinking so much of being blameless in the sight of man or demons as he is of being "blameless in his sight" at His coming (R.V.). We have already noted that in Christ we are seen as blameless. "There is therefore now no condemnation to them which are in Christ Jesus" (Rom. 8:1). Only upon this ground could we be taken into God's family. Because of our blameless standing in Christ, we should seek to live a blameless life before Him. Then He will have only things for which He can commend us in that day when we stand at His judgment seat. "That ye may be blameless in the day of our Lord Jesus Christ" (I Cor. 1:8). You ask, "Are you trying to teach us that we should live without sin before the Lord?" That is exactly what we are trying to teach, but we are sorry to add that we do not expect you to attain to it. We must all say with the apostle Paul, "Not as though I had already attained, either were already perfect: but I follow after," etc. (Phil. 3:12-14).

XXX

PAUL AND HIS EPISTLES

(II Peter 3:15, 16)

3:15. "And account that the longsuffering of our Lord is salvation; even as our beloved brother Paul also according to the wisdom given unto him hath written unto you."

The first part of this verse is somewhat of a repetition of verse 9. The reason for the seeming delay in the coming of these events is not slackness on the part of the Lord, but manifests His longsuffering and is meant for the salvation of the sinner. In the latter part, he brings in a nice touch concerning Paul. He calls him "our beloved brother," and says that the letters he wrote to these Asia Minor Christians were written by wisdom given unto him by the Lord.

"The Longsuffering of Our Lord"

We have written concerning the longsuffering of the Lord in connection with verse 9. We sometimes marvel that He does nothing to sinners who oppose Him and insult Him day by day. Men would not dare abuse the names of their neighbors the way they do the name of the Lord. On all sides today we have unmentionable impurity and uncleanness, and fornication and adultery are rampant. All sin is a direct thrust at the throne of God, but He allows it to go on without a word. It would be easy for Him to quickly mete out judgment, but His sword stays in its scabbard.

"Salvation"

The mockers had said because He had not come, He would never come and would never punish them for their sins. The Christians know that this is not so, and that the cause for this seeming delay in His coming is that He desires to see sinners saved. His longsuffering should be an indication to all that the Lord is willing to save. Why are not wicked men suddenly cut down in their sins? The Lord desires to yet show them mercy and to save their souls. We have seen men saved who lived terrible lives for many years. Think of Saul of Tarsus, how he hated the name of Christ, and persecuted Christians, but the Lord saved him. Paul tells of this longsuffering on his behalf in I Tim. 1:16, "That in me first Jesus Christ might shew forth all longsuffering." We know a sinful man who went through the thick of battle in World War I. He was about the only one of his company to come back. Afterwards he was saved. O, the longsuffering of the Lord, how we should thank Him for it.

Be Patient

The Christians have trials and troubles in this world and consequently often long for the coming of the Lord. The reason the Lord does not come at once for us is that there are yet more to be saved; the church is not yet complete. He is not unconcerned about our difficulties, but He is concerned about the souls of sinners. "For this is good and acceptable in the sight of God our Saviour; who will have all men to be saved, and to come unto the knowledge of the truth" (I Tim. 2:3, 4).

"Our Beloved Brother Paul"

We like the affectionate way Peter speaks of Paul. He calls him "our beloved brother." There seems to have been no enmity or jealousy amongst the early Christian workers. Peter, at one time, was at fault in that for fear of prominent Jews, he refused to eat with the Gentiles. For this Paul withstood him to his face (Gal. 2:11, 12). If Peter held any ill-will because of this, he certainly got over it, and here shows affection and high regard for Paul. Reproof should not embitter a true child of God, but cause him to leave his folly. "Faithful are the wounds of a friend" (Prov. 27:6). Peter might have taken further offense because Paul mentioned his failing in his letter to the Galatians, and the Galatians were included amongst those to whom Peter is now writing (I Pet. 1:1). In spite of this there is no evidence of malice in Peter's epistles.

Honor All Servants

Some of us are servants of Christ. Even though some do not speak well of us, we should, like Peter, speak well of them, and show them affection. Let us honor and love all those who preach the gospel even though we may not be able to agree with them in all they say or do.

"BROTHER PAUL"

Peter titles Paul simply as "brother Paul." This lovely title speaks of nearness and affection. We are linked in close relationship to every other Christian by the blood of Christ. They are all our brothers and sisters in Him. Kindly notice what he does not call Paul. He gives him no flattering titles, but calls him simply "brother." Many a preacher today would be insulted if called by no greater title than this.

"THE WISDOM GIVEN UNTO HIM"

In the writing of his epistles, Paul had wisdom given him of the Lord. The Lord is the source of all true wisdom. "If any of you lack wisdom, let him ask of God" (James 1:5). Although Paul was a man well-taught in the schools of men, Peter does not say Paul got his wisdom from Gamaliel, but suggests that it was a super-natural gift of God. Paul also says that his wisdom came from the Lord. "According to the grace of God which is given unto me, as a wise master builder, I have laid the foundation —" (I Cor. 3:10).

WISDOM FROM GOD

Solomon was a very wise man; his wisdom came from the Lord (I Kings 3:28). Bezaleel also received his wisdom from the Lord in connection with the building of the tabernacle (Ex. 31:3). Joseph received wisdom from God, or he would not have been able to stand before Pharaoh (Acts 7:10). Daniel received wisdom in order to interpret Nebuchadnezzar's dreams (Dan. 2:20, 21). The Lord Jesus promised to give wisdom to His disciples (Luke 21:15). If we are to be wise, we too must get it from the Lord and His Word. We should study the Word diligently and then ask Him to give us wisdom in the understanding of it, and in the ministering of it to others.

"WRITTEN UNTO YOU"

Paul had written to the same Christians in Asia Minor to whom Peter was now writing. Peter especially mentions Galatia (I Pet. 1:1) and Paul's epistle to the Galatians was sent to the Christians there. Paul also sent letters to the Ephesians and Colossians, and both Ephesus and Colosse are cities in the Asia section of what is now Asia Minor. Asia is also included in the countries to whom Peter is writing (I Pet. 1:1). The epistle to the Hebrews may also have been sent up to these countries. We believe both of Peter's epistles were written later than Paul's. Paul may have been already executed at the time when Peter wrote. Peter seems to indicate in our verse that all of Paul's epistles were already written, and that he and the Asia Minor Christians were well acquainted with them. No doubt Paul's epistles were widely spread during the time of the early church.

Paul and Peter Wrote of the Same Things

Both in this verse and the next Peter is suggesting that he and Paul wrote in absolute agreement and of the same things. Peter evidently believed Paul's letters were of inspired authority. Although some seemed to deny Paul's apostleship, and belittled his teachings, Peter certainly did not. He puts him on a level with himself and the other apostles. While both Peter and Paul wrote some distinctive things, for the most part their writings are about the same things.

3:16. "As also in all his epistles, speaking in them of these things; in which are some things hard to be understood, which they that are unlearned and unstable wrest, as they do also the other scriptures, unto their own destruction."

In this verse Peter continues to commend Paul's epistles, putting them on the same level with all other Scriptures. He first says that Paul's epistles contain the same teachings as his own. He admits that there are some things in them which are difficult to understand, not because of any obscurity on Paul's part, but because of the grandeur of some of the themes, and the frailty of many readers. He continues, that some unlearned and unstable wrest or twist some of these difficult portions in such a way as to bring destruction upon themselves.

"All His Epistles"

The expression "all his epistles" would lead us to believe that many and perhaps all of Paul's epistles were already written, and that Peter and many of his readers were well acquainted with them. They may have already been the common property of many of the churches. While they were first of all letters written for certain churches, or private individuals, history tells us that soon they were considered inspired of God and distributed from church to church. They must have been in the hands of some who professed to be teachers of the Word, or they could not have been accused of wresting or twisting them.

"Speaking In Them of These Things

When Peter says, "speaking in them of these things" he was inferring that the things written by himself in his two epistles could also be found in Paul's epistles. We have noticed, in connection with our studies on the first epistle of Peter, that he seems everywhere to be trying to show that the things which Paul had taught them were true. As in I Peter, most of what we have in II Peter can also be found in Paul's epistles. Both everywhere insist on godly Christian living, not to obtain salvation, but as a fruit of it (Eph. 2:10, Titus 3:8). Both teach the truth of the inspiration of all Scripture (II Pet. 1:19-21, II Tim. 3:15, 16). Both speak of false prophets and teachers (II Pet. 2, II Cor. 11:13-15). They both also speak of the coming again of Christ (II Pet. 3:4, I Thess. 4:13-18), the day of the Lord (II Pet. 3:10, I Thess. 5:2), of the dissolution of all things in this scene (II Pet. 3:7-12, Heb. 1:10-12). These are but a small part of what they have in common.

"Some Things Hard to be Understood"

Again we would say, it is not because Paul was an obscure writer that some things in his epistles are hard to understand. It is rather that his subjects are so sublime and so profound that they are difficult for the human mind to fully grasp. His teachings deal with much which the natural mind cannot understand at all. Even the carnal minded Christian finds many things very difficult. In order to understand some of these things even the spiritual minded Christian needs special enlightening by the spirit of God.

Depths of Scripture

Some portions of Scripture have depths which will never be fully plumbed by any man in this scene. No one ever knows it all; there is always more to learn. We who are mortal can never fully understand the ways of the infinite God. Paul, in writing of Melchisedec, says to the Hebrews, "of whom we have many things to say, and hard to be uttered, seeing ye are dull of hearing" (Heb. 5:11). We too, often are "dull of hearing." Some of the truths of Paul's letters are not pleasing to the flesh, and consequently, there is not much desire on the part of some to understand them.

Difficulties in Paul's Epistles

There are a number of things which appear contradictory to the natural mind in Paul's epistles. For instance, many do not know that a man's standing in Christ is different from his actual state. In Christ the Christian stands "clean every whit" with all his sins put away, but his state may be far from perfect. Sometimes Paul is writing of our standing and sometimes, of our state. It takes spiritual discernment to understand the distinctions. The subjects of law and grace have confused many, also the gospel and election, the flesh and the spirit, faith and works, the old nature and the new. Eternal life and apostasy has been a difficulty to many, while prophetic things have been confusing to others. Paul uses the word "law" in seven different ways in the book of Romans. Some things which he wrote passes knowledge. To understand all which he wrote would be to understand the ways of the Almighty God.

We Know but Little

There is much round about us in this world concerning which we know but little. For instance, what do we know about life, whether it be plant, or animal, or human life? What do we understand of electricity, or magnetism, or chemical action? What do we know of the cause of the movements of our earth, or the moon, to say nothing of our solar system, or yet scores of other solar systems? Nothing in nature or science is fully comprehended by us, so why think it strange when some things in the Bible are beyond our comprehension? We may not be able to fully understand, but we can believe.

Not Only Paul's Epistles

Not only parts of Paul's epistles are difficult, but some of Peter's are too. In fact, there are difficult portions in all parts of the Scriptures. Think of the miracles of our Lord Jesus, and the many miraculous things in the Old Testament. Perhaps the most difficult of all is the book of Revelation. These difficulties should not deter us, but stir us on to an ever greater knowledge of the Word of God. We should delight to climb the steeps, and to fathom the depths. We believe the Lord meant that they should enliven interest in the Word. How wonderful to be reading along and to suddenly find a new gem in the mine of the Word.

Not All Hard

Some might conclude from our remarks that Paul's epistles are very difficult. This is not so. Only "*some things* are hard to be understood." As in all the Scriptures, the way of salvation is very plain. Neither is the manner of life which the Lord expects His people to walk difficult to comprehend. Some cast aside the whole Bible because of its difficulties. An infidel was eating dinner in a train diner with a preacher. The infidel asked, "What do you do with the parts of the Bible which you cannot understand?" The preacher replied, "Just what I do with the bones of these fish; lay them aside and enjoy the meat." Some foolishly choke on the bones. Do we have to know the ingredient of every dish before we will partake of our dinner? Let us not starve spiritually because we do not understand every part of the Bible.

"Unlearned"

The word "unlearned" is translated "ignorant" in the Revised Version. Many profess to be Bible teachers who are not even saved. A friend of ours was often plagued by a teacher of a false cult. He was always talking to him about the kingdom, or eternal punishment, or some prophetic subject. Although this man was a good customer of his, our friend sickened of it all, and finally asked him, "When were you saved, and when were you born again?" The man could give no satisfactory answer. Our friend said, "You remind me of one who is trying to teach higher mathematics, when he has not as yet passed out of the first grade."

Divisions or strange sects come from a man or men often unsaved, misunderstanding some doctrines and then strongly advocating them. It is often easy for such to gain simple followers. One woman, after listening to an oratorical quack, said, "He is a wonderful man; he even mentioned the name of God." So easily are some led astray.

NOT MERELY FLESHLY LEARNING

Because one is wise in the ways of the world, even though saved, does not qualify him as a fit Bible teacher. Besides being saved, one must be well instructed in the Word before attempting to teach others. Even then he must not be a man who knows the Bible in a mental way only, but must be taught in the school of fellowship with the Lord. Only as one sits at the feet of the Lord like Mary, and is willing to be taught by the Holy Spirit will he be useful as a teacher of God's Word.

"UNSTABLE"

There are always unstable souls who are easily beguiled (ch. 2:14). Many are not thoroughly grounded, thus easily swayed. They are "tossed to and fro and carried about with every wind of doctrine" (Eph. 4:14). They are like Reuben "unstable as water" (Gen. 49:4), ready to run some place else if given the least excuse. Some are like the weathervane, which faces another way everytime the wind blows from another direction. Especially likely are they to turn if the new way is easier on the flesh. These unstable souls are ever ready to twist the Scriptures to suit their new found fancies.

"WREST"

The unlearned and unstable "wrest," or "twist," or "distort" the Word of God to make it say things the Lord never intended. The original word is often used in connection with winding on a windlass, and sometimes, in connection with torture especially by twisting. Many today wrest the Scriptures even as a wrestler twists his opponent. We were amazed recently to see on the television (shame on us), how these wrestlers twist each others arms, legs, and even each others necks and backs. It is a wonder they do not break each others bones. Even so, some twist and distort portions of the Scripture until they completely lose the purpose for which they were written.

Why Wrest the Scriptures?

Why were they wresting the Scriptures already in Peter's day, even as they do today? Why were Paul's epistles especially open to this treatment? We believe one of the reasons was and is today that some want to be classed as Christians, but do not want to live a clean life for the Lord. So they look for a way to excuse their sin. This was true of the false teachers of Peter's day. They were twisting the teaching of Christian liberty, especially taught by Paul, to mean that it gave license to live as one pleased (II Pet. 2:19). Some try to justify their sins by saying David was guilty of murder, and Peter, of denying his Lord, and Jacob, of deceit. They forget that these actions were thoroughly condemned by the Lord, and repented of and forsaken by the guilty parties.

Other Reasons

Sometimes it is not a matter of morals, but a desire to bring some new sensational thing in order to obtain followers. We believe this is one of the reasons for the vast number of sects today. Sometimes it comes from one unlearned, as our verse suggests, seeking the office of teacher before being thoroughly taught or firmly grounded in the Word.

It Is Easy to Wrest the Scriptures

A tramp came to a Christian's door and asked for some odd job to do. While at his job the woman tried to preach to him. He said, "Lady, don't you know that the Bible says there is no God?" She would not believe him, but he asked for a Bible and turned to Psalm 14, and sure enough there it was, "There is no God." However, he failed to read and tried to cover the line ahead of it, which says, "The fool hath said in his heart, There is no God" (Psalm 14:1).

Read Carefully and Prayerfully

To keep from twisting the Word, we must be very careful to read every part in the light of its context, and to read it carefully and prayerfully. We must notice to whom it is written and why. As we come to the Scriptures, we must not put into them our own preconceived ideas, but let the Lord speak to our hearts. If we come humbly and with a desire to know His will, the Spirit will teach us correctly. If we come to a portion which does not seem too clear, let it rest for a time and study some plainer portions. These portions which are easier to understand will eventually throw light on the more obscure parts.

MUCH TEACHING HAS NO FOUNDATION

Much which is passed for truth is not based on Scripture at all. As a young Christian we were stunned to find that there were no Scriptures which teach the baptism of little children. Much ceremony and ritual, which some churches look upon as almost essential to salvation, has no basis in Scripture at all. This is true of a great deal which the Catholic Church teaches and practices. Many Protestant churches are far from guiltless in this matter.

DO NOT WITHHOLD THE WORD

The Catholic clergy today discourages Bible reading, because they claim the unlearned (those who are not the clergy) cannot understand the Word, and that many wrest it to their own destruction. It is to be noticed that the apostles did not on that account refrain from giving the people the Word of God. All the more reason to bring it in all its purity to the people.

"THE OTHER SCRIPTURES"

The term "Scriptures" means "writings," and practically always when used in the New Testament refers to the inspired books of the Old Testament. This is the only place where we have any indication that the apostles considered the writings of any New Testament author as part of the Scriptures and so, inspired of the Lord. The word "other" in the expression "the other scriptures," tells us that Peter considered Paul's epistles on a level with the Old Testament Scriptures, and so, a part of the Word of God. In order to know that Paul's writings were inspired, Peter must have been inspired himself. The early church would be far more likely to consider Peter's writings inspired than they would Paul's, because there was no question as to Peter's apostleship. This testimony of Peter would therefore bear great weight as to the truthfulness and inspiration of Paul's writings.

INSPIRATION

We conclude from our verse that the early church considered Paul's and also Peter's letters as part of the Scriptures, and thus, inspired. "All scripture is given by inspiration of God, and is profitable for doctrine, for reproof, for correction, for instruction in righteousness" (II Tim. 3:16). It is therefore necessary to believe and to obey all the Scriptures, Paul's, Peter's and all the rest.

WE MUST RIGHTLY APPLY SCRIPTURE

Of course, we must note to whom each portion is written and why. Much of the Old Testament was written to a special people, in a special land, with special ceremonies, etc. Many lessons can be learned from the Old Testament, but all does not directly apply to us. Much of even the Old Testament is of an eternal nature, written to all of God's saints of all ages. Some things in the New Testament are for the unsaved, some for the babes in Christ, some for the mature Christians, but remember, all is the Word of God and inspired by Him.

"THEIR OWN DESTRUCTION"

To wrest Scripture is a very dangerous thing. Our verse says, by doing so they bring on their "own destruction." This is the sad part of warping and twisting Scripture; by it the twisters destroy their own souls and the souls of others too. False cults so undermine the Word that they take away every chance of salvation from all who believe and follow them. They belittle the seriousness of sin, and so, rob their hearers of the sense of the need of salvation, or they belittle the work and person of Christ and so, rob them of any chance of faith in Him who alone can save. It is not Paul's fault that they come to destruction, nor is it the fault of any part of the Scripture. The Word, if read with a meek spirit, will bring destruction to none, but only salvation, and joy, and peace. It is not the Scriptures which bring the destruction, but the wresting of them. How important then to teach sinners the right way of salvation.

AN ILLUSTRATION

The story is told of a woman who was riding in a train with her baby. A fierce blizzard was raging outside, and she was concerned about getting off at the right station. The conductor assured her that he would inform her as to when to get off. A man sitting near her said, "Don't worry, I know exactly when we come to your station; I will tell you when to get off the train." Soon he said to her, "The next stop will be your station." When the train stopped she got off. It soon started up again and not long after the conductor came along and asked, "Where is that woman with her baby?" The man said, "She got off at the last stop." "Got off at the last stop? Why man, that was not a station at all, we just stopped to make a slight repair on the locomotive." The next day the poor woman and her baby were found frozen to death. She was a victim of counsel from one who thought he knew, but did not. It is far worse to give souls wrong counsel, and to have them be lost forever.

XXXI

FINAL EXHORTATIONS

(II Peter 3:17, 18)

3:17. "Ye therefore, beloved, seeing ye know these things before, beware lest ye also, being led away with the error of the wicked, fall from your own stedfastness."

We now have a warning for the Christians. Knowing about those who wrest the Scriptures, they were to be on guard lest some of these false teachers lead them astray also. He does not suggest that they would lose their salvation, but that they might fall from their lofty condition in Christ.

"Ye Know These Things Before"

The Revised Version has, "Knowing these things before hand, beware." The apostle is forwarning them about these perverters and false teachers so that they might not fall into their traps. The Scriptures are full of red lanterns warning the Lord's people of dangers which lie in their path. "For there shall arise false Christs, and false prophets, and shall shew great signs, and wonders; insomuch that, if it were possible, they shall deceive the very elect. Behold, I have told you before" (Mat. 24:24, 25).

"Beware"

Peter would have the Christians to be very much on guard and to watch very carefully, as the original word for "beware" implies. How often we are warned by the word "beware" in the Word. "Beware of false prophets, which come to you in sheep's clothing" (Mat. 7:15). "Beware of dogs, beware of evil workers, beware of the concision" (Phil. 3:2). "Beware lest any man spoil you through philosophy and vain deceit, after the tradition of men" (Col. 2:8). None are so advanced or so strong that they dare for one moment let down their guard. The enemy will be quick to thrust in his darts. My stedfastness in Christ is a pearl of great price; may I guard it with utmost care.

LITTLE SINS GROW. ILLUSTRATION

We need to beware lest little sins creep into our lives. Each sin is like a little snake which, if not immediately killed, may grow into a giant serpent. A naturalist found a baby python. He nourished it, raised it, trained it to do tricks. At the climax of his stage act his giant python would coil about his body and then look into its trainer's face. One day at the end of a performance, the python was wrapped around his body. He told it to recoil, but instead it began to squeeze with its powerful muscles. As the curtain went down the audience could hear the man's bones cracking in the vice of this pet serpent. Sin is like that. If played with, it will crush a man spiritually.

"LED AWAY"

"Led away" would be better translated "carried away." How quickly and easily some are carried away with a strange doctrine. Let a clever talker come along with a display of oratory and gone they are. "For they that are such serve not our Lord Jesus Christ, but their own belly; and by good words and fair speeches deceive the hearts of the simple" (Rom. 16:18). Many are like "a wave of the sea driven with the wind and tossed" (James 1:6). We would counsel immature Christians to keep out of earshot of that which they know to be wrong, lest they be scarred by it. Not only seducers from without will lead astray, but unless we are on guard the flesh within will do the same.

"THE ERROR OF THE WICKED"

Error and wickedness usually go together. "Wicked" would be better translated "lawless." A lawless one is a criminal, so we could read this part of our verse, "the error of the criminal." He who leads one astray so that his soul is lost is the worst kind of a criminal. The word "error" has the sense of fraud in it. This means that these criminal men deceive in order that they may defraud their dupes out of material things, or perhaps defraud them of salvation. This is just what those wicked men of chapter 2 were doing. It was for gain that they were bringing false doctrines, and in it all, were defrauding their followers of everlasting life. While those really saved would not lose their souls if led astray, they would certainly lose their Christian testimony, and usefulness, and reward in glory.

"FALL"

It is an awful thing to fall. Many a Christian has run well in this Christian race, only to stumble and fall. We thank God when such get up and run again, but many never lose the scars from these falls. Peter had an awful fall when he denied his Lord, but he repented of his sin and then ran better than ever before. David had an awful fall, when he sinned with Bathsheba, and arranged for her husband to be killed in battle. He too, repented of his sin and rose to run again, but the scar of this fall never left him or his immediate family. Judas had an awful fall too, but we fear that poor man never really knew the Lord, for he went out and hanged himself. The Scripture says, "He went to his own place."

WHAT CAUSES ONE TO FALL?

Many things may cause one to fall from his stedfastness in Christ. Afflictions sometimes cause it, or personal injury by other Christians. Worry takes some down, and sometimes the lust of the flesh. Our verse says deceitful workers will do it. Underlying it all is unbelief. Wrong thoughts of the Lord are sure to bring wrong actions. Real faith in Him will keep us from falling.

TO KEEP FROM FALLING

How now shall we keep from falling? We believe Peter answers this question in chapter 1:5-10. He says in 1:10, "If ye do these things ye shall never fall." The things which he refers to are the virtues listed in 1:5-7. If we add these things to our faith, there is little likelihood of our falling. An additional help to stedfastness is continual prayer. One who is in constant fellowship with the Lord is not likely to fall or be deceived. Real earnest Bible study in true meekness will also assure stedfastness in Christ. Shun sinful associates, and keep company with ardent, strong Christians. Seek to be active in Christian service. One has said, "If you fall asleep in the woods mosquitos will feast upon you, but if you keep busy chopping wood your activity will keep them away." Keep humble and watchful; "Let him that thinketh he standeth take heed lest he fall" (I Cor. 10:12).

"FALL FROM YOUR OWN STEDFASTNESS"

"Stedfastness" here is in contrast with the "unstable" of verse 16. Like a soldier facing danger, we should be strong and hold our ground. It will be a struggle to walk close to our Lord. "Hold that fast which thou hast, that no man take thy crown" (Rev. 3:11). "Therefore my beloved brethren; be ye stedfast, unmoveable, always abounding in the work of the Lord, forasmuch as ye know that your labour is not in vain in the Lord" (I Cor. 15:58).

3:18. "But grow in grace, and in the knowledge of our Lord and Saviour Jesus Christ. To him be glory both now and for ever. Amen."

This last verse might well be called the text for Peter's whole second epistle. He desired that the Christians would advance in the things of the Lord, both in their lives for Christ and in their knowledge of Him. His whole epistle is either advice on how to grow, or warnings against things which would hinder growth. He winds up his epistle with a doxology of praise and honor to our Lord Jesus Christ.

"GROW"

When Peter tells his readers to grow, he presupposes that they have life, since dead things cannot grow. To receive this new life from God is of utmost importance. This is imparted to every soul who puts his trust in the Lord Jesus. However, the impartation of this life is only the commencement of the Christian life, even as the birth of a child is only the start of his human life. After we receive this life, we must live it and continue to grow in it. A literal rendering for our word "grow" is, "keep on growing." Some translate it "grow continually."

ALL LIFE GROWS

All living things, whether plant, animal or human, grow. The human body grows from a tiny infant to a mature man. A man we are acquainted with weighs nearly 300 pounds, but was only 3 pounds at birth. We know very little about growth. Why, when we put a seed in the ground, it springs up and grows into a beautiful flower, or bush, or tree, we do not know. Why a baby grows into a man, we cannot tell either. Who knows why a youth becomes a certain height and then quits growing? Growth, like life itself, is a mystery, indeed.

Helps to Growth

While we cannot cause growth, we can help or hinder it. We feed an infant in order that he may grow. We do not cause a seed to grow, but we can plant it in good soil, fertilize it, and water it. Growth in our spiritual life is very similar. We cannot make it grow, but we can help or hinder it. The food this new life needs above all else is the Word of God. "As new born babes, desire the sincere milk of the word, that ye may grow thereby (I Pet. 2:2). Paul says, "I have planted, Apollos watered, but God gave the increase" (I Cor. 3:6). We can plant the good seed in the hearts of men, and when it starts to grow, we can water it with the Word of God. We can tend it, cultivate and prune it, but only the Lord can make it grow.

Grow in Christ-Likeness

Our verse puts the responsibility for growth upon the individual Christian. It especially mentions that we should "grow in grace, and in the knowledge of our Lord and Saviour Jesus Christ." We have heard it put this way. "We should grow roots of humility downward, shoots of love to Christ upward, and branches of usefulness to mankind outward." These branches should be loaded with the fruits of the Spirit, to bring joy to the heart of man and God. Day by day we should grow more like our Lord Jesus.

"Grow in Grace"

Peter says that we should especially "grow in grace." Grace is hard to define. It is generally said to be "unmerited favor," but it often means far more than this. One has said, "Grace is love which passes beyond all claims to love." Another has put it this way, "Grace is redeeming love ministering to the unlovely, and endowing the unlovely with its own loveliness." To give you some idea of the comprehensiveness of the word, we here give you what the dictionary gives. "Grace, favor, good-will, divine influence, mercy, pardon, privilege, natural or acquired elegance; beauty; embellishment."

SAVED BY GRACE, THEN GROW IN GRACE

First of all we are saved by grace. "By grace are ye saved through faith" (Eph. 2:8). Only the loving favor of God has brought salvation to us. We deserved nothing from Him but judgment. Yet out of His heart of love, He sent His Son to die for us, and now the guiltiest sinner can be saved. Now that we stand in this grace, we are to grow in it. In other words, we are to seek to manifest this same loving-kindness in our lives. To grow in grace means to grow in meekness, gentleness, patience, goodness, usefulness, etc. It is said of the child Jesus, "And Jesus increased in wisdom and stature, and in favour with God and man" (Luke 2:52). Perhaps to grow in grace means just that; to increase "in favour with God and man." Let us note carefully all His lovely character, and ask Him to create the same loveliness in us.

SOME EFFECTS OF GROWTH IN GRACE

If we grow in grace, we will be in no danger of being carried away with the error of the wicked as verse 17 suggests. We will be happy Christians; "Singing and making melody in your heart to the Lord" (Eph. 5:19). One has said, "Grace is like oil which keeps the light shining throughout the night." If we grow in grace we will keep shining for Him no matter how the storm may rage around us. If we grow in grace we will certainly be serving Christians. This will be the way in which we will grow in favor with man and God. Little deeds of kindness to all we contact is an evident token of real growth in grace. "Whosoever will be great among you, let him be your minister (servant)" (Mat. 20:26).

"GROW — IN KNOWLEDGE"

Knowledge" is a favorite word with Peter, especially in this second epistle. We have it five times in the first chapter alone and once in the second chapter. Five of these times he uses it in connection with our Lord Jesus. Some already then were boasting of superior knowledge, but Peter is careful to say that only knowledge of Christ is of any worth. The literal rendering is "full knowledge." We need to go on to know more and more of our Lord Jesus. The day upon which we first met Him, we could say we knew Him, but we must increase in that knowledge. It is wonderful to know much of His character, person, and work, but to know Him is more. To know one well we must meet him personally and converse with him, yea, better still, live with him. "I count all things but loss for the excellency of the knowledge of Christ Jesus my Lord" (Phil. 3:8).

We Know Only in Part

At best we will only know Him in part in this scene. A great Bible student said, "I feel as if I have investigated a small garden, and there is a whole continent yet before me." We know only a small part of our world, but there are vast universes entirely unknown. When we know all we ever will of Christ and His Word while in this world, we will still only know a small part of that which there is to know. Even the great apostle Paul says, "Now I know in part, but then shall I know even as also I am known" (I Cor. 13:12). How utterly ridiculous then for some young Christian to talk as though he knows it all.

"Our Lord and Saviour Jesus Christ"

We like the way Peter winds up his epistle with the all comprehensive name, "our Lord and Saviour Jesus Christ." This is the third time in this epistle that he uses it (1:11, 2:20). How dear to his heart our Lord had become. His blessed name was ever in his mind and on his lips. He obeyed Him as Lord, he loved Him as Saviour, he adored Him as the greatest human, Jesus, he worshipped Him as the mighty anointed Son of God, Christ.

"To Him be Glory"

Peter was ever anxious to bring glory to the name of the Lord Jesus. He ever honored the Son even as he did the Father. "That all men should honour the Son, even as they honour the Father. He that honoureth not the Son honoureth not the Father which hath sent him" (John 5:23). "Worthy is the Lamb that was slain to receive power, and riches, and wisdom, and strength, and honour, and glory, and blessing" (Rev. 5:12).

"Both Now and For Ever"

This is literally "unto the day of eternity." Almost all the New Testament writers burst forth with similar doxologies of praise to our Lord Jesus, but only here is it put exactly in this way. Not only now in this scene did Peter want Christ glorified, but throughout a long eternity, and we know it shall be so. Eternity will be none too long to express our thanksgiving and praise to Him, who did so much for us. How wonderful to think that we shall share that glory with Him through a long eternity. We shall see Him as He is and be like Him forever more (I John 3:2). "Unto him that loved us, and washed us from our sins in his own blood, and hath made us kings and priests unto God and his Father; to him be glory and dominion for ever and ever. Amen" (Rev. 1:5, 6).

"AMEN"

"Amen," so ends this great doxology and this wonderful epistle. May we, indeed, give unto our Lord Jesus Christ praise, and honor, and worship already now in this scene as well as in glory. So be it, Lord.